D0464344

Cottrell, Robert.
   The end of Hong Kong : the secret diplomacy of
imperial retreat / Robert Cottrell. -- London : John
Murray, 1993.
   xi, 244 p., [8] p. of plates : ill., 1 map, ports. ;
25 cm.

Includes bibliographcal references (p. 224-238) and
index.
06812643   ISBN:0719549922

1. Hong Kong - History. 2. Hong Kong - Politics and
(SEE NEXT CARD)

The End
of Hong Kong

The End
of Hong Kong

The Secret Diplomacy
of Imperial Retreat

ROBERT COTTRELL

JOHN MURRAY

© Robert Cottrell 1993

First published in 1993
by John Murray (Publishers) Ltd.,
50 Albemarle Street, London W1X 4BD

The moral right of the author has been asserted

A catalogue record for this book is available from the British Library

ISBN 0-7195-4992-2

Typeset in 11/13 pt Times
Printed and bound in Great Britain
at the University Press, Cambridge

For my mother

Contents

Illustrations

The author and publisher wish to thank the following for permission to reproduce photographs: Plates 1, 2, Hong Kong Government Public Records Office; 3, ITN/Rex; 4, 5, 6, 7, 8, 9, 11, Hong Kong Government Information Services; 10, 12, 13, 14, 15, New China News Agency.

Acknowledgements

The very high degree of confidentiality surrounding modern Sino-British diplomacy has meant that this book is at best a mere sketch of the more recent events which it depicts. But since the detail of those events will probably not be generally available until the declassification of official papers twenty to forty years hence, and since Hong Kong itself will be passing from British to Chinese rule barely four years hence, a sketch may yet be of some interim value.

The same confidentiality has dictated that much of the information and most of the opinions in the pages which follow are attributed, if at all, to unnamed 'officials' and 'diplomats' without clue even as to nationality. I take no pleasure in this mystification, I apologize for any frustration which the reader may feel, and I wish that the codes of official secrecy and official practice allowed of more transparency. But they do not, and without bowing to them I could not have progressed at all.

Against that background, I cannot properly thank here by name the many people with past or present involvement in official or public service in Britain, Hong Kong or China who agreed to talk to me on the understanding that they would not be identified in anything which I might then write. I thank them nonetheless for giving generously and without exception of their time, their patience, their recollections and their insights.

I have no such inhibition in expressing my indebtedness to the editors of the publications for which I served as a correspondent during the 1980s, and on behalf of which I began my exploration of Hong Kong and its future: I think especially of Sir Geoffrey Owen, Nicholas Colchester and Alain Cass at the *Financial Times*, of Derek Davies and Philip Bowring at the *Far Eastern Economic Review*, and of Andreas Whittam Smith, Matthew Symonds, Stephen Glover and Michael Fathers at *The Independent*.

For allowing me access to their libraries in Hong Kong, I am grateful to the *South China Morning Post*, the *Far Eastern Economic Review* and the China Club. For their advice, assistance and encouragement during the writing of this book, I thank Freddie Balfour, Claire Barnes, Jan Bradley, Ian Buruma, George Cardona, Michael Charnock, Frank Ching, Anthony Dicks, John Greenwood, Clare Hollingworth, Dominic Lawson, Bruce Palling, David and Gail Pirkis, Nicholas Ruffer and his colleagues at Kim Eng Securities, Lucretia Stewart, Jon Swain, Stephen Vines, Simon Winchester and Anna Wu. Finally, in every aspect of this endeavour, I have been sustained by my wife, Teresa Ma, whose understanding of Hong Kong will always be far deeper than my own.

Errors and omissions are, however, those of the author.

Author's Note

For China, names of people and places are romanized using the pinyin system. This includes some place-names for which other forms of romanization are still in common use, notably Beijing (Peking) and Guangzhou (Canton).

For Hong Kong, names of places are rendered according to prevailing local usage. Names of people follow, where possible, *Who's Who in Hong Kong* (1984 and 1988 editions).

Chinese-language publications are identified by an English title where one is in established use, for example, *People's Daily, New Evening Post*.

Translations from Chinese-language newspapers and magazines are, where not otherwise credited, taken from the BBC 'Summary of World Broadcasts' series.

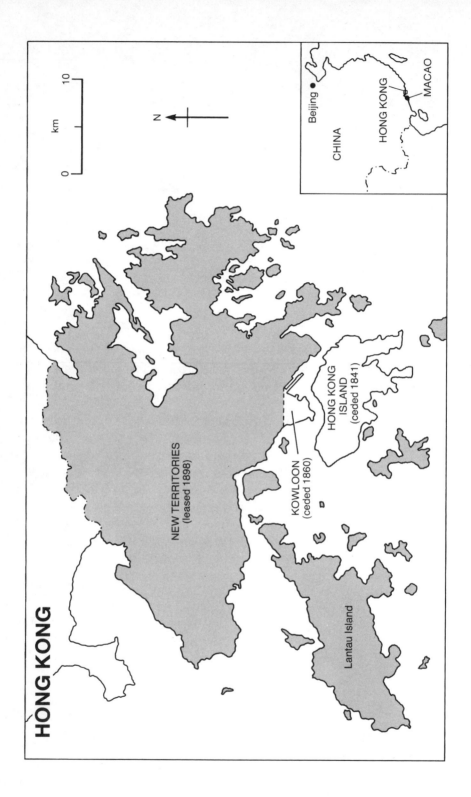

1

The Legacy
of History

ONE of the few vestiges of its nineteenth-century history which
Hong Kong has yet to dismantle or destroy is the Peak Tram,
the sleek funicular which climbs from a lower terminus –
really no more than a platform and a ticket office – on Garden Road,
by the Central Government Offices, to an upper terminus on Victoria
Peak, the crest of the range of hills spanning the width of Hong Kong
Island.

The tram was, like most things in Hong Kong, conceived as a speculation, in this instance by a syndicate of businessmen wishing to
increase the prospective traffic of customers to the hotel which they
planned for what is now the upper tram terminal, a thousand feet
above sea-level. Scottish engineers supervised the laying of a track so
uncompromising that it rose in its mid-section to a 1 in 2 gradient, up
which the cars have climbed daily since 1888, locked like lizards on to
the rock-face.

The upper terminus gives out on to Lugard Road, winding west-
ward round the Peak where the air is hill-station air, cool and quiet but
for the hum of traffic rising from the streets below. From here, at
nightfall, extends a view across Hong Kong harbour which no city
elsewhere in the world can match: a panorama within which the inter-
play of light and hills, shimmering water and tropical sky induces
something closer to hallucination than to common experience. If the
Devil had only possessed a spectacle of riches such as *these* with which

to tempt Christ from the mountain-top, then how different a course the universe might have taken.

A single sweep of the eye reveals the essential geography of the place: an island, ten miles wide, standing off the southern edge of a ragged peninsula to form a long sheltered harbour in the strait. One row of hills rises across the centre of Hong Kong Island; a second runs like a curtain along the northern edge of the peninsula, Kowloon, dividing Kowloon from its semi-rural hinterland, the 'New Territories', which sprawl northwards for another twenty miles to form a border with China along the Shenzhen River. It was the harbour which first brought the British to Hong Kong, and it is the harbour which still lies at Hong Kong's heart today, seven miles of deep sheltered water offering the finest haven between Singapore and Shanghai. Through this narrow conduit races the commerce of half a continent, spinning the city around it like a dynamo. Nothing stops, nothing sleeps, nothing yields. Every minute of every day is consumed with the jostle for space, for food and for money.

A hundred ships lie at anchor in the roads, unloading to lighters or waiting their turn to slip up the narrow inlet between west Kowloon and Tsing Yi Island to berth at the container port of Kwai Chung. Night and day the lights of Kwai Chung blaze out across the Rambler Channel, cranes swinging and truck engines roaring as containers are stacked and shunted and loaded and dumped and shuffled between ships and trailers and docks. This is not just Hong Kong but half China at work: computers, toys, clothes, books, clocks and whatever else goes into the billions of dollars of Gross National Product packed into steel boxes and funnelled down to the port for shipping off to the markets of Japan, Europe and the United States.

On either side of the harbour, the aspect is one of unrelieved and yet somehow exhilarating urbanism. In the very densest of the press, commanding the apex of the harbour on its island shore, the skyscrapers of the Central business district rise in a vitrified forest of pink granite and grey steel, hung with curtain walls of gold and silver and midnight blue. As befits a city which considers itself the financial capital of the Far East, the very tallest and newest and smartest buildings are those of the dominant banks, conceived with an ostentation worthy of the Medicis: the pinnacles and twisted flashing triangles of I.M. Pei's Bank of China, the brown ziggurat of the Standard Chartered Bank, the grey skeleton of Sir Norman Foster's Hongkong and

Shanghai Banking Corporation headquarters, its atrium the size of a cathedral nave. Lower and lumpier are the buildings of the grand old trading houses, Jardine Matheson and Swire pre-eminent among them, the renown of which owes as much now to history as it does to commerce. Hong Kong cherishes them in its folklore as Gibraltar does its Barbary apes;[1] but the swashbuckling taipans of old have long since given way to the hearty red-faced desk-men who would rather own a cargo ship than sail it.

Around the banks and towers of Central huddle the grubbier commercial districts of Wanchai and Causeway Bay, their streets by day a turmoil of markets and traffic jams and pavements solid with browsing crowds, by night an open jewel box of shimmering red and green and sapphire-blue neon signs crowding the skies with their invitations to buy, drink, dance, dine or dally. They vie for the tourist trade with the more up-market hotels and shopping arcades of Tsimshatsui, across the water on the southern tip of Kowloon, where the camera salesmen and restaurant waiters, car jockeys and food-hawkers treat their customers with that peculiar blend of efficiency and contempt which supplies so much of Hong Kong's not always very lovable personality. Beyond Tsimshatsui, a mile and another world away in the northern reaches of the Kowloon peninsula, the factories of Kwun Tong and Kowloon Bay spew their filth into the air and the harbour as yet another night-shift works its way through yet another ten thousand shirts or jerseys to be finished, dyed, packed and dumped into waiting lorries.

Go down among these streets, and the heat and bustle will make of them a zoo, a beehive, a bedlam; view them from the cool distance of the Peak, and they are a perpetual wide-screen ballet of movement and colour, an un-still life achieving an almost allegorical completeness. Even the heavens frame a choreographed display of jumbo jets queuing and circling to land at Kai Tak airport in the armpit of Kowloon. Slashed open along the axis of its harbour, Hong Kong reveals itself as a furious cross-section of the human condition in one of its more strenuous manifestations, a place where the totality of twentieth-century city life could be caught in a single time-stopped moment.

It is surely, in its way, an Atlantis for our time, this city which has come bursting out of the ocean to plant its sprawl of glittering skyscrapers across the wild hills and shores of southern China. With its gaudy colours and its sharp edges and its ceaseless clatter, Hong Kong is itself the ultimate Made-in-Hong-Kong object, the emanation of its own spontaneous ingenuity. A century and a half ago, there was little more to distinguish this place than a few clusters of huts, a waterfall, a shipyard and a trade in sandalwood. Today, there is a magical and extravagant city-state of six million people, seemingly at the peak of its history. A century and a half, even a decade and a half hence – who can say? The beauty of Hong Kong lies in its plasticity, its fertility, its capacity to invent and reinvent itself a dozen times within a single generation. Tomorrow, there might be anything here, or nothing.

It is a Chinese city, but like no other city that has ever existed on China's shores. It is a British colony, but one where Britishness is more often than not a decorative veneer, a trick of the light, a polite fiction. For Hong Kong was created not by Britain and China, but by Britons liberated from the obligations of Britain and by Chinese liberated from the obligations of China. Its population has been self-selected from successive waves of migrants and refugees impelled by ambition or desperation. Here, they have been free to make of themselves what they would. It is not only the city which reinvents itself, but also its people.

Amid this transience and urgency, such of a past as Hong Kong possesses holds no mystique. It is certainly not a commodity to be mentioned in the same breath as the present, still less to be weighed against the future. Most of the buildings in Hong Kong are less than thirty years old; but then so, too, are most of the people. The 1960s and 1970s, the formative years of the modern city, were decades during which the young devoured the old and Father Time arrived not with a scythe but with a wrecker's ball. Hong Kong seemed determined to slough off its own small endowment of history as a snake leaves behind its skin.

But history, for all Hong Kong's efforts, was only effaced, not escaped. Its people were hostages to the past, more so than those of cities with a hundred times Hong Kong's antiquity – for this was, to adapt Han Suyin's (and, later, Richard Hughes's) phrase, 'a borrowed place, living on borrowed time'. It was a colony which had survived longer than most into the post-colonial era; and it was territory which China had repeatedly claimed as Chinese, and which it had declared its intention of resuming when the time was 'ripe'. It lived as it did only on China's tolerance.

4

There was, moreover, a factor which promised to turn Hong Kong's uncertainty about its future from a chronic into an acute condition: the composition of Britain's titles of possession. Though Britain had forced China's nineteenth-century Qing rulers to sign separate treaties ceding Hong Kong Island and the Kowloon peninsula in perpetuity, the New Territories had been transferred on a 99-year lease running from 1 July 1898. As the 1970s gave way to the 1980s, the mathematics of that lease began to grow uncomfortably precise. Unless the New Territories lease could be extended, or some alternative formula found, that part of Hong Kong would fall once again under China's undisputed sovereignty on 1 July 1997. And, since China denied the legal validity of all three treaties by which Britain had acquired Hong Kong, leased and ceded portions alike, and since Britain was now a relatively small, weak and distant power, incapable of defending Hong Kong militarily or sustaining it through a blockade, China might very well decide that 1997, when it would in practice be obliged by Britain to address the issue of the New Territories, would also be the point at which it demanded the return of the rest of Hong Kong to which it in theory laid equal claim.

Despite the knowledge that the uncertainty of 1997 would have to be resolved in some way, sooner or later, it was in Hong Kong's nature to repress the question as long as possible; and, if confronted with it, to dispute it, to deny its complexion, to assert instinctively that China would agree to be bargained down from its entitlement. The characteristic Hong Kong view, at least among the bankers and businessmen who saw things primarily in financial terms, was that China should not, would not, could not afford to take Hong Kong back and so lose its services as an entrepôt for capitalism. A deal would be done and face would be saved.

And, in a way, they were right. A deal *was* done. Face *was* saved. But it was very far from being the sort of formula which Hong Kong's conventional wisdom had been expecting, and the face which was saved was that of Britain as much as that of China. Formal negotiations between Britain and China began, at Britain's request, in September 1982, and ended exactly two years later. They yielded a treaty which bound Britain to withdraw its government from the whole of Hong Kong on 30 June 1997, and which provided for China to resume exercise of sovereign and administrative power over Hong Kong from 1 July. China promised to grant a 'high degree of autonomy' to the local government in Hong Kong, to declare Hong Kong a 'special administrative region', and to leave its social, legal and economic systems substantially unchanged for at least fifty years.

The agreement of 1984, known as the Joint Declaration, was widely praised as a remarkable diplomatic achievement, the product of great pragmatism on both sides. But it did not and could not override China's sovereign rights. For all Britain's and China's declared intent that Hong Kong should preserve both its prosperity and its freedoms after 1997, China, as poor and as totalitarian as Hong Kong was rich and free, would when that time came be able to treat Hong Kong exactly as it wished. Now, almost a decade later, as the 1997 transition draws closer, the uncertainty of its aftermath fills even the most prosaic aspects of Hong Kong with a fugitive, even a romantic, excitement: the uncertainty as to whether, in the next century, the city will glitter still more brightly out into the Chinese night, or whether the skyscrapers of today are the high-water mark of an existence from which, once touched, Hong Kong will slip slowly back into the ocean from which it sprang. It is impossible to imagine a gulf of this magnitude opening before any other city of comparable importance to the world – Paris, say, or Los Angeles. Yet, in the Hong Kong of 1993, it is happening.

THE STRONG LINES of Hong Kong's topography, the theatre-scenery of the natural setting, make it relatively easy to airbrush away in the mind's eye the cityscape of the late nineteenth and twentieth centuries and to imagine the harbour and island as they must have appeared to the British merchants who first coveted Hong Kong in the 1830s, perceiving that the acquisition of a piece of defensible territory would greatly improve the comfort and security in which they might pursue their business interests on the China coast. Since the closure of China's ports to overseas trade in the mid-eighteenth century, their position had been tenuous. The imperial Chinese government had authorized foreign merchants to do business only at Guangzhou, and only during the winter months, where they were confined to foreigners' compounds and required to deal solely with an official import monopoly known as the Co-hong. The summers they would spend eighty miles down the Pearl River at Macao, which had been governed by the Portuguese since the mid-sixteenth century.

The legal trade in furs, cottons and woollens from the West and teas and silks from China brought the foreigners a dull if steady income. But it was the smuggling of opium, brought from Bengal and sold for silver, which made them rich. They were not in principle concerned by the illegality of the trade in Chinese eyes; indeed, they had no particular desire to see the drug legalized at all in China,[2] since they had invested heavily in the corrupting of officials along a thousand miles of coastline to establish their own distribution channels, and legalization would simply have brought competition, taxation and regulation in its wake. Illegality, nonetheless, exposed them – and, more particularly, their stocks – to occasional retributive action by provoked or zealous mandarins.

The ideal solution, the merchants saw, would be to possess a permanent base on the China coast under the protection of the British flag, where their own interests would be pre-eminent and where opium would be tolerated. Their newspaper, the *Canton Register*, proclaimed this manifesto in April 1836:

If the lion's paw is to be put down on any part of the south side of China, let it be Hong Kong: let the lion declare it to be under his guarantee a free port, and in ten years it will be the most considerable mart east of the Cape. The Portuguese made a mistake: they adopted shallow water and exclusive rules. Hong Kong, deep water and a free port forever!

It was, ironically, the most determined of Chinese attempts to suppress the opium trade which finally delivered Hong Kong into the merchants' hands – a sequence of events which began in March 1839 when an Imperial Commissioner, Lin Zexu,[3] blockaded the foreigners in their compounds at Guangzhou and demanded that they surrender their opium stocks for destruction. After an interlude of defiance, some 1,400 tons of opium were duly surrendered, the blockade was lifted, and the merchants retreated to Macao. But fearing a fresh blockade or an attack by Lin, the British left Macao by sea to regroup across the Pearl River estuary in Hong Kong harbour under the protection of two Royal Navy frigates, which skirmished with Chinese war-junks.[4]

By February 1840, rumours of confrontation on the China coast were rustling through the British Parliament. The Foreign Secretary, Lord Palmerston, decided on a belligerent response, vigorously encouraged by the richest of the Hong Kong opium-smugglers, William Jardine, a partner in the firm of Jardine Matheson and Company, who had recently retired from the China coast to London. Palmerston and Jardine saw the chance not only to avenge a Chinese 'insult', but also to achieve the general re-opening of Chinese ports to British trade by force. On 21 February the Foreign Secretary sent an order to India that an expeditionary force be prepared for China, intending that his chosen course should be as close as possible to a *fait accompli* by the time he revealed it to Parliament.

Three times during March, Palmerston deflected Opposition demands for a statement on China. Finally, on 7 April, Sir Robert Peel's Tories secured their debate by moving a vote of censure against the government's competence in foreign policy. The fiercest critic of Palmerston – and of the opium trade – was the young William Gladstone, who declared that the Chinese had 'the right to drive us from their coasts on account of our obstinacy in persisting in this infamous and atrocious traffic'. He did not, he said, know of 'a war more unjust in its origin, a war more calculated in its progress to cover this country with permanent disgrace', than that which Palmerston proposed.

But the Foreign Secretary was impassive. Opium, he said, was China's problem. If China wanted to halt the trade, so be it; but it should not expect Britain's help. 'I wonder what the House would have said to me', he taunted, 'if I had come down to it with a large naval estimate for a number of revenue cruisers to be employed in . . . preserving the morals of the Chinese people, who were disposed to buy what other people were disposed to sell them.' His concern was with free trade, and with British interests. He had been told by British traders that 'unless measures of the government are followed up with firmness and energy, the trade with China can no longer be conducted with security to life and property or with credit and advantage to the British nation'. The censure motion was defeated by nine votes. 'Firmness and energy' became the order of the day, and Palmerston's fleet duly sailed.

When the British expeditionary force, led by sixteen warships and carrying four thousand troops, arrived off the China coast in June 1840, it brought letters to Emperor Daoguang demanding an apology for the treatment of the merchants at Guangzhou, compensation for their opium and the opening of China's five principal coastal ports to

foreign trade; failing which, the soldiers were to seize and hold territory along the China coast until such time as the Emperor yielded.
Overwhelming China's coastal defences as they went, the British
sailed north as far as Tianjin, seizing the island of Zhoushan. The
Emperor dispatched a malleable mandarin, Qishan, Governor of
Qili,[5] to negotiate with the invaders and, as a first step, to dissuade
them from advancing any further towards Beijing. This Qishan suc-
ceeded in doing, by promising the commander of the force, Admiral
George Elliot, that all British demands would be satisfied through
negotiations at Guangzhou. As his reward for deflecting the enemy,
Qishan was promoted to Imperial Commissioner and sent to
Guangzhou to make good the settlement which he had promised.

Admiral George Elliot fell ill, and the job of negotiating devolved
upon his cousin, Captain Charles Elliot, the British government's
Superintendent of China Trade, who concluded an agreement with
Qishan which had very little in common with the terms of Palmerston's
letter to the Emperor. The Convention of Chuanbi, named after the
village near Guangzhou where it was signed on 20 January 1841,
ignored the more general opening of China's ports to trade, but promised a cession of Hong Kong to the British Crown, an indemnity of
six million dollars[6] by annual instalments of one million, and a
resumption of trade at Guangzhou.

The compromise was not what either Palmerston or the Emperor
had had in mind, the Emperor having rather assumed that Qishan was
seducing the barbarians back to Guangzhou in order to attack them
there and inflict the signal defeat which the Emperor had been given to
expect was in his power. Elliot and Qishan were rudely dismissed by
their respective governments, both of which repudiated the Convention of Chuanbi. But these were still the days in which dispatches
travelled by ship; and in the seven months which were needed for
Elliot to report his achievement to London, and for Palmerston's note
of dismissal to arrive in reply,[7] a British flag had been planted on
Hong Kong Island and a new British settlement was quickly sinking its
roots.

James Matheson, the business partner of William Jardine, began
building his first warehouse on the north shore of Hong Kong Island
in February 1841, within a month of the seizure. In June, Charles
Elliot conducted his first land sale. By November, a main road,
Queen's Road, was well advanced along the harbour front. In

December, Elliot's newly arrived successor as British Plenipotentiary and Superintendent of Trade, Sir George Pottinger, took the view that Hong Kong had 'already advanced too far to admit of its ever being restored to the Emperor'.

Thus, when a second British expeditionary force, this time under Pottinger's command, succeeded in imposing a second treaty on the Emperor more in line with Palmerston's wishes,[8] Pottinger elected to insert into the new treaty a clause securing Hong Kong's cession for a second time – 'The only point', he later wrote, 'on which I intentionally exceeded my . . . instructions, but every single hour I passed in this superb country convinced me of the necessity and desirability of possessing such a settlement'. Forgiven, unlike Elliot, his excess of enthusiasm, Pottinger was named a Knight Commander of the Order of the Bath and Hong Kong's first governor.

The priorities of the new colony were quickly established: the Hong Kong Club opened in 1846, a year before the laying of the foundation-stone of St John's Cathedral. The population of the island, estimated at 5,000 to 7,000 before Britain's seizure, rose tenfold in the following fifteen years. The colonists had barely tamed the foreshore when they began thinking about the prospects for expansion. Their goal was the peninsula of Kowloon, the southern tip of the Chinese mainland half a mile away across the harbour, possession of which would perfect the security of their shipping.

The opportunity to pursue that goal came in 1858, when yet another British expeditionary force, this time under Lord Elgin, arrived to launch a second 'Opium War' against China – the ostensible *casus belli* being a dispute over China's right to search a ship flying a British flag in a Chinese port, compounded by a wrangle over the right of foreign ambassadors to reside in Beijing, a concatenation which provoked Karl Marx, writing from London for the *New York Daily Tribune*, to wonder whether 'the civilized nations of the world will approve this mode of invading a peaceful country, without previous declaration of war, for an alleged infringement of the fanciful code of diplomatic etiquette'.

One of the Allied Commissioners then based in Guangzhou, Harry Parkes, arranged to lease the Kowloon peninsula as a temporary encampment for Elgin's soldiers. The army, having once possessed the place, showed its customary reluctance to relinquish it, and the temporary lease was converted into a lease 'in perpetuity' in March

1860. Then, when Elgin had concluded his hostilities in October by entering Beijing, burning the Emperor's Summer Palace and securing the imperial assent to yet another treaty, the Convention of Beijing, the terms of that document were fixed to include the conversion of the lease over Kowloon into an outright cession to the British Crown, 'with a view to the maintenance of law and order in and about the harbour of Hong Kong'.

Britain claimed the peninsula on 19 January 1861. Chinese officials – probably acting on behalf of the Imperial Customs – marked the separation by erecting a bamboo fence eight feet high along the width of the new frontier. The ceded territory of Hong Kong was now complete. It might, by the prevailing standards of British colonial grandeur, have been a very modest possession. It was certainly too distant, too small and too hot for comfort. But in strategic terms, it was a declaration of intent: 'a notch cut in China', remarked a contemporary commentator, 'as a woodsman notches a tree, to mark it for felling at a convenient opportunity'.

Yet, though the tree tottered, it was not allowed to fall. For the rest of the nineteenth century, Britain and a succession of other foreign powers hacked ever deeper into China's sovereignty, but left a residue of power with the Manchu court. Extraterritoriality placed foreign nationals out of reach of China's judges; foreign bureaucrats, under the eventual command of Sir Robert Hart,[9] created the Imperial Maritime Customs, assuring the revenues with which the Chinese court might at some date in the infinite future hope to make good its war reparations; foreign soldiers, led by Frederick Townsend Ward and Charles Gordon, helped defend Shanghai from the Taiping rebels; and a foreign diplomat, Anson Burlingame of the United States, was even hired by China as its own roving ambassador in 1868, following advice from Sir Robert Hart that this was the way to win friends in the West.

Under the volatile and malevolent Dowager Empress Cixi, the imperial court sank ever further into its mephitic twilight. Japan, having inflicted a crushing military defeat on China in the war of 1894–5, secured the cession of Taiwan and lodged another huge indemnity claim against the Beijing government. It withdrew a demand for southern Manchuria only because Russia, Germany and France sprang jointly to China's defence. But these three 'friendly' powers then promptly claimed concessions of their own from China as

11

the price of their support. 'The European governments', observed Lenin, 'have begun to rob China as ghouls rob corpses'.[10] In the scramble for concessions from November 1897 to May 1898, Germany, Russia and Britain seized harbours on the North China coast, France on the South China coast.[11]

One last bite remained to be taken. France was demanding not merely possession of Guangzhou Bay, but also an undertaking from China that no further territory in the most southerly provinces would be ceded to other powers. Britain, which had been ruminating for almost a decade on an extension to Hong Kong, decided to act while the way ahead was still clear. On 2 April 1898, the British minister in Beijing, Sir Claude MacDonald, informed the Chinese foreign ministry, known as the Zongli Yamen, that Hong Kong wished to extend its boundaries 'for defensive purposes'. The acquisition of the New Territories, a small enough matter by the standards of the time, was thus put in train.

MacDonald, a soldier by profession and an Africa veteran, was considered no great ornament to Beijing by the foreigners of longer residence. G.E. Morrison, *The Times*'s correspondent, called him 'the type of military officer rolled out a mile at a time and then lopped off in six foot lengths'. Sir Robert Hart wrote that 'MacDonald's appointment will be interesting to watch. Those of us who have succeeded so badly by treating Chinese as educated and civilized ought now to be ready to yield to a man versed in negro methods and ignorant of the East.'[12]

Having been told to secure an extension to Hong Kong, MacDonald briskly set about it. The fact that at the outset he lacked even a map of the proposed cession did not seem to bother him – one eventually arrived on 13 April, more than a week after he had opened talks with the Zongli Yamen – nor did the absence of any very clear reason of which he was aware for presenting the demand. He had been supplied with a four-year-old memorandum from Hong Kong explaining why the extension was wanted, but had found it useless. 'These documents', he wrote in a dispatch to London,

contained sundry arguments in favour of an extension of Hong Kong territory, such as the necessity for a new rifle range, exercise ground for the troops, the inadequacy of cemetery accommodation at Hong Kong and the like. But in view of the fact that as far as I can estimate, the area demanded would amount to some 200 square miles, I did not think it desirable to put forward that consideration in presenting the case.[13]

In one important respect only did MacDonald depart from his initial instructions. He had been told to obtain a cession of what came to be called the New Territories; he emerged with a lease, following the precedent set by Germany which, when taking Jiaozhou Bay in Shandong, had done so on a 99-year lease, and which had since been followed by France at Guangzhou Bay, by Russia's taking of a 25-year lease over Port Arthur and by Britain's taking of a lease over Weihaiwei 'for so long as Russia occupies Port Arthur'.

MacDonald sympathized with the argument put to him at the Zongli Yamen, that for Britain to press for an outright cession of the New Territories would be to risk provoking France, Germany and Russia into demanding the conversion of their own leases into cessions. MacDonald suggested that Britain take a lease with a view to converting it into a cession at a more propitious time.

MacDonald later gave the Foreign Office this account of his negotiation with the Zongli Yamen:

The question of the nature of our title to the extension of the territory was more troublesome. I tried to obtain an absolute cession, but could not resist the force of argument that all other nations who have obtained leases of territory would follow suit, which might be inconvenient for ourselves. The principle of a lease having been admitted, a term of 99 years seemed sufficient.[14]

The Foreign Office in London agreed. 'If the Chinese object strongly to a lease only determinable by mutual agreement,' instructed Arthur Balfour, in a telegram dated 30 April 1898, 'we would take a 99-year lease as in the case of Kiaochow [Jiaozhou].'[15]

Though he had no legal training, MacDonald drafted the lease himself. It made no mention of rent and gave no precise delineation of the territory to which it referred. On 9 June, the 'Convention Respecting an Extension of the Hong Kong Territory' was signed at the Zongli Yamen by MacDonald for the British government and by Li Hongzhang, the doyen of China's diplomats, on behalf of the Emperor. The acquisition was met with general applause in Hong

Kong, where the military establishment looked forward to firing ranges and naval exercises, the civilians to vastly improved opportunities for hunting and golf. 'Another wedge of civilization driven into Kwangtung [Guangdong]', declared the *Hong Kong Weekly Press*.

The temporary nature of the possession was scarcely even remarked upon, save by the law officers in London and Hong Kong whose job it was to turn MacDonald's loosely phrased assertions into good statutory form. Their initial concern was with finding a means by which Britain, though it had leased the New Territories from China for a term of 99 years, could properly administer it as a integral part of Hong Kong, the balance of which had been ceded in perpetuity. The Colonial Office did not, after all, have it in mind to give the New Territories *back* to China; it had merely been prevailed upon to accept the form of a leasehold for foreign-policy reasons.

The means adopted to fix the basis for British rule over the leased area was that of an Order in Council, a declaration made in the name of the British Crown which recorded for the purposes of British law what the British government considered to be its rights over the New Territories. China's view of the Convention, and of Britain's rights, was not relevant to the exercise.

The Order in Council, dated 20 October 1898, stated that the territories leased from China, 'within the limits and for the term described' in the Convention, would form 'part and parcel of Her Majesty's Colony of Hong Kong in like manner and for all intents and purposes as if they had originally formed part of the said Colony'. (A second Order in Council, issued on 27 December 1899, removed a provision in the first Order which had reserved to China jurisdiction over the cluster of buildings making up the so-called 'Walled City of Kowloon'.)

By virtue of the Orders in Council, the New Territories acquired the *ad hoc* legal status of, as it were, a temporary cession. The Hong Kong government was able to draft its own land law for the New Territories, declaring the land there 'to be the property of the Crown during the term specified in the Convention of the 9th day of June 1898'. The convenience of this formulation was that it allowed the British, when they issued sub-leases to owners and purchasers of land in the New Territories, to issue these sub-leases in the name of the Crown, rather than of the Chinese Emperor, who remained the sovereign as far as

China was concerned;[16] it also enabled them to proceed with their own local land reform, establishing title among the 100,000 villagers whom they had acquired along with the land.

The relatively large number of New Territories villagers posed a second and more substantial problem. They had not been consulted in advance about their incorporation into Hong Kong, and they were much less enthusiastic than Hong Kong about the union. Their resistance was violent, organized and supported by Chinese irregular troops. On 17 April 1899, a British army force confronted a mob several thousand strong in what came to be known as the Battle of Tai Po and dispersed it with casualties on both sides. A relative calm returned, during which James Haldane Stewart Lockhart, the Colonial Secretary, was able to travel through the countryside addressing village groups, confiscating arms and removing fortifications.

Evidently, not all the villagers were admirers of the British Crown. But on the question as to whether they were, nonetheless, British subjects, and as to whether they had ceased to be Chinese subjects by virtue of living on land which had been 'temporarily ceded' to Britain, the 1898 Convention of Beijing was silent. MacDonald had neglected to address the topic when drafting it, and the Foreign Office had neglected to ask him to do so. In 1899, when a New Territories resident asked the Hong Kong government to certify him as a British subject so that he could enter British Columbia without paying a tax demanded from Chinese nationals,[17] the Colonial Office's legal advisers reported that the New Territories villagers were indeed British subjects, as would be anyone else born in the New Territories during the balance of the lease.

'To hold that the very day after the cession', ruminated Sir W.E. Davidson, legal adviser to the Foreign Office, in 1905, 'every Chinaman [in the New Territories] without any choice, or knowledge even on his part of the antecedent circumstances, became a British subject, seems to me unreasonable and unusual, although it may in strict law be technically arguable and defensible.'[18] But there the matter would have to rest. The New Territories were British, at least in British law; their inhabitants were British, or so the Colonial Office said; and so it was deemed to be for the next 99 years, a period so far exceeding the purview of any one generation of civil servants that it approximated to permanence for all practical and official purposes.

BY THE TIME that Margaret Thatcher, the British Prime Minister, came to raise the question of Hong Kong's future with Deng Xiaoping, China's *de facto* leader, in Beijing in September 1982, the history of Hong Kong's colonization claimed little if any place in the British national consciousness. Even in relatively specialized works on the history of the British Empire, it commanded only a few paragraphs. The acquisition had not, by the British reckoning, been any great matter for glory or for shame. There had been no stirring military victory; rather, the affair had been a prosaic adventure of essentially commercial interest, and the object of it at first thought so poor a catch – a 'barren island', in Palmerston's famous phrase – that the British tended to view 1841 as being a sort of Year Zero before which Hong Kong might as well not have existed at all.

Thus, far from having the notion that they had deprived the Emperor of China of a valuable possession, Britons of the Palmerstonian caste had seen themselves in the 1840s as generously, even altruistically showering upon China the priceless gifts of free trade and Christianity, resistance to which on the part of the Chinese could only be explained by a centuries-deep incrustation of ignorance and incompetence; a viewpoint which had, by the 1980s, altered more in the details than in the underlying logic. China was still seen to be profiting from a Western presence in Hong Kong, but with Christianity losing its place in the pecking-order of largesse to be replaced by technology, management skills and foreign exchange. In British eyes, Hong Kong, one of the 'miracle' economies of Asia, was working wonderfully well *for China* under British management, and that was the basis on which to begin talking about Hong Kong's future; it would be only logical for China, as the substantial, even the principal, beneficiary of a British-run Hong Kong, to demonstrate an appropriate complicity in maintaining the existing arrangements into the indefinite future. This was something of a self-serving perspective, but it was not a duplicitous one, for the British really did believe that they had in Hong Kong produced something both valuable and unique, one of the very rare acts of colonialism for which, even in the post-colonial era, no apology need be either sought or offered. They were, in consequence, somewhat taken aback by the response which they received from China.

For if Britain had reduced Hong Kong's past to a more or less picturesque matter, to China the colonization of Hong Kong was still very much live and unfinished business. In the Chinese perspective, shaped not only by an opposing nationalism but also by the dicta of Marxism, the arrival of the British imperialists in 1840 and the humbling of the Qing emperors had been the determining events with which the slow, painful birth of modern China had begun, the events which compelled China's emergence from the age of feudalism through a confrontation with the power of the industrialized world. Hong Kong was a great city, yes; but it was also the enduring symbol of an era of anger and shame, emotions which still burned fiercely a century and more later. It was, in the rhetoric of the time, a 'blood-debt' which had still to be liquidated.

The Communist analysis of the Opium Wars was rooted in Karl Marx's own contemporary comments. As a journalist in London, he had followed Britain's adventurism with a keen interest, arriving at the view that:

> The English cannons in 1840 . . . broke down the authority of the Emperor, and forced the Celestial Empire into contact with the terrestrial world. Complete isolation was the prime condition of the preservation of old China. That isolation having come to a violent end by the medium of England, dissolution must follow as surely as that of any mummy carefully preserved in a hermetically sealed coffin, whenever it is brought into contact with the open air.[19]

In 1939, Mao Zedong listed the Opium Wars as the first of the twelve 'historical landmarks' of the 'struggle by the Chinese people against imperialism and its lackeys'.[20]

A modern history of the period, *Imperialism and Chinese Politics*, written by a leading Communist Party academic, Hu Sheng, illustrates how Marx's analysis was developed to identify the foreign powers as the objective allies of the Qing court, united in their oppression of the Chinese people:

> Many writers on the modern history of China have, consciously or unconsciously, presented events in the wrong light. They describe the imperialists' policy of aggression against China in such simple terms as to make it appear that the Qing government was little less than a wretched victim, continually at the mercy of,

and humiliated by, the imperialist powers. This description con-
tradicts historical facts . . .

At the beginning of the [First Opium] war, the foreign aggressors had regarded the Qing government as an obstacle to their
having a free hand in China. The outcome of the war convinced
them, however, that it was vulnerable to the threat of force and
could be coerced into submission . . . This new situation took
clear shape in the events that occurred in the twenty years after
the Opium War and indeed these twenty years may be taken as a
distinct period in the history of China. When the period ended
. . . the foreign aggressors were working hand in glove with the
feudal rulers in applying force against the Chinese people.[21]

Thus, if Britain had seen itself, and to an extent still saw itself, as
China's benefactor, China saw Britain, together with other foreign
powers, as 'aggressors' dedicated to the subjugation and plunder of
the Chinese people, 'hand in glove' with the decadent Qing. Chinese
accounts of the Opium Wars also dwelt, unsurprisingly, on the bloodi-
ness of the British conquest and on allegations of gratuitous brutality
which received little weight in accounts written from British sources.
Hu Sheng remarks, for example, that 'the British forces, when they
landed on Chinese soil, massacred and looted in the usual fashion of
colonial wars'.[22] 'The Opium War', a pamphlet in the *History of
Modern China* series, published in Shanghai for general and educational use within China, depicts a relentless campaign of murder and
looting, of which this paragraph is representative:

The British took Tinghai on July 5th [1840]. The pirates began
plundering the city as soon as they landed. According to an eyewitness account by an invading officer, when the troops landed
and the Union Jack was unfurled, a horrifying scene of pillage
and rapine followed. The men forced their way into every house
and ransacked every drawer and chest, and the streets were
strewn with books, paintings, furniture . . . The plundering only
stopped when everything of value was gone.[23]

Such were the echoes which China heard when Britain spoke of
Hong Kong.

Small wonder, then, that when the time came for Britain formally to raise the future of its colony, it found that China took a slightly more equivocal view of Hong Kong's *raison d'être* than did Britain itself. And still smaller wonder that Thatcher reaped a whirlwind of condemnation from China when, after meeting Deng Xiaoping in September 1982, she publicly asserted the validity of the treaties establishing Hong Kong, and spoke warmly about the course of nineteenth-century Sino-British relations. The Hong Kong Communist newspaper *Wen Wei Po* accused her of:

> indulging in dreams about the British Empire of the past when she spoke impudently about the 'friendship' shown by Queen Victoria to China a hundred years ago, the prosperity which the British brought to Hong Kong in the nineteenth century and the 'legitimacy' of unequal treaties which 'should be observed' . . . The fatuous rulers [of imperial China] have all become historic criminals. Chinese people have already stood up for a long time. They will never tolerate imperialists who attempt to bully them . . . Repeated mention of the unequal treaties is tantamount to a violation of Chinese territories and sovereignty and an insult to the national dignity of the Chinese people.[24]

In his own mind, Deng Xiaoping could have had no real choice about Hong Kong, and he was visibly shocked to discover that Thatcher could have conceived otherwise. Hong Kong belonged to China, he told her. It had always done so. He could not and would not surrender it a second time, and so be reviled by succeeding generations as his own generation reviled Li Hongzhang for signing the New Territories lease in 1898. China would certainly be resuming the whole of Hong Kong, said Deng. The only real question was whether that resumption would take place with or without Britain's co-operation.

2

The Limits
of Possession

THE idea that 1997 was, after all, not really such a very long time away seems first to have troubled the Hong Kong government in the mid-1920s. It fell to Sir Cecil Clementi, who arrived as Governor in 1925, to raise with London for the first time what would simply become known as 'the lease question', the Damocletian sword which Hong Kong was slowly raising its head to discern.

Clementi was a graceful, clever man, a former Colonial Secretary of Ceylon whom Rabindranath Tagore described after lunching at Government House as 'one of the most cultivated Europeans I have ever met in the Orient'. He was also one of the most aggressive, on paper at least, in advocating the entrenchment of Britain's position in the New Territories, provoking a Foreign Office minute that the lease question should be kept constantly in view, for fear that problems might be created around it 'not only by the Chinese, but by Governors like Sir C. Clementi'.[1]

The basic questions which Clementi raised in the 1920s were essentially those which would still be confronting the British and Hong Kong governments fifty years later. Could Britain's tenure of the New Territories be extended? Was there a way in which the Hong Kong government could sell sub-leases over New Territories land which did not, as did all such sub-leases which it had so far issued, end three days before the fatal date of 30 June 1997? And, if not, could other means be found to maintain the long-term confidence of investors?

It is probable that Clementi's interventions marked the last point at which Britain might plausibly have sought to secure permanent title to the New Territories by the crude use of military action or diplomatic pressure to compel China to convert the lease into a cession – as was, in fact, Clementi's objective. Alternatively, and less traumatically, with the New Territories still largely untouched by the British, the physical development of the colony might still at that date have been truncated in such a way as to provide for the ceded areas of Hong Kong Island and Kowloon to survive the New Territories' eventual reversion to China.

Instead, it fell to the Foreign Office to decide that a cession should not be engineered, and to the Colonial Office to advise Clementi that development of the New Territories should nonetheless proceed. The officials concerned fully appreciated that a serious potential problem existed in respect of the New Territories, and that they were merely deferring its resolution to a succeeding generation. But, as a Colonial Office assistant under-secretary, Sir Gilbert Grindle, noted in the 1928 Hong Kong file: 'It is difficult to be quite so sure what the position will be in Hong Kong 69 years hence.'

Clementi had made his initial proposals regarding the New Territories in a letter to the Colonial Secretary, Leo Amery, in January 1927, following a wave of Nationalist-led strikes and boycotts against the British throughout China in 1925–6 which had paralysed Hong Kong. Expressing his concern for Hong Kong's security, Clementi wrote that it would be 'fatal to this colony' if the New Territories were ever to be handed back to China. He proposed two possible courses of action.[2]

Clementi's first proposal was that Britain demand that China cede the New Territories in perpetuity as a retrospective quid pro quo for having agreed at the Washington Conference of 1921–2 to withdraw from Weihaiwei.[3]

His second and somewhat disingenuous plan was that Britain should profit from any further anti-British manifestations in southern China, following those triggered by the May 30th incident in Shanghai in 1925, when British police shot dead at least nine demonstrators. At Guangzhou, where more Chinese protesters were shot by British and French soldiers in June 1925, the Nationalists' provisional government had organized a crippling strike and boycott against Hong Kong from July 1925 to October 1926. If Britain found it 'necessary' to take any 'war-like action' to protect its own interests in southern China,

Clementi wrote to the Colonial Office, then it should make the cession of the New Territories a 'condition of the resumption of friendly relations' with China.

Amery replied cautiously:

> It would be exceedingly dangerous to call attention to the lease, in view of the strength which the present movement for the restoration of Chinese sovereign rights has attained . . . To show the Chinese we are nervous about the New Territories when it is clearly for us to assume that the lease will run its normal course would be to expose a weakness which they would not be slow to exploit and which might well lead to a campaign for the rendition not only of the leased area but even of the colony itself.[4]

In the course of a leave taken in London that summer, Clementi developed his argument, telling the Colonial Office that, quite apart from the defence of Hong Kong, the New Territories lease was starting to raise questions of public spending and town planning. Was it sensible for the government to invest in the development of those parts of Hong Kong which could eventually be returned to China, rather than those parts which would remain permanently British, or to put Hong Kong's aerodrome and reservoirs on land which it might later lose? And yet how, without expansion into the New Territories, could Hong Kong ever hope to relieve its increasingly congested urban areas? Already, he asserted, the uncertainties associated with 1997 were sufficient to influence the considerations of private investors. So if Britain did intend to hold on to the whole of the colony after 1997, as he believed it must, then the Hong Kong government should show its determination and reassure investors by selling New Territories land leases running beyond that date.[5]

The issue of land leases, however esoteric, was – as Clementi foresaw – at the heart of the matter for any investor. With the exception of a freehold site granted almost by accident for the Cathedral of St John on Garden Road, and a few outright sales which were later reversed, all land in Hong Kong had been sold by the government on leasehold terms since 1841. The first leases were for 999-year terms. Then, as the government recognized the potential for future income from reversion, most sites came to be offered on 99-year terms. In the New Territories, the standard lease was for 75 years, with the option to renew for a further 24 years less 3 days, but with all tenure deemed to date from 1 July 1898. The effect of this formula was that all New Territories leases issued by Britain would expire three days before the expiry of the head lease granted by China to Britain under the terms of the 1898 Convention of Beijing. This was the limit which Clementi now felt posed too much of a constraint on Hong Kong's development, and through which he wanted to break, if necessary by defying the terms of the treaty.

Invited to comment on Clementi's desire to offer land leases to investors in the New Territories extending beyond Britain's own head lease, Sir John Risley, legal adviser to the Colonial Office, wrote:

> It is impossible to grant leases on such terms as will at the same time lead –
> i.   China to infer that we mean to give up the [New] Territories in accordance with the agreement of 1898; and
> ii. The lessees to infer that we shall retain them . . .
> If the most important thing is to avoid offending Chinese susceptibilities, I would issue leases for the unexpired period; if to avoid discouraging intending lessees, I would [issue] 75-year leases and leave HMG to protect or compensate the lessees when the Territories are given up.[6]

A further attempt to resolve the land-lease question was made in November 1928, when Clementi was once again in London, and a one-day conference on Hong Kong was arranged jointly with the Foreign Office. Clementi argued, according to a Colonial Office minute, 'That the lease [of the New Territories] from Government to Government was not merely a land lease, but a lease of all sovereign rights. This would include the right to dispose of land and allot leases well beyond the term of the head lease.'[7] The Foreign Office, worried more about Britain's international relations than about Hong Kong's attractions to property developers, opposed the idea for precisely the reason that Clementi advanced it. It would create, said Sir Victor Wellesley, Foreign Office deputy under-secretary of state, 'the danger of encouraging Hong Kong to think that we were going to keep the New Territories for ever'.

Yet that was just what the Colonial Office did think. And, though Amery allowed the Foreign Office to rein in Clementi, his officials agreed with the Governor's basic stand that the New Territories were not to be surrendered. It was simply that they, unlike Clementi, thought that advertising such a view would create more problems than it solved. An unsigned summary note attached to the Colonial Office's 1927 Hong Kong file stated: 'It is of course quite clear . . . that Hong Kong and the New Territories stand or fall together, and that there can be no question of giving up the latter if we are to retain the former. It is unthinkable that we should ever consent to return Hong Kong or the New Territories to China . . .'

In a literal sense, of course, this was a gross overstatement of the situation in 1927–8. The New Territories had been part of Hong Kong for less than thirty years and still comprised mostly green fields. The force of the Colonial Office position lay in its presumption that, if the indivisibility of Hong Kong *was* accepted, then, since Britain held Hong Kong Island and the Kowloon peninsula in perpetuity, Britain would also have to find a way of holding the New Territories in perpetuity. The possibility that this logic could be inverted, and that the indivisibility of Hong Kong might serve to bind the whole colony to China rather than to Britain, was, in 1927, as the Colonial Office honestly if poignantly recorded, 'unthinkable'.

IMPORTANT THOUGH THE question of 1997 had suddenly seemed to Sir Cecil Clementi, it was nonetheless doomed to drop back down the Whitehall agenda for almost half a century; not because it had been resolved, but because, as the Sino-Japanese and Pacific Wars gave way to Chinese civil war and to the founding in 1949 of the People's Republic, there were other, far more immediate issues preoccupying those whose job it was to worry about Hong Kong.

The Pacific War had ended in a flurry of telegrams between London, Washington and the Allied headquarters in China at Chongqing about the modalities of Hong Kong's surrender. Had President Franklin D. Roosevelt lived beyond April 1945, he might well have thrown the weight of the United States behind the claim of the Chinese Nationalist leader, Chiang Kai-shek, to take Japan's surrender in Hong Kong, and to assume the continuation of government there in place of Britain. But Harry Truman, who succeeded Roosevelt, yielded to Britain's insistence that Hong Kong should, in the first instance at least, be returned to British rule. By 16 September 1945, the date of Japan's formal surrender, Britain had already re-established a makeshift colonial government in Hong Kong under Franklin Gimson, whose misfortune it had been to arrive there as Colonial Secretary just a fortnight before the colony's fall to Japan at Christmas 1941, and who had spent the war in internment.

The speed with which entrepreneurial activity returned to post-war Hong Kong astonished the British teams sent to assist its reconstruction. Within a week of the *South China Morning Post*'s reappearance as a single inky sheet announcing the arrival of a British fleet under Admiral Harcourt on 30 August 1945, it was carrying its first advertisements for restaurants and film-shows and its first peevish Letters to the Editor about the shortcomings of the military administration. But the sporadic signs of normality overlaid vast economic problems. The cost of living in 1945 was five times its level in 1941; within a few months of the end of the Japanese occupation, the population of Hong Kong had risen from 600,000 to a million; there were just six working buses in the whole of the territory, and the harbour was cluttered with wrecks.

Broadly based economic recovery gathered pace in 1947–8, when external trade tripled, a supply of rice was assured at a stable price and government revenues showed an unexpected surplus due mainly to the introduction of direct taxes on salaries and profits. But the crisis was far from over. The Chinese civil war was producing its own torrent of refugees, pushing up Hong Kong's population from one million in 1945 to almost two and a half million in 1950. The hillsides were packed with squatter huts and the rudimentary social services were hopelessly overwhelmed. Yet still there seemed no end to the numbers who would rather be in Hong Kong than in China.

The year of the Communist victory, 1949, was among the most dramatic in Hong Kong's history; but the truly astonishing aspect of it was what *failed* to happen there. With the Communist armies sweeping southward through China from mid-1948 onwards, it seemed that Hong Kong's days as a British colony must be nearing their end. Chiang Kai-shek had only narrowly failed in his bid to reoccupy Hong Kong at the end of the Pacific War; it was scarcely conceivable that Mao Zedong's Communists, with their far fiercer doctrinal antipathy to imperialism and capitalism, would leave the job unfinished. Yet, when Lin Biao's army finally arrived in southern Guangdong in mid-October 1949, its main units halted twenty-five miles short of the Hong Kong border. The Chinese commanders passed word to the

British that their orders were to keep the peace and to prepare for the resumption of trade and the re-opening of the Kowloon–Guangzhou railway; and in Hong Kong itself there was no breath of the strikes and riots which might have been expected as 'softening up' for a Communist take-over. The Chinese, against all apparent logic, really did seem prepared to leave the British colonialists in place.

China has never given any specific rationale for its sparing of Hong Kong in 1949. It may be that Mao and his generals decided that possession of the colony was not worth the military confrontation which an advance by the People's Liberation Army would undoubtedly have provoked: for, though it has since become commonplace to say that China could 'take Hong Kong with a telephone call', the British government of 1949 was in a bellicose mood, the fall of a near-defenceless Hong Kong eight years earlier to Japan still fresh in its mind. It raised the strength of the Hong Kong garrison from 5,000 to 30,000 as the Communists drew near, with token contingents of Australian and New Zealand troops signifying those countries' joint commitment. Harold Macmillan told a tense House of Commons that the colony was 'the Gibraltar of the East'. Clearly, given the geography of the prospective battle and the logic of numbers, the People's Liberation Army could have taken Hong Kong with a bloody, drawn-out action; but it could not have counted on a low-cost 'lightning' victory, and that prospect may have been enough to stay its hand.[8]

An alternative, or supplementary, explanation is that the Communist leaders foresaw the strategic benefits which could accrue to China from leaving a British-run Hong Kong in place as a 'window' on the West. They had, for example, observed in fairly recent times Hong Kong's value as an external supply-base, the Kowloon–Guangzhou railway having proved crucial to the provisioning of Chinese resistance during the early years of the Sino-Japanese War. They may also have reckoned that the presence of a British colonial government in Hong Kong would provide them with an important source of political leverage in future relations with Britain, and perhaps even a wedge to drive between the interests of Britain and its great ally, the implacably anti-Communist United States.

Whatever factors influenced Mao Zedong's action, his judgement was rewarded more quickly than perhaps even he had foreseen. It was to Hong Kong that China turned in 1950 to build its reserves of petrol, chemicals, rubber, motor-vehicles and machinery for the war in

Korea; and, when that war led to United Nations and United States trade embargoes against China, it was Hong Kong and Macao – policing the embargoes with mixed feelings and no very great efficiency – which provided China's principal routes for sanctions-busting. Not until thirty years later, in 1980, did China openly admit what had taken place: Zhao Guanji, a State Council official, said that Hong Kong had been 'China's lifeline'.[9]

If Communist China's initial attitude towards Hong Kong was shaped mainly by pragmatism, it soon evolved into a more fixed policy 'line': the British presence would be tolerated, provided that Britain managed Hong Kong in such a way as to avoid any embarrassment or inconvenience to China. This was the burden of the message given by Zhou Enlai, the Chinese Prime Minister, to the Governor of Hong Kong, Sir Alexander Grantham, who paid a private visit to Beijing in October 1955 and saw Zhou 'unofficially' for a three-hour conversation. Accounts of that meeting vary,[10] but it is certain that Zhou signalled China's willingness to tolerate the British presence in Hong Kong by proposing that China station an official representative in the territory, a suggestion which Britain rejected, but which was to recur several times in succeeding years.[11] It has also been reported that Zhou identified certain 'rules of conduct' for Hong Kong, for example that Britain should not steer the territory towards democracy or self-government; that foreign powers should not use it as a military base; that Nationalist subversion should be prevented and the safety of Chinese officials protected; and that China's economic interests should not be obstructed.[12]

The *entente cordiale* prescribed by Zhou endured through the late 1950s and early 1960s, despite the political and economic ructions, including the disastrous Great Leap Forward, which afflicted China internally. Mao gave his own blessing in 1959 by saying: 'It is better to keep Hong Kong the way it is, we are in no hurry to take it back, it is useful to us right now.'[13] The Communist Party's Central Committee issued a directive in 1960 stating that the resources of Hong Kong and Macao should be 'fully utilized in the interests of long-term planning'; Zhou urged Chinese provincial governments to co-operate economically with the enclaves, leading Guangdong Province to reach an agreement to supply Hong Kong with water, as it already did Macao.[14] The over-arching message was that, although resumption would come, it was not imminent. 'We must first resolve the most important problem, Taiwan . . . Then, at the opportune moment, we will claim Macao and Hong Kong,' said Chen Yi, China's foreign minister, in 1966.[15] But the most enduring and often repeated formula of all was the one first advanced by the *People's Daily*, the Communist Party's principal national newspaper, in March 1963. The question of Hong Kong, it said, would be 'settled peacefully through negotiations' when conditions were 'ripe'. Until then, the status quo would prevail.

BARELY, HOWEVER, HAD Hong Kong grown used to the emollient promise of the *People's Daily* when it began to hear the first distant rumblings of the turmoil which would prove the greatest post-war threat to its survival as a colony: the Cultural Revolution.

The first wave of unrest hit Hong Kong in the summer of 1966, in what were called the 'Star Ferry riots', which – though attributed by a public inquiry to locally organized hooliganism – were undoubtedly spurred on by the new mood of restless violence sweeping through the youth culture of the mainland. But it was only with the shocking spectacle of the Macao riots of December 1966 that the true danger and its causes were perceived.

The Macao riots began on 3 December with an attempt by police to demolish an illegal extension which had been built on to a 'leftist' (Communist-affiliated) school. Students who tried to prevent the demolition claimed that they were brutally beaten by the police. The next day, students joined with the Macao Federation of Trades Unions to organize street demonstrations which degenerated into bloody riots. By 5 December, five people were dead, the city was under curfew, and seven Chinese gunboats had entered its waters. The student leaders demanded punishment of the local police chief and compensation for the wounded; then Chinese representatives inter-vened to extend the demands, calling for the surrender of 'Nationalist agents' in Macao and for general restrictions on police powers. The Governor of Macao capitulated, signing a humiliating series of pledges in the offices of the Chinese Chamber of Commerce under a portrait of Mao Zedong. Macao became from that moment more of a condominium than a colony, with the external show of Portuguese authority cloaking the real power of China.

Hong Kong's own experience of the Cultural Revolution began with a labour dispute at a plastic flower factory in May 1967, which esca-lated into a series of demonstrations and riots continuing through

June. Thin lines of policemen struggled bravely to restrain mobs besieging Central District, while loudspeakers blared down from the Beijing-owned Bank of China building urging the rioters on. 'The British will not be here much longer,' amplified voices taunted the police below, 'do you think they will take you with them when they leave?'

In July, after a series of police raids on leftist organizations and the closure of three newspapers, the radicals retreated from open confrontation to urban terrorism. A thousand bombs were planted during the following six months in streets, shops and schools. Assassination lists circulated; television news-readers were threatened with acid attacks; the Post Office received letters from Guangzhou addressed to 'Get-Out-Imperialists City'. Though the flow of water from China continued, additional amounts to help Hong Kong cope with a chronic drought were refused, and food supplies were halted for four days.

Periodically during the turmoil, the Hong Kong government was receiving private reassurances from Beijing, carrying the authority of Zhou Enlai, who remained Prime Minister, to the effect that the rioters were not being encouraged by the Chinese government, and that it was not Beijing's intention to dislodge the British. But even if Beijing was, in a strict sense, withholding its formal sponsorship from the violence in Hong Kong, the *People's Daily* was fulminating against the British in terms which were scarcely calculated to cool tempers, accusing them of 'fascist atrocities' and 'moribund, savage imperialism'. On 20 August 1967, it declared:

We must tell the British imperialists that not only have Chinese peasants the right to till the land in the 'New Territories', but the whole of Hong Kong must return to the motherland . . . How can it be imagined that Hong Kong will always be under the rule of British imperialism? Of course it cannot: it is absolutely unthinkable . . . Hong Kong is an inalienable part of Chinese territory.

Even here, however, no imminent date was being specified for resumption. The British suspected the Chinese of aiming, in fact, less for their ousting than for a repeat of the more insidious triumph which had been achieved in Macao, where the colonial government was retained largely to do the Communists' bidding. But whatever the outlook, it was certainly grim enough for many of Hong Kong's more distinguished citizens to conclude that they would be better off elsewhere. The list of public figures taking extended summer vacations was exceptionally long that year, the rich were suddenly to be found in Canada and Taiwan, and property prices fell sharply. By the end of 1967, when the violence finally burned itself out, the Cultural Revolution in Hong Kong had left 51 dead and 800 injured.

That Hong Kong did survive 1967 more or less intact was due primarily to the discipline of its police force. Leftist attempts to shatter police morale, through both political propaganda and acts of terrorism, fell short of their mark. It was also apparent, through the failure of strikes, the fall in sales of leftist newspapers and the willingness of neighbourhood associations to co-operate with the police, that the violence of the leftists found very little popular support. In December, the leftists finally switched tactics to launch what was termed a 'smile' campaign, attempting to win back goodwill through food distribution and other small acts of public service.

The result was a vindication both of the Hong Kong government's unyielding attitude during the troubles and of the support which it had received from the Colonial (now briefly known as the 'Commonwealth') Office in London. For the main business of the Colonial Office was not diplomacy but municipal government in exotic climes, and it took the view that if Hong Kong faced a serious threat to public order, then the remedy lay in a rigorous insistence upon the rule of law. The Cultural Revolution might be a political matter in China; but it was a criminal one in Hong Kong.

The Cultural Revolution thus crystallized perhaps the last serious collision of traditional interests between the old Colonial Office and the Foreign Office, before the former was merged into the latter by Harold Wilson's Labour government in 1968. For the priorities of the Foreign Office – which had no special organic link with Hong Kong – lay with the welfare of Britons and the maintenance of British interests in China, and with the long-term nurturing of Sino-British relations. And while Sir David Trench, Governor of Hong Kong from 1964 to 1971 and the last Colonial Office appointee to hold that post, had seemed determined almost to caricature imperial sang-froid during 1967 by maintaining his weekly game of golf and even taking his summer leave as planned at the height of the riots, Britons – and particularly British diplomats – in China were being subjected to appalling abuse and physical assault, much of it in explicit retribution for the firm line taken by Trench's administration in Hong Kong. After the imprisonment in Hong Kong of two journalists employed by the official New China News Agency, a British journalist, Anthony Grey of Reuters, was placed under house arrest in Beijing. In August, China's Ministry of Foreign Affairs issued an ultimatum to the British chargé d'affaires in Beijing demanding that Hong Kong release its leftist prisoners and permit the re-opening of banned newspapers. When this ultimatum was rejected, the office of the British legation was burned, and the residence of the chargé was sacked by a mob. At least twice, visitors from the Beijing mission urged Trench to find ways of speeding the release of leftists from prison, in order to rebuild relations with China, only to be told that Hong Kong was British soil where the law was the law – though Trench did eventually agree, in 1969, to the early parole of one leftist journalist, when this was the last obstacle to Grey's release.

If, when the violence ebbed away, Hong Kong was only too keen to forget the traumas of the Cultural Revolution, those days were etched for ever in Foreign Office memories – including those of diplomats involved at a senior level in the negotiation of the Hong Kong settlement in the 1980s. They had been made painfully aware of the vulnerabilities and conflicts inherent in maintaining a British colony on Chinese soil; they had tasted the degree to which Hong Kong, and the legacy which it represented, could canalize and divert, even poison, the broader flow of Sino-British relations; and they carried with them the knowledge that Chinese political behaviour, when passions were unleashed, did not necessarily halt at the limits of courtesy, or reason, or even self-interest. All of which is not to suggest that the Foreign Office would indulge any active desire, a decade or so later, to 'let Hong Kong go' in a way that the Colonial Office might have resisted had it endured. Rather that, when the chaos of the Cultural Revolution, late Maoism and the Gang of Four had finally subsided, and when a 'window of opportunity' presented itself at the end of the 1970s to open a dialogue about Hong Kong's future with an apparently rational regime in Beijing, it was hardly surprising that the Foreign Office should have felt so strongly that the opportunity should be seized, even blindly, for fear that it might neither persist nor recur.

31

IN HONG KONG itself, as calm returned, the Cultural Revolution succeeded the Communist victory of 1949 as the *locus classicus* for those who argued that China could have no real inclination to take back the colony – for, if it did, then surely 1967, with British authority stretched thin, fanaticism in command and the inhibitions of conventional behaviour cast to the winds, would have been the time to strike. The rich repatriated themselves and their money with a new sense of self-confidence, even of immunity. The Hong Kong Stock Exchange's Hang Seng Index, a crude but potent measure of sentiment, rose from a low of 59 in 1967 to 1,775 in March 1973, one of the greatest 'bull runs' in world stock-market history. An energetic new governor, Sir Murray MacLehose, had arrived in 1971; the Connaught Centre, Hong Kong's first skyscraper of Manhattan proportions, rose on the harbour front; and world trade in the pre-oil crisis days was booming. Against such a backdrop, there was certainly little disposition within Hong Kong itself to waste much time worrying when, on 8 March 1972, China wrote formally to the United Nations Special Committee on the Declaration on Decolonization, asking the committee to remove Hong Kong from its decolonization agenda on the grounds that:

> The questions of Hong Kong and Macao belong in the category of questions resulting from the series of unequal treaties which the imperialists imposed on China. Hong Kong and Macao are part of Chinese territory occupied by the British and Portuguese authorities. The settlement of the questions of Hong Kong and Macao is entirely within China's sovereign right and does not at all fall under the ordinary category of colonial territories. Consequently, they should not be included in the list of colonial territories covered by the declaration on the granting of independence to colonial countries and peoples. With regard to the questions of Hong Kong and Macao, the Chinese government has consistently held that they should be settled in an appropriate way when conditions are ripe.[16]

The burden of the letter, signed by the foreign minister, Huang Hua, was that China rejected British and Portuguese claims to the territories of Hong Kong and Macao and would decide for itself how and when they would be recovered. But the terminology was sufficiently vague for Britain to confine its disagreement to the sending of a note to the UN Secretary-General saying that the Chinese letter 'in no way affect[ed] the legal status of Hong Kong'.

Did Britain's restraint amount to a half-nod in the direction of China's stand? There is a suggestive accident of timing, in that Huang Hua's letter was followed five days later, on 13 March, by the communiqué announcing that Sino-British diplomatic relations were to be normalized, the fruit of a year of formal negotiations between the two governments. It is hard now to imagine that the future of Hong Kong was not a major element in the haggling over normalization: but British diplomats insist that it was not, and there appears to be no evidence in the public domain to suggest otherwise. Officially, the main issues to be resolved were those concerning China's representation at the United Nations; the status of the British consulate at Tamsui on Taiwan; and the British government's view of the legal status of Taiwan.

With hindsight, nonetheless, it can be appreciated that the normalization of Sino-British relations crucially changed the *données* of the Hong Kong question, even if Hong Kong had not been made part of any specific bargain. The more cordial and close the alliance between China and Britain became, the more anachronistic the colonial status of Hong Kong would appear and the more difficult it would be for Britain to resist at least discussing its eventual return to China. Thus, if the timing of the Huang Hua letter was simply a coincidence, then it was a happy one: and the message which it was intended to convey was presumably the one more explicitly stated by Zhou Enlai in an interview with Louis Heren of *The Times* in October 1972. Heren, writing in reported speech, recorded Zhou as saying that:

> The future of Hong Kong would have to be decided. A state must enter into negotiations when a treaty expires. Now that full diplomatic relations existed between the two countries, Britain would naturally have to negotiate at the appropriate time. Territories taken from China were bound to be returned . . . It was not Chinese policy to embark upon such matters with undue haste . . . In a changing world this matter would have to be settled, but it did not have to be considered now.[17]

The politeness born of normalization was quickly apparent in the blurring of the public profile of Britain's relationship with its colony.

The word 'colony' itself began to disappear from the official rubric, to be replaced by the word 'territory'. The Colonial Secretary of Hong Kong became the Chief Secretary, and the Colonial Treasurer became the Financial Secretary. British ministers, when obliged to make reference to British sovereignty over Hong Kong, adopted the deliberately opaque formula that Britain's position on the sovereignty of Hong Kong was 'well-known', to avoid offending China by reasserting explicitly the validity of the nineteenth-century treaties, which China insisted were 'unequal' and thus invalid. The Colonial Office might have taken umbrage at such double-talk, but it was no longer there to do so: Hong Kong now answered to the Foreign Office, overseen by the same senior diplomats who oversaw relations with China.

There is evidence that the British government, or at least its Prime Minister, Edward Heath, by the time that Sino-British normalization occurred, took the view that Hong Kong very probably *was* going to be reclaimed by China in 1997, and that Britain would have to reach some sort of accommodation. It is all but certain that Heath intended to raise the issue with China's leaders during the official visit which he was scheduled to make to China as Prime Minister in 1974, anticipating Thatcher by almost a decade. But though Heath did go to China, and did discuss Hong Kong with Chinese leaders, a general election had by then intervened to unseat his government, and it was as Leader of the Opposition that he arrived in Beijing; consigning, perhaps sadly, to the realms of speculation the question of what deal might have been reached in respect of Hong Kong by a prime minister viewed as a trusted friend by China, at a time when China was far less confident than it would be a decade later of its capacity to run Hong Kong without Britain's help.

3

'A Window of Opportunity'

In the late 1970s, as the period before the termination of the New Territories lease continued to shorten, concern about the future of Hong Kong began to be expressed both in the territory itself, and among foreign investors. In particular there was increasing realization of the problem posed by individual land leases granted in the New Territories, all of which were set to expire three days before the expiry of the New Territories lease in 1997. It was clear that the steadily shortening span of these leases and the inability of the Hong Kong government to grant new ones extending beyond 1997 would be likely to deter investment and damage confidence.

The British Government had by this time, following a detailed examination of the problem conducted in consultation with the then-Governor, concluded that confidence would begin to erode quickly in the early-to-mid-1980s if nothing was done to alleviate the uncertainty caused by the 1997 deadline. Accordingly, when the Governor of Hong Kong visited Peking in March 1979 at the invitation of the Chinese Minister of Foreign Trade, an attempt was made, on the initiative of the British Government, to solve the specific question of land leases expiring in 1997. These discussions did not result in measures to solve the problem.

The 'Joint Declaration' White Paper, 1984[1]

THE task of attempting to translate the normalization of Sino-British relations into a closer working relationship between Hong Kong and the People's Republic of China fell to the new Governor, Sir Murray MacLehose, who had been appointed to the territory with effect from November 1971.

MacLehose had served in China and Malaya, in Hong Kong as Political Adviser to Sir Robert Black in 1959–62, and then as British ambassador to Saigon and to Copenhagen. With the disappearance of the old Colonial Office, he was the first governor of Hong Kong to be appointed by and from the Foreign Office. Yet, if Hong Kong had expected a figure of elegant abstraction, it discovered a tall, domineering Scot who set about the weighty and often mundane tasks of his administration with a zest that many of his Colonial Office predecessors had all too visibly lacked. The practical achievements of his governorship included major improvements in the quality and quantity of public housing, construction of Hong Kong's underground railway system and the eradication of systematic corruption from the police force.

MacLehose's diplomatic agenda was subtler, but in its way no less radical. According to one senior Hong Kong civil servant:

He arrived with two ambitions. One was to be a total contrast with his predecessor, the other was to reconcile Hong Kong with the Chinese Communist Party. I remember talking to him at his Queen's Birthday garden party in 1973. I said to him, 'Sir, very good party. Why don't you invite some representatives of the New China News Agency?' And I got five minutes straight from him on the subject. 'I have plans for that. Obviously they cannot come right now, but it is a priority. We have got to get this right.' Murray was in favour of reconciliation. You could see it.

Since China still had no formal representative in the territory, its further requests to station one having been refused by Britain, it had since the mid-1950s conducted its diplomatic business through officials posted to the Hong Kong branch of the official New China News Agency. The agency's director was China's barely camouflaged chargé d'affaires. It was also generally accepted, though more discreetly, that he headed the Hong Kong and Macao 'Work Group' of the Chinese Communist Party – even though no such political organization had been officially registered in Hong Kong, as the law would strictly have required.

At the core of the internal 'normalization' pursued by MacLehose in Hong Kong was, therefore, the establishment of a close working relationship between the Chinese representatives operating from within the New China News Agency and the office of the Hong Kong government's Political Adviser – the Political Adviser being an official seconded from the Foreign Office to Hong Kong to supervise relations with China. Previously, the NCNA's contacts with the Hong Kong government had been channelled through the press and public relations officers of the Hong Kong government's Information Services department, in conformity with the fiction that the NCNA's vocation was journalism. The Political Adviser's office also became, under MacLehose, the focus for a deepening of contacts with Guangdong Province, particularly as illegal immigration became an ever more serious problem. And, in a move of significant psychological impact, senior Hong Kong civil servants ceased to receive the daily intelligence briefings on 'leftist' activities in Hong Kong which treated the Communist presence as inherently subversive.

The process of mutual confidence-building reached its culmination in 1978, when MacLehose himself stood alongside Wang Kuang, the New China News Agency's then-director, exchanging toasts at the NCNA's China National Day celebration in Hong Kong, a result which was the more precious for having been achieved against a backdrop of wild and often baffling political shifts within China itself.

For, across the border, the relative calm which had characterized China during the early 1970s, and which had accompanied the general thawing of relations with Britain, the United States and Japan, had relapsed by 1975–6 into the chaos of late Maoism. As Mao himself grew too weak mentally and physically to rule, power was abrogated by his wife, Jiang Qing, and the ultra-leftist Gang of Four. Zhou Enlai died in January 1976, Mao in September. Zhou's moderate protégés, notably Deng Xiaoping, were dismissed and disgraced. Then, to the general amazement of foreign observers, the struggle took a fresh turn. In December 1976, Jiang and the Gang of Four were arrested; Hua Guofeng, an otherwise undistinguished protégé of Mao, was appointed titular Communist Party leader; and in July 1977, Deng made a sudden return to political life, his rehabilitation supported by factions of the People's Liberation Army command. In the succeeding year, the new balance of power slowly resolved itself until, in November and December 1978, the Communist Party Central Committee held a landmark conclave, the Third Plenum of the 11th

Central Committee, at which Deng's 'reformist' policies were overwhelmingly endorsed. To the relief of the West, the Communist Party
appeared to have regrouped around a new paramount leader, Deng,
whose aim was to redirect its energies away from internecine ideological struggles and back towards the rebuilding of the national
economy.

The external effects of China's changing political climate were felt
first in Hong Kong. In the spring of 1978, Beijing-controlled companies made high-profile forays into the Hong Kong property market,
spending some US$40 million, a very large sum for those days, on
industrial and commercial sites. Guangdong provincial authorities
began to talk about creating what they called a 'special export zone',
a term later amended to 'special economic zone', just across the
border from Hong Kong at Shenzhen, where foreigners would be
encouraged to invest in joint-venture companies manufacturing for
export; and, in the autumn of that same year, they proposed a series
of moves to restore communications links between Hong Kong and
China. The resumption of direct air services was authorized after
a hiatus of thirty years, beginning with twice-daily charter flights to
Guangzhou in October to bring businessmen to the autumn trade fair.
A Hong Kong–Guangzhou hydrofoil service began along the Pearl
River in November. Hong Kong-registered trucks were allowed to
cross the border to collect goods from Guangdong Province, obviat-
ing cumbersome transhipment at border checkpoints. Discussions
also began about electrifying and double-tracking the Kowloon-
Guangzhou railway line. It was, MacLehose said, as though 'an arti-
ficial screen' between Hong Kong and Guangdong were at last being
removed.

It was clear, too, that China's new pragmatists saw an important
role for Hong Kong as a provider of investment and expertise to
support the process of economic modernization to which the central
government in Beijing had committed itself. In December 1978,
China's foreign trade minister, Li Qiang – dressed, the *South China
Morning Post* marvelled, 'in a pin-stripe banker-type suit accented
with a "jazzy" tie in bright colours' – paid an informal visit to Hong
Kong. At the Far East Stock Exchange, one of four then operating in
the city, he enquired how China could go about floating a bond issue
in Hong Kong. At a dinner for Hong Kong property tycoons, he asked
them for 'help in speeding up China's modernization programme'. He

lunched at Government House, and concluded with a press conference, the first ever given by a Chinese official in Hong Kong, at which he declared, to the surprise of bankers around the world, that China would 'require tens of billions of dollars in foreign credits to support its modernization programme, in which Hong Kong will play a part'.

This was music to the ears of Hong Kong which, though it had been founded as an entrepôt for China trade, had suffered a quite unnatural isolation from its hinterland during the economic and ideological vicissitudes of the Communist era. It had continued to buy its food and other basic commodities from China, but it was able to sell very few of its own goods to China in return, while the re-export trade between China and third countries via Hong Kong, the true entrepôt function, had all but vanished.[2] If China did now want to tap Hong Kong's resources in support of its own development, then it would find tremendous pent-up enthusiasm which only a few kind words from Beijing would be needed to unleash.

Deng's gospel of 'reform and the open door' brought trade missions and ministers from further afield pouring into Beijing through the winter of 1978 and the spring of 1979. Another senior Hong Kong official, since retired, recalls a visit during that heyday from a British government minister:

I said to him, 'What do you really expect?' He said, 'We want nothing less than what the French have got. The French have got this and this and it adds up to fourteen billion dollars.' The figures were always used very loosely. Only some of the deals were actually signed. I remember keeping a little tally of all these overseas 'deals', what the various countries were expecting to get, and when it started ascending into the hundreds of billions I thought 'This has got to stop. We are going too fast.' But the great attitude of the day was that we [in Hong Kong] were sitting on a platinum mine. It was a very nice thought, but it was really a sort of euphoria. Everything was going to take a much longer time to happen than people seemed to accept.

If the British government's own Departments of Trade and Industry were excited by the new, open, friendly mood of China's government

under Deng Xiaoping, then so too was the Foreign Office, as it considered its obligations to Hong Kong. It now perceived a – by its own
criteria – rational interlocutor in Beijing; and, equally importantly,
it saw China embarking upon a process of economic modernization
for the success of which China would need Hong Kong to remain as
it was then, a capitalist city, a source of foreign exchange and international expertise. The British were conscious, moreover, that
Deng was already in his mid-seventies, and that it was impossible
to forecast who or what might succeed him. With fewer than twenty
years left before 1997, the conclusion was, for the British, inescapable: the 'window of opportunity' had opened before them in Beijing
during which it would be folly not to raise the question of Hong
Kong's future at the very highest level should the opportunity present
itself.

Such, then, was the background against which MacLehose found
himself considering an unexpected invitation, issued informally by Li
Qiang over his lunch at Government House in December 1978, to visit
Beijing. The verbal invitation had been followed by a written one, the
first letter ever addressed to a governor of Hong Kong by a minister of
the People's Republic of China. As the Governor himself saw the
offer:

> It was a serious initiative, issued against the background of the
> modernization programme. Everybody agreed: of course I
> should go. We wanted to know what China's economic plans
> were – communications, resources, power, industrialization,
> and what Hong Kong could do to help. I asked for a thorough
> briefing on all these things, and this approach clearly fitted in
> very well with their own concept of the visit.

China's modernization and Hong Kong's role in it were thus the
main focus. But in the telegrams between London, Hong Kong and
Beijing that December, a second theme was being confidentially discussed.[3] If, as seemed possible, MacLehose was granted an audience
with Deng himself, would this be the occasion on which to raise the
question of 1997 in some form or other? The British were not sure how
the ground might be prepared, or whether it could even be prepared at
all. As one official, who was closely involved with the process,
explained: 'We just did not have the sort of contacts which you needed

to discuss these things at a lower level. We thought the best way was to start at the top and try to get the man at the top to say "There is a problem." If you fed your question in at the bottom, it would just vanish, nothing would happen.'

So it would be a leap in the dark, but one which, by the time MacLehose left for Beijing in March, the British had persuaded themselves to take.

THE FOREIGN OFFICE could not have justified a high-risk Hong Kong initiative simply on the basis of its own perception that an approach to China might be opportune. Hong Kong was a big, articulate place, with an identity and interests of its own which the British were pledged to respect. It was necessary to establish that circumstances in Hong Kong also argued for such an initiative to be undertaken. And, as the 1984 White Paper on Hong Kong recorded, the Foreign Office did indeed arrive at such a conclusion. It found that 'concern about the future of Hong Kong began to be expressed' by investors during the late 1970s, and that 'confidence would begin to erode quickly' within a few years if nothing was done to alleviate 'the uncertainty caused by the 1997 deadline'.

In retrospect, it must be said that the signs tell a more equivocal tale. The Hang Seng Index, for example, which had crashed spectacularly during the first oil crisis of 1973, rose steadily from 350 at the end of 1975, to 495 at the end of 1978 and 879 at the end of 1979. Nor was investor anxiety observable in the behaviour of the property market over that period: on average, prices of small Hong Kong flats also roughly doubled between 1976 and 1979. More telling still, land in the New Territories actually grew more expensive relative to land in Kowloon between 1976 and 1979 – indicating that investors were, all other things being equal, growing less rather than more worried about the lease question during those years.[4] Indeed, the Hongkong Land Company, the territory's leading property developer, went so far as to decide in 1979 that it would depreciate its properties in the New Territories on the same basis as those in the rest of the colony, on the grounds that the property market as a whole seemed to make no meaningful distinction. 'Commercial decisions are being taken on exactly the same basis for the whole of the colony,' explained the company's finance manager, Robin De Morgan. 'Identical sites in both parts of Hong Kong are being priced on exactly the same basis.'[5]

41

Among financial institutions which lent against residential property, the Hongkong Bank group, including its Hang Seng Bank subsidiary, was by far the territory's largest mortgagee. In the view of Sir Michael Sandberg, who was then the banking group's chairman: 'Apart from the general thought that "some time or other we have got to get this settled", I don't think there was any great pressure. In those days, 1978, there were still nearly 20 years to go, and who in Hong Kong had a ten-year mortgage?'

The average repayment period for a residential mortgage in Hong Kong in the late 1970s was five to seven years. Had banks decided that they were after all worried about the value of their collateral five to seven years on, it was open to them to respond by reducing their valuations. There was no 1997-related problem in the residential property market in the late 1970s, at least, which could not have been resolved by purely commercial judgement;[6] and Tom Welsh, the Hongkong Bank's general manager for Hong Kong, later painted this similarly straightforward picture of corporate lending: 'So far 1997 has not become a legal or documentation problem for us. Until recently, no lending was done here except on the basis of five years. That was enough for most people. Then the Mass Transit Railway Corporation came along for 10-year money. That was considered exceptionally lengthy, and it still is.'[7]

Indeed, the banks themselves, to judge by their own investment programmes, proved to be some of Hong Kong's most aggressive optimists, whatever their accountants and lawyers might have been saying about the legal niceties of 1997. In 1980–1, when the lease question was still no closer to resolution than it had been in 1978–9, Bank of America committed HK$1.4 billion to a new head office building; Citibank HK$600 million; and the Hongkong Bank HK$6 billion.

At the time, there were, of course, some voices warning of the danger ahead: the Hong Kong Society of Accountants, taking the contrary view to that later adopted by the Hongkong Land Company, was re-examining depreciation policies in the territory; and Jimmy McGregor, a former civil servant who headed the Hong Kong General Chamber of Commerce, had spoken powerfully of the 'run-down of investment' which he believed awaited Hong Kong in the early 1980s if the lease question had not by then been resolved. But even if investors should have been worrying about the lease question in the late 1970s, it is not clear that they did so to the extent that the Hong Kong government perceived. By the turn of 1978–9, it seemed to be the case that, while China's new political climate was encouraging the Foreign Office in London to think about raising the problem of Hong Kong's future, that same new climate was encouraging investors in Hong Kong to think that the future might not be such a problem after all.

This was the background against which the British and Hong Kong governments concluded, after their 'detailed examination', that action needed to be taken on the lease. It would, arguably, have been just as plausible for them to have found, had it suited their purposes, that there were, on the contrary, no immediate problems associated with 1997, such that the issue could be left to one side a little longer. But Hong Kong's vote was cast, nonetheless, in favour of raising the issue

It is tempting to say that what Britain really wanted from Hong Kong was less an answer than an alibi. For, though the Foreign Office had decided for its own analytical reasons that the 1997 question should now be raised, political prudence dictated that the action should be ascribable primarily to Hong Kong's own indigenous 'concern' to have the question raised, since it was on Hong Kong alone that the consequences of this very considerable gamble, be they miraculous or catastrophic, would fall.

A more candid and complete survey of the British motivations would also have been obliged to take into account the British government's own worries about Hong Kong's uncertain future, to which it could not admit publicly for fear of fuelling the very confidence crisis which it hoped to pre-empt, but which were rapidly acquiring a disturbingly financial character. Britain was, notably, beginning to write a series of loan guarantees for the construction of a new complex of power stations at Castle Peak in the north-west of the New Territories by a privately owned Hong Kong company, China Light and Power. To win contracts for British manufacturers, the government's Export Credit Guarantee Department would agree between 1978 and 1981 to guarantee loans totalling more than £800 million, with repayment schedules running from 1991 until 2002, the first international project-financing in Hong Kong to extend beyond 1997. Foreign bankers, presuming that Britain must know more about Hong Kong's future than anybody else, were so impressed by its willingness to guarantee the core loans for Castle Peak that they eventually agreed to grant US$300 million in subsidiary loans, also repayable after 1997, *without* government guarantees.

In reality, the British government had no 'inside' information of a positive character about Hong Kong's future at all in 1978, and not much more in 1981. It guaranteed the loans because Britain needed the export orders and Hong Kong needed the power station. But if Hong Kong investors might not be thinking long-term, Britain was becoming obliged to do so. The closer 1997 drew, the more financing packages would spill over into the void. There would be more power stations, more bridges and tunnels, there was talk of a new port and a new airport. And, unless and until the issue of 1997 was resolved, thus removing the uncertainty and redefining Hong Kong's legal status, the pressure would build on the Hong Kong and British governments to guarantee loans for projects which might well be on Chinese soil by the time they were finished. For that reason if for no other, Britain needed to clarify China's intentions. But how?

THE RANGE OF possibilities was wide. There were even those who argued that a perfectly satisfactory way for Britain to resolve the uncertainty would be by doing nothing whatsoever. The popular version of this thesis was no more than a continuation of the old argument that, since Hong Kong was useful to China, China itself would find a way of not taking it back even when the time was 'ripe', and that the best thing the British could do was to avoid drawing attention to what was really a Chinese problem, not a British one. A more refined reasoning depended upon a legal – or legalistic – view of Britain's rights and obligations, based upon the proposition that, since China did not recognize the validity of the New Territories lease, it could scarcely recognize its expiry; and that, since Britain's authority to govern the New Territories was founded, in British law, not on the Second Convention of Beijing but on the subsequent Order in Council, then that same authority could be extended beyond 1997 by amending the Order in Council without formally involving China in a renegotiation of the underlying treaty.

The most learned exposition of this argument came from Professor Peter Wesley-Smith of the University of Hong Kong's Department of Law, who theorized that even a new Order in Council could be foregone, if China also took no action:

Let us assume that Britain decides to remain in the New Territories after the term of her lease has expired. She has thus made a decision to extend her jurisdiction (or to maintain a jurisdiction already exercised for nearly a hundred years). This is an act of state. How, on 1 July 1997, do the courts recognize it? Not by the Order in Council, unless it has been amended; not by the [Convention of Beijing], for it no longer takes effect. The courts would be bound by an Act of Parliament, but no such Act would have been passed . . . When the issue is raised in the courtroom, the Chief Secretary can provide an executive certificate which states that the New Territories remains part of Hong Kong – and in subsequent cases, the judges could rely on that precedent. The executive certificate is as sufficient for that purpose as the Order in Council or the treaty itself.

What if there is no executive certificate? The determination of the government to stay on in the New Territories will be obvious by the simple fact that it has not departed. It is neater and more satisfying and more apparently 'legal' to have a formal document announcing the decision, but if the political circumstances do not permit formal documents, the courts can look for other indications of government intent. 'Business as usual' is enough.

Thus there is no need for the UK to issue a new Order in Council or negotiate a new treaty. There is no legal or constitutional obstacle to the maintenance of British jurisdiction in the New Territories after 1997 though no new documents are prepared. If China would prefer to do nothing, let her. If amending the Order in Council is politically dangerous, let it be. 1997 is the kind of problem which, if ignored, will go away.[8]

Alternatively, and perhaps more realistically, the British might have chosen to make a first approach to China through an intermediary, a stalking-horse, who could raise the question in a way which engaged neither government. In the view of Sir Michael Sandberg:

It would have been far better to have used a non-government person, a Lawrence Kadoorie or a John Keswick who could have gone up to Beijing and simply made a few remarks.[9] If they had been told, 'No chance', it would not have mattered. The government could have had nothing to do with it. And if there had been an encouraging response, then things could have moved on from there.

Perhaps the most elegant gambit would have been the one suggested to MacLehose at the start of 1978 by Lo Tak-shing, a solicitor and a member of the Legislative Council of Hong Kong. Lo was also a member of the Advisory Committee on Diversification, a body appointed by MacLehose to reflect on the long-term options available to the Hong Kong economy. It was in this latter context that Lo suggested a means of addressing the constraint posed by the diminishing tenure of New Territories land leases:

> I said, 'Why not get a junior officer in the [Hong Kong government] Land Department to give to a Chinese corporation – a minor corporation, or a subsidiary – a lease which extended beyond 1997, for example by five years. Now, if the Chinese don't like it, they can say, 'You have made a mistake. You cannot go beyond 1997. We do not want this lease.' They might ask through diplomatic channels, 'What are you doing?' You look them straight in the face and say, 'The clerk made a mistake.'
>
> But if nothing happens with that first lease, then maybe you try a second one, extending it by one year more. Then you extend one to a company which is not a Chinese state-owned company but maybe an associated company. Then you do another one, playing it by ear. And gradually, you have fuzzed the date and you have fuzzed the whole thing.

Lo's scheme resonated for some months afterwards through the private and semi-private thoughts of the Hong Kong government. What appeared to be a variant of it, for example, occurred in a *Financial Times* feature published in November 1978, which suggested as a possible course of action:

> that a bold governor would, in 1981 or 1982, quietly order his legal officers to write individual leases for developers . . . in the New Territories running beyond 1997. The lawyers would protest that Britain had no legal right to give away land not hers by treaty. But the answer to this would be that only China could properly protest, and that China's acquiescence would be secured by prior diplomacy.[10]

Such were a few of the options which the British, in the end, rejected. They were not, notably, even prepared to think about the option of amending the Order in Council without an explicit agreement from China, let alone of approaching 1997 with no legal safety-net whatsoever. In the words of Richard Margolis, who arrived in Hong Kong as Deputy Political Adviser in 1981:

Theoretically, the British might have amended the Order in Council to say, for example, that it was valid 'until such time as revised arrangements should be agreed between the United Kingdom and the People's Republic of China'. But that is just paper. It would only work if Britain had the power, in the latter half of the twentieth century, to extend its jurisdiction over a piece of China 7,000 miles away without bothering to consult the Chinese government on the subject . . .

If we had presented a solution like that to Hong Kong, we would have been awarded one out of ten for creativity, and then people would have asked 'Did you consult Beijing?' And we would have said, 'This is a unilateral document, we can do what we like.' And we would have been laughed out of the room.

The British took the view, moreover, that to test China's intentions 'unofficially', whether by the use of an intermediary or, as Lo Tak-shing had suggested, by a technical device, was not what they required. They positively wanted to engage China on an official, explicit level, and they wanted to arrive at a formal resolution of the 1997 question which, whatever else it might be or do, was legally unambiguous, which provided a clear framework for the ownership of land and other assets in Hong Kong beyond 1997, and which contained a clear understanding with China about who ran the territory. On this last point, they were not prepared to share power informally with China, as Portugal had done in Macao.

Self-evidently, by using the MacLehose visit to raise the question of 1997 in Beijing, the British would create the circumstances in which some form of a rebuff might occur. But they intended to keep the whole exercise secret; and, even if a rebuff did ensue, they would at least have engaged Deng's mind, placed 1997 on the agenda, and – as they hoped – opened the way to further talks at lower levels in which their logic might prevail. For the absolute 'worst-case' scenario in

47

British eyes was not even that China might declare, in 1979 or 1982, its intention of re-taking Hong Kong in 1997. It was that China might refuse to discuss the matter at all, or relapse into a post-Deng chaos, and then abruptly declare in 1996 or even 1997 that it had decided to tell Britain to go. By raising the issue well in advance, the British could be sure that the writing, whatever it said, would be on the wall for some years, and that if there were going to be a transition, then Hong Kong would have plenty of time to prepare for it.

This was not simple altruism. Quite apart from the financial costs to Britain and British interests of a precipitate withdrawal, British governments had by the late 1970s acquired an almost neurotic fear of further large-scale 'non-white' immigration into Britain, and they were all too aware that chaos in Hong Kong would threaten to bring to British ports and airports tens of thousands of ethnically Chinese Hong Kong citizens. Though the Commonwealth Immigrant Act of 1962 had stripped Hong Kong passport holders of their legal right to land in Britain, they would have a powerful moral claim to do so in time of crisis.[11] The British fear of a refugee influx from Hong Kong remained a powerful background factor throughout the subsequent process of negotiation and settlement.

Yet beyond those harsh imperatives, British motives were by and large benign. Hong Kong was casting, as it were, a rosy after-glow on the memories of empire. Its achievements brought prestige and stature to Britain in the Far East. It was, in many ways, a better advertisement for British skills and values than Britain itself. It did not yield large sums for the British Crown in the way that Hong Kong popular gossip, and the Chinese government, often suggested; but the intangible benefits, and the profits of British-linked companies, were large enough to make running it worth Britain's while. If Hong Kong wanted Britain to stay, and China agreed, then Britain would do so. And if not, then it was a matter of political convenience and professional pride to Britain that this model of colonialism should end in an orderly and honourable withdrawal.

IF ONE WERE to seek a point at which the process of Hong Kong's rendition, as it was eventually conceived, had its origin, then these first weeks of 1979 would be the candidate: not only because it was with the preparations for the MacLehose visit that the 1997 question began its journey towards the ear of Deng Xiaoping, but also because it was at this juncture that the cast of diplomats began to assemble which was to dominate the evolution of British policy throughout the subsequent negotiations and settlement.

The first of them was MacLehose himself, who occupied Government House in Hong Kong until the spring of 1982, and to whose advice Margaret Thatcher and her ministers would give much weight after his return to London. The second was Sir Edward Youde, who vacated the British Embassy in Beijing in 1978 to return to the Foreign Office as Chief Clerk, the archaic title of the senior deputy under-secretary, with overall responsibility for Far East policy. Youde would later succeed MacLehose as Governor in Hong Kong, assuming the responsibility of representing Hong Kong's interests in the negotiations between Britain and China. The third was Sir Percy Cradock, who succeeded Youde as ambassador to Beijing, and who was, as leader of the British team for the first half of the formal Sino-British negotiations in 1982–3, and as foreign policy adviser to the Prime Minister in 1984, to be the intellectual author of Britain's most important tactical decisions. The fourth, then at a more junior level in the hierarchy, but with a brilliant intellectual reputation, was Dr David (later Lord) Wilson, Political Adviser to MacLehose in 1979 and something of a protégé of Cradock. Wilson would lead the British working party responsible for drafting the detailed text of the Joint Declaration in 1984; in 1987, he would return to Hong Kong as Governor himself, in succession to Sir Edward Youde.

In the weeks before his departure for Beijing, MacLehose professed some brief hesitation about the value of his raising the Hong Kong question with Deng. He thought it would be 'dangerous' if a negative answer were received and the fact of that answer somehow became public. But in February 1979, the Foreign Secretary, Dr David (later Lord) Owen, intervened decisively, telling MacLehose that he intended to discuss the question of Hong Kong's future with China's leaders during a visit which he was planning to make to Beijing in April. He wished to make use of the Governor's visit, therefore, to prepare the ground for the approach which he himself would be making soon after.

In his memoir, *Time to Declare*, Owen has since linked his wish to pursue a Hong Kong settlement with the newly announced restoration of diplomatic relations between China and Portugal, on terms which appeared to provide for confirmation of the status of Macao as

Portuguese-administered territory. But since it was not clear to the Foreign Office at the time what Portugal actually had agreed privately with China in respect of Macao, and since Britain did not want a 'Macao-type' solution for Hong Kong *per se*, the perception was presumably no more than that China might now be willing to talk about Hong Kong, having talked about Macao.

Owen himself was thinking in terms of proposing to Deng a pre-emptive concession of British sovereignty over the whole of Hong Kong, together with a legally binding formula providing for continued British administration on a renewable 'rolling' basis. Thus, if sovereignty were conceded in 1992, then the new treaty might provide for British administration until 1997, renewable in 1993 to secure administration until 1998, and so on.[12]

The vagaries of British politics were, as it happened, going to prevent Owen from pursuing a Hong Kong settlement, much as they had frustrated Edward Heath five years before him. Instead of visiting Beijing in April, Owen was to find himself fighting a general election in which his own Labour government would be defeated. The idea of a 'rolling treaty' did not take root in the Foreign Office, and did not survive Owen's departure. But all this was still some time away, as telegrams passed between London, Beijing and Hong Kong finalizing the details of the Governor's brief.

The view eventually taken by the Foreign Office was that, particularly with the Owen visit now in prospect, it would be neither necessary nor desirable for MacLehose, should he meet Deng, to attempt to raise directly the question of whether China wished to discuss arrangements for continued British rule of Hong Kong after 1997. Instead, the Foreign Office evolved what some there called the 'sidelong approach', the essence of which was that MacLehose would raise the question of property leases as a purely commercial matter. As one Hong Kong official recalled:

To tackle the lease question itself was going to be very difficult. Two crucial issues were identified. The first was the British right to administer Hong Kong. The second was whether a way could be found to start issuing sub-leases beyond 1997. It was decided that the administration question, the Governor's powers, the Order in Council, all that could be tackled much nearer the time. But the land question needed to be tackled sooner. And, what was more, it could be a relatively painless way of getting at the problem. On the one hand, it would have been difficult for China to say anything in a formal way about the head lease; and, under British law, it would have been perfectly legal to issue sub-leases which extended beyond the tenure of the head lease.

The Foreign Office's lawyers were, in fact, keen that the Governor should raise the possibility of varying the Order in Council, seeking Deng's consent for Britain to extend its own terms of authority over the New Territories. But Owen vetoed this idea, because, he thought, 'It seemed very legalistic, and, if we ever reached that stage, I could not see who would challenge any continued administration by the Governor or any other body. I therefore decided that the Governor should not raise the need for an Order in Council in Beijing or even hint at any potential legal problem.'[13]

The instruction eventually given the Governor was that he should raise only the question of land leases in the New Territories, and that he should present the issue as a commercial problem rather than a political one, specifically emphasizing that Britain was not at this stage seeking to address the question of British rule beyond 1997, but was merely trying to facilitate long-term investment in the interests of Hong Kong itself. MacLehose was then to ask whether the expiry date of 27 June 1997, which was written into all New Territories sub-leases sold by the Hong Kong government, could be replaced with a statement that such leases were valid 'for so long as the Crown administers the territory'.

This, the British thought, had a reasonable chance of success. Then, if Deng did agree, they would have set things moving in the right direction. The next step might be for Owen to put forward ideas for a general review of treaty arrangements, or – as his officials had in mind – a much more modest approach to China simply for its acquiescence in a suitably anodyne amendment to the Order in Council. But one step at a time: the important thing was to open the dialogue *tout court*.

The final factor which preoccupied the British as they prepared for the MacLehose visit was the need which they had identified for absolute confidentiality. As one party to that discussion saw it: 'It all had to be done in such a way that if it failed – as, sadly, it did fail – there would be nothing to show what had happened.'

The trip itself could not be other than a matter of public record. It was being celebrated long in advance by the press as conclusive evidence of Hong Kong's new intimacy with, and importance to, China. But the intention of raising the question of land leases, known only to a handful of civil servants in London and Hong Kong, was to be kept secret even from most of the Governor's inner 'cabinet' of advisers, the Executive Council.

The Executive Council ('Exco') was made up of half a dozen civil servants, known as its 'official' members; and six to ten representatives of the private sector, who were known, in the conventions of colonial terminology, as its 'unofficial' members. At its weekly meetings, the Governor was constitutionally required to consult the Executive Council on all important policy matters, and he would almost invariably accept its advice. For the Beijing trip, however, only Sir Yuet-keung Kan, the Council's senior member, who was accompanying MacLehose on the trip, was briefed. This was in itself a potentially controversial decision. In the view of one unofficial who joined the Executive Council some time later: 'It was wrong. If I had been on Exco at the time and had found out later that I had not been told, I would have been most upset . . . I assume [MacLehose] must have been told not to tell Exco. But if he was told, he could have replied "I cannot be Governor of Hong Kong and not tell my cabinet what is going on." ' In the contrasting view of a Hong Kong civil servant:

The fact is that Murray consulted the senior member of Exco, Sir Y.K. Kan, and that was it. That was his style. You can argue that he should have consulted more widely. But bringing Exco into something like that would have been a major departure. It would have involved overcoming large amounts of resistance [from London] on the normal bureaucratic grounds – security, vetting and so on – and so, for reasons which he had every right to consider valid, he decided not to do it. Obviously, when Exco unofficials discovered later how much had gone on without their being consulted, they were quite upset . . . Much of the criticism of Murray's visit stems from people who were upset about how little he had told them. And after the Thatcher visit to Beijing, when the negotiations began in earnest, Exco was briefed much more fully. But you have to transplant yourself to 1979. It had never been done.

The secrecy was so extreme because, if the British were worried about the long-term consequences of a rebuff from Deng Xiaoping, they were much more worried about the short-term consequences of any such rebuff becoming known in Hong Kong, sowing confusion and dismay among investors. No expectations relating to 1997 were to be allowed to build up around the visit; and any speculation that the Governor *might* raise the lease question was to be discouraged, as directly and as disingenuously as it was in the power of the Hong Kong government to do.

Clare Hollingworth, the eminent China specialist of the *Daily Telegraph*, felt – justly – confident enough to write in the newspaper of 5 March 1979 that 'The principal objective of the historic [MacLehose] visit is to discuss the future of the colony.' But readers of the *South China Morning Post*, Hong Kong's own 'establishment' newspaper, were being told with equal assurance on 7 March that 'Certainly, no one in Government feels [the visit] heralds talks on the lease of the New Territories . . . Officials point out that this would be a matter between China and Britain rather than China and Hong Kong.'

The official line, with some fine tuning, slowly prevailed. On 23 March, the day before the Governor left for China, the *Financial Times* declared simply: 'The issue of the expiry of the New Territories lease in 1997 will not be discussed when Sir Murray MacLehose makes the first official visit to China by a Hong Kong Governor.'

This was not quite a manifestation of the lie direct in Whitehall and Hong Kong briefings. In a strict sense, *the* New Territories lease, the one issued to the British Crown in 1898, was indeed not on the British agenda. The Governor was going to talk about the sub-leases issued by the Hong Kong government to private investors. But the distinction was a fine one, and the effect of insisting upon it thoroughly misleading. Which was, of course, the wished-for result.

THE HONG KONG Governor's party left for China by hydrofoil on 24 March 1979. Its principal members were Sir Murray and Lady MacLehose; Dr David Wilson, the Hong Kong government's Political Adviser; and Sir Yuet-keung Kan, the senior member of the Executive Council. After a banquet and an overnight stay in Guangzhou, they proceeded to Beijing, where their first two days were filled with relatively minor engagements, including a banquet given by the Governor's official host, the Minister of Foreign Trade, Li Qiang, and a return banquet hosted by Sir Percy Cradock, the British ambassador.

On the programme sent in advance to the Hong Kong party, the morning of 29 March had been set aside for 'sightseeing'. But this was a recognized convention within Deng Xiaoping's personal protocol. His appointments with visitors were never confirmed until the last moment. It was only on the evening of 28 March that MacLehose was told that Deng would indeed be receiving him the next day. He told Kan over breakfast the next morning. Then, joined by Wilson and Cradock, they made their way to the Suzhou Room of the Great Hall of the People, on Tiananmen Square, for the ten o'clock meeting.

They were seated there in conventional Chinese style, a horseshoe of chairs with Deng and MacLehose at the centre and interpreters at their shoulders. The Hong Kong party ranged off to the right, with Cradock next to MacLehose, then Kan and Wilson beyond him. Deng was accompanied by Li Qiang and Liao Chengzhi, the latter a veteran expert on reunification policy with family ties to Hong Kong.

After an initial exchange of greetings, Deng led off the conversation with a loosely prepared statement which, somewhat to the surprise of the British, made reference to the question of Hong Kong's future. A version of this statement, since published semi-officially by China, conforms in its essential points to what others record Deng as having said more discursively, namely that:

It has been our consistent view that the People's Republic of China has sovereignty over Hong Kong, while Hong Kong also has its own special position. A negotiated settlement of the Hong Kong question in the future should be based on the premise that the territory is part of China. However, we will treat Hong Kong as a special region. For a considerable length of time, Hong Kong may continue to practise its capitalist system while we practise our socialist system.[14]

Deng asked MacLehose to encourage Hong Kong businessmen to invest in China, and in particular to assist the development of Shenzhen, the border town where the special economic zone was planned. 'We think we can build up a great city,' said Deng, 'there will be great exchanges between Shenzhen and Hong Kong.' MacLehose asked whether the frontier between Hong Kong and Shenzhen would crumble. Deng replied: 'No, there must be a frontier between

Shenzhen and capitalism. But capitalism in Hong Kong and socialism in China can continue well into the next century.'

Twice, Deng repeated his point that Hong Kong would continue to enjoy a 'special position', even though it was part of China. He said that China had not decided exactly when it would resume its exercise of sovereignty over Hong Kong – that this might happen before 1997, or it might not happen until the next century. The decision would be for China to take. But whatever China decided, it would 'continue with present realities', and the interests of investors in Hong Kong would be protected.

Deng's reference to the interests of investors provided MacLehose with the cue which he sought to raise the British proposal on leases. He told Deng that, purely as a commercial matter, the approach of 1997 might soon begin to cause problems for investors in the New Territories by virtue of the diminishing term of the land leases which Britain was able to offer. He explained to Deng the British proposal for removing the expiry date of 1997 from such leases and substituting the formula that they would run 'for so long as the Crown administers the territory'.

This was, for Britain, the crucial moment: and it appears – recollections differ – that it was marred by imperfect translation, Deng's interpreter being heard to render MacLehose's remarks as though the Governor were suggesting an alteration to the terms of the head lease held by Britain under the Convention of Beijing, rather than the sub-leases issued by the Hong Kong government. Wilson, the best linguist of the British delegation, intervened to clarify the point. But the atmosphere had suddenly grown heavier, and the momentum of discussion was being lost. Instead of nodding the acquiescence for which the British had hoped, Deng halted. According to one of those present, 'Either he was very fuzzy and he did not understand quite what was being asked of him, or he was very wily and he understood all too well.' He then deliberately turned aside the question, adopting an *ex cathedra* tone to counter it with a formula of his own. Investors, he said, should be told to 'set their hearts at ease'.

MacLehose made a second run at his objective. He responded that the reassurance which Deng had given, though welcome, would not address the particular short-term anxiety created by the diminishing term of the land leases; and he repeated the British formula for blurring their expiry date. This time, Deng's reply was more considered, and more categorical. Whatever wording was used for land leases, he said, it must avoid *any* reference to 'British administration'. He was not going to say that Hong Kong's political situation would remain unchanged in the future; he was only going to say that its capitalist system would remain unchanged in the future, and that investors would not suffer.

The meeting ended. If it had not gone as the British had hoped, there were at least some very substantial reassurances from Deng about Hong Kong's economic future, and a message – 'set your hearts at ease' – which would be well received by investors. There was, however, still one last blow to come that day. When the party returned to the British Embassy, a telegram from London was awaiting them. The Labour government had lost a vote of confidence in the House of Commons, and an election would ensue. Owen would not be making his planned follow-up visit to Beijing. His officials, it seemed, would have to tidy up as best they could the loose ends which their meeting with Deng had left hanging.

THAT AFTERNOON, MACLEHOSE saw Huang Hua, the Chinese foreign minister, who said it had been 'inappropriate' to raise the question of land leases with Deng. When MacLehose replied that the problem was a real one which was not going to disappear unless specific action were taken, Huang said that Deng's reassurance should be sufficient. To ask for any more would be 'legalistic'. An evening meeting with Liao Chengzhi yielded no new information. On that note, MacLehose was obliged to leave Beijing and continue his tour of China, before returning to Hong Kong on 4 April.

When he did arrive back in the territory, it was to make public Deng's formula, 'set your hearts at ease', which proved more than enough meat to satisfy the local hunger for news from Beijing. Under the headline 'Don't Worry, Deng Tells Hong Kong Investors', the *South China Morning Post* recorded on its front page of 7 April that 'Deng Xiaoping has asked the Governor, Sir Murray MacLehose, to tell investors in Hong Kong to "Put their hearts at ease" . . . "It was a most realistic and helpful comment for the record," said Sir Murray.'

In its leader columns that same day, the *Post* offered this warm gloss:

Perhaps the most significant statement made to Sir Murray was by . . . Deng Xiaoping, who 'formally requested [the Governor] to ask investors to put their hearts at ease'. Bearing in mind that no discussions were expected on the lease and that in any case no Chinese official today would presume to bind his successors to any formal long-term undertaking with regard to Hong Kong, this must be a substantial encouragement to investors seeking security for the short- and indeed even the medium-term future . . .

In Hong Kong's experience, a statement such as that made by Mr Deng, backed as it is by the knowledge that his words carry great weight, is as near as one is likely to get to a guarantee. And the realist who decides to invest in Hong Kong can write his own small print knowing as he must the realities of the political situation.

Most of the realities, at any rate. For, from the moment at which MacLehose proclaimed Deng's message, Hong Kong was divided in two: between the very small group of people which knew that there was more to it than that, and the very large group which did not. The very small group, at first no more than half a dozen people in the Hong Kong government and a handful more in the New China News Agency, slowly grew to include businessmen who cultivated their contacts in Beijing, and who were given to understand that China had been both perplexed and irritated by what it saw as a British 'manoeuvre'. But as the confidence of domestic and foreign investors-at-large soared, their hearts all too clearly 'at ease', the businessmen in the know simply kept quiet and made their profits while they could. The average price of a small flat in Hong Kong leapt by 67 per cent in 1979, and again by 30 per cent in 1980. By some measures, Hong Kong property became the most expensive in the world. The Hang Seng Index exactly doubled in 1979–80, in a boom financed largely by credit. If Deng Xiaoping was testing China's ability to sustain confidence in Hong Kong by its own intervention, then he could scarcely have hoped for a better result.

4

'One Country, Two Systems'

WHEN he received Sir Murray MacLehose in March 1979, Deng Xiaoping was flanked by Liao Chengzhi, the Communist Party's chief strategist for Taiwan, Hong Kong and Macao affairs. Liao's job was to bring about China's reunification.

Reunification was an ideal which transcended political boundaries. It was supported as fervently by the government in Taipei as by that in Beijing, though obviously the two differed as to which held legitimate sovereignty. For Deng, as he consolidated his leadership of the Communist Party in 1977–8, reunification supplied a political complement to his over-arching commitment to economic reform. Reform was a potentially controversial endeavour which was sure to encounter resistance from the Party's more conservative members; but reunification was a binding force within the Party, a touchstone of patriotism from which dissent was unthinkable. If Deng could deliver on reunification, which even Mao Zedong had not achieved, then his position would be secure however divisive his economic policies might prove.

Hong Kong was a point at which Deng's twin ambitions overlapped. A successful resumption of the territory, leaving intact its capacity to channel capital and expertise into the rest of China, would be a triumph for both reunification and the cause of economic reform. The central government anticipated Hong Kong's heightened importance by setting up a new department, the Hong Kong and Macao Affairs Office of the State Council, in 1978, with Liao Chengzhi as its director – though the existence of this office was not made public until 1982, presumably to avoid provoking speculation in Hong Kong about China's intentions.

In the priorities of reunification, however, Hong Kong still ranked far behind Taiwan, the redoubt of the Nationalists since their defeat by the Communists in 1949. Not only was Hong Kong infinitely less threatening than Taiwan, politically and militarily, for the mainland; it was also a problem which, thanks to the expiry of the New Territories lease in 1997, would slowly resolve itself in China's favour even without positive action on China's part. Mao Zedong himself was recorded in Party lore as having said that the Hong Kong question would be addressed after that of Taiwan; Chen Yi, then China's foreign minister, had said the same thing in 1966; Liao Chengzhi repeated the formula in 1977.

By late 1978, there was, moreover, an additional reason for China to hope that the Taiwan question might be resolved in the relatively near future. Motivated primarily by their shared antipathy to the Soviet Union, China and the United States were preparing to normalize diplomatic relations. In November 1978, the US proposed a draft normalization agreement. From 13 to 15 December, Leonard Woodcock, the US representative in Beijing, worked closely with Deng on a final wording. As soon as the differences had been resolved, the United States President, Jimmy Carter, announced on 15 December his intention of restoring full diplomatic relations with China from 1 January 1979.

The United States was Taiwan's most important diplomatic ally and supplier of arms. Though Washington issued a separate statement relating to Taiwan, saying that the United States 'continues to have an interest in the peaceful resolution of the Taiwan issue and expects that the Taiwan issue will be settled peacefully by the Chinese themselves', a US delegation sent to Taipei on 27 December 1978 was pelted with red paint and vegetables, while demonstrators trampled peanuts underfoot as an insult to Carter. In Beijing, hopes surged that the closure of the United States Embassy in Taipei, coupled with the termination of the US-Taiwan Mutual Defence Treaty and the withdrawal of US troops from the island, would arouse a sufficient sense of vulnerability within the Nationalist government to make it more susceptible to overtures from the mainland, if these could be cast in a suitably friendly and generous form. The Chinese Communist Party Central Committee recorded in its December 1978 communiqué: 'With the normalization of Sino-US relations, the prospect of having our country's sacred territory of Taiwan return to the embrace of the motherland and achieving the magnificent goal of reunification has already emerged more clearly before us.'

China still did not formally renounce the possibility of retaking Taiwan by force. But to assist its 'soft sell', the Communist Party also ruled in December 1978 that its propaganda would cease to call for Taiwan's 'liberation' and would instead look forward to the 'peaceful reunification of the motherland'. In a 'Letter to Taiwan Compatriots', published at the 1979 New Year, the Beijing government set out the 'principles' of this new policy. These included promises that Beijing would 'respect Taiwan's status quo . . . adopt reasonable and rational policies and methods, and . . . refrain from causing Taiwan people to suffer losses'.

This same basic message was repeated in more sweeping terms when Deng received a delegation from the United States Senate Military Affairs Committee on 9 January 1979. Taiwan, he said, would be able to retain autonomy 'for so long as the people of Taiwan so desire' after reunification; administrative power would remain with the Taipei government; the existing economic and social systems there would be preserved; and local security forces could be maintained.[1]

This, in embryo, was the new reunification policy which Liao Chengzhi was beginning to elaborate on Deng's behalf – the policy which would come to be known, three years later, as 'one country, two systems'. Its innovatory feature was a willingness to compromise between form and substance. If Taiwan would only bow to Beijing's sovereignty, then the Beijing government would promise to concede a very high degree of administrative autonomy to the Taipei authorities. The 'two systems', Communism on the mainland and capitalism on Taiwan, could then co-exist within a single country. This new approach was something of a gamble by virtue of the political legitimacy which it implicitly yielded to Taipei. But Deng was in an adventurous mood that winter.[2] He was new to power; and, at 77, was by no means assured of many more years in which to leave his mark.

When Deng met MacLehose in Beijing on 29 March, the policy of 'one country, two systems' was thus in its formative stages, and it was being devised specifically for Taiwan. Clearly, it could have potentially important implications for Hong Kong, but there was also in Hong Kong the additional problem of a foreign colonial government with which to deal. This was the background to Deng's remarks that day; and it is a matter for speculation how differently the Hong Kong question might have been handled had the British mind not been focused so closely on the question of land leases, and had Deng's broader signals been interpreted rather more clearly.

Though Deng stopped short of making an explicit comparison with China's offer to Taiwan, his repeated references to Hong Kong's future 'special status' were a way of saying that some deal of the sort made by possible by the 'one country, two systems' principle could in due course be offered to Hong Kong. He evidently meant this as a reassuring message for Hong Kong, even though, logically, there could be not possibly be any place for Britain in a 'one country, two systems' arrangement. That Deng did expect Britain to go, and was speaking on this premise, was apparent from his reaction to the Foreign Office proposal for using 'Crown administration' as a new basis for New Territories land leases. But whatever happened, he was saying to MacLehose, Hong Kong would not simply be folded back into the mainland. Whatever happened, the interests of investors would be protected. 'One country, two systems' would enable Hong Kong's economy to continue on its present course. Beyond that, Deng did not want to be drawn into any new and detailed discussion of Hong Kong's future while China was preoccupied with Taiwan. When MacLehose's insistence on talking about land leases beyond 1997 took him by surprise, Deng's response was not evasive, but logical within its limitations. He merely re-stated, in much blunter terms, the message which had been contained in his earlier, more discursive comments. China was not yet ready to discuss Hong Kong as such, but investors should not worry; China would sort it out.

SIR PERCY CRADOCK had concluded the business of the MacLehose visit by returning to the Chinese Ministry of Foreign Affairs with a written version of the British proposal to grant New Territories land leases 'for so long as the Crown administers the territory'. A taste of China's response came informally in May, when Song Zhiguang, an assistant foreign minister and a former ambassador to Britain, told visiting French journalists that Hong Kong 'is part of China', and that 'when the lease expires, an appropriate attitude will be adopted in settling the question'. There may have been an important nuance in Song's remarks, if he was intentionally suggesting that China had already decided that the Hong Kong question would be resolved in 1997 'when the lease expires', rather than, as China had previously insisted, 'when the time is ripe'. But of more immediate relevance to Britain was Song's underlining of China's disinclination to take any action whatsoever in respect of Hong Kong at the present time or in the near future. This disinclination was reconfirmed when Song finally gave his ministry's formal answer to Cradock in September. He said that China viewed the proposed change to New Territories land leases as 'unnecessary', and that China 'hoped' Britain would not act as the Foreign Office had proposed.

Wishing to hear more, the British kept an ear open to Hua Guofeng, who though nominally the Chinese Prime Minister was in reality now a very marginal figure, when he visited London in November 1979. Hua dined at 10 Downing Street with its new master, Margaret Thatcher, but the conversation was leaden, and Hua was unable to offer any new information about Hong Kong. The legacies of the visit were purely formal ones: the first, that it implied a return visit by Thatcher to Beijing at some future date; the second, that it yielded a communiqué in which Thatcher and Hua referred to their common interest in the 'stability and prosperity' of Hong Kong, a bland formula to which Chinese and British diplomats would return incessantly in the difficult years ahead.

In December 1979, Lord Carrington, the British Foreign Secretary, received his Chinese counterpart, Huang Hua. Huang was closer to the centres of power than Hua Guofeng, but discussion of Hong Kong during that visit was 'bleak' in the British recollection. Huang told Carrington, much as he had told MacLehose the previous March, that Deng had already made 'an authoritative statement' on Hong Kong and that 'both sides should believe this to be sufficient'. In May 1980, James Callaghan, Thatcher's predecessor as Prime Minister, returned from Beijing with the view that China had put the Hong Kong question 'on the back burner'.

The Foreign Office remained, nonetheless, determined to pursue its dialogue with China, the Deng-MacLehose meeting having only increased its discomfort and its sense of urgency. Britain's formal raising and China's formal rejection of a proposal for unblocking the land-lease question had now ruled out any possibility of Britain experimenting with some unilateral action along similar lines. And yet, at the same time, the Chinese were clearly envisioning some sort of change in Hong Kong's arrangements, which they felt under no obligation to disclose until much later in the day – exactly the situation which Britain had hoped most keenly to pre-empt.

Hong Kong was not an issue to capture the imagination of Thatcher herself, preoccupied as she then was with the struggle at home to impress her own very different values on the country which she had inherited from Callaghan. Carrington accepted his civil servants' advice to pursue the Hong Kong question when he paid his own visit to Beijing in April 1981, but he found that Huang Hua now simply refused to discuss the territory at all. Huang told Carrington to raise the matter with Deng; but when Carrington saw Deng the next day, he found that even Deng would do no more than repeat, word for word, his earlier assurance that investors should 'set their hearts at ease'. Instead, Deng wanted to talk at length about his reunification hopes for Taiwan, and to draw to Britain's attention the new and detailed proposals for achieving that goal which were then in the final stage of drafting.[3]

The British knew that they were being stonewalled, if relatively politely. But much blunter messages, stripped of diplomatic circumlocutions, were being delivered by Beijing officials to influential Hong Kong visitors. When Fung King-hey,[4] one of Hong Kong's leading financiers, breakfasted with Liao Chengzhi in Beijing in March 1981 and asked about Hong Kong's future, Liao was categorical. 'The British want us to show our hand,' he said. 'They are forcing the issue. But we will not be forced. *Zhongguoren bu wei biao tai*. China will not be forced into making public its position.'

And, even if Deng had been disposed to talk about Hong Kong, he – like Thatcher – had more pressing matters on his mind. In February 1980, he was managing the final purge of hard-core Maoists from the Central Committee, to be followed in succeeding months by the forced standing-down of a much broader spectrum of the old guard. His principal lieutenants, Hu Yaobang and Zhao Ziyang,[5] were being manoeuvred into place as Party leader and Prime Minister respectively. Then, in November 1980, he authorized the three-month public trial of the Gang of Four, sending shock-waves through the Communist Party as the failings of Mao Zedong were implicitly denounced.

The initial shine was fading, meanwhile, from some of Deng's own achievements. The first wave of economic reforms in 1979–80 had been launched without adequate expertise or controls, and 'open-door' euphoria had led China to sign contracts to spend billions of dollars which it did not possess. As to Taiwan, the hopes for reunification raised at the start of 1979 had greatly diminished. The normalization of diplomatic relations with the United States had quickly been offset in April 1979 by the passage of the Taiwan Relations Act;[6] the government of Chiang Ching-kuo in Taipei showed no inclination to negotiate, even on the basis of its own retained autonomy; and the election of Ronald Reagan as US President in 1980 had given Taipei a new and more reliable friend in Washington.

It was a difficult period, but Deng – again, like Thatcher – held his ground. In June 1981, the Central Committee formally approved a new Party hierarchy dominated by Deng's allies, and endorsed the further implementation of the policies of reform adopted in 1978. It pushed forward, under Deng's impetus, the Party's thinking on such matters as the special economic zones, foreign exchange earnings, foreign trade and foreign investment; and in doing so, it may have set the stage for a shift in the pattern of China's reunification policy which was to take place over the next six months. As *Ming Pao*, the most respected of Hong Kong's non-partisan newspapers, reflected presciently:

> Over the past year, the leaders in China simply did not have time to give any thought to the issue involving Hong Kong's future. What little time they had to spare was used in dealing with the Taiwan issue, in which President Reagan was involved, the dispute with Vietnam, the situation in Cambodia, the Sino-Soviet feud and the crisis in Poland.
>
> The Sixth Plenum has given its final approval to the political line and the economic policy to be followed in China. Deng Xiaoping and Hu Yaobang are no longer to be bothered by the ultra-leftists. While many difficulties still lie ahead, they are confined to how to enforce the lines which have already been laid down.
>
> To China, the question of Hong Kong's future is a question of economic policy-making . . . Diplomacy is also involved, but it is of lesser importance. Hong Kong's future is not a difficult problem for China. There is no Gordian knot to be cut. It should be

easy now for Deng and Hu to spend a little time on the Hong Kong question, give it some thought, and resolve it.[7]

Liao Chengzhi's long task of drafting a definitive proposal for reunification with Taiwan was meanwhile being completed. His proposals, grouped under nine main headings, and commonly called the 'Nine Points', which Deng had commended in draft form to Carrington in March, were published as a speech by Marshal Ye Jianying, chairman of the standing committee of the National People's Congress, on 30 September 1981, the eve of China's National Day. In language which foreshadowed the terms of the eventual settlement to be offered Hong Kong, Ye said that:

- Talks should be held between the Communist Party and the Kuomintang [Nationalists] . . . to accomplish the great cause of national reunification;
- The two sides should . . . facilitate the exchange of mail, trade, air and shipping services, visits by relatives and tourists, and academic, cultural and sports exchanges;
- After the country is reunified, Taiwan can enjoy a high degree of autonomy as a special administrative region and it can retain its armed forces. The central government will not interfere with local affairs on Taiwan;
- Taiwan's current socio-economic system will remain unchanged, so will its way of life . . . Private property, houses, land, enterprises or foreign investment will not be encroached upon;
- People in authority . . . in Taiwan may take up posts of leadership in national political bodies . . .;
- When Taiwan's local finance is in difficulty, the central government may offer subsidies . . .;
- Industrialists and businessmen in Taiwan are welcome to invest and engage in various economic undertakings on the Mainland . . .;
- The reunification of the Motherland is the responsibility of all Chinese.[8]

But even as Ye was issuing these promises and exhortations, it was apparent that Taiwan had no intention of taking them seriously. The radical new approach to reunification, conceived in the optimism of late 1978, had reached a temporary impasse. The 'Nine Points' were no longer a speedy way forward, but represented for China a way of temporarily signing off with a public declaration of its new secular policy, to which Taiwan could respond as and when it chose.

BETWEEN SEPTEMBER AND December 1981, China's reunification policy underwent a silent but momentous change. Prior to that period, Beijing had treated Taiwan as the priority, and Hong Kong as an issue to be deferred. After that period, from New Year 1982 onwards, a new order was apparent. The reunification of Hong Kong was to be achieved with all possible speed, both for its own sake and in the hope that it would provide an example sufficiently encouraging to embolden Taiwan to follow suit.

China has never officially disclosed the timing of, or the background to, its decision to move so abruptly in late 1981 towards the resolution of Hong Kong's future. But the contributing factors may be deduced readily enough. Deng felt both the weight of history and the exigencies of politics pressing down upon him. There was little prospect of progress on reunification with Taiwan. Yet there was, conversely, a demonstrable anxiety on the part of Britain to reach some sort of settlement for Hong Kong. Indeed, the British just would not stop raising the matter. There was, moreover, in the 'Nine Points' for Taiwan, a ready-made set of policies which could be applied, with modifications, to Hong Kong. By switching his attention to Hong Kong, Deng could be all but guaranteed a tangible triumph of reunification, albeit on a slightly reduced scale, within a short space of time. Then – who knew? – a successful deal over Hong Kong might just encourage Taiwan, and its American friends, to regard the 'one country, two systems' concept with rather more confidence than they did at present. Deng and Liao shifted direction, towards the more accessible target.

Beijing entertained a flurry of Hong Kong delegations and businessmen in November and December 1981, not at this stage to brief them explicitly about China's intentions, but rather to build contacts and confidence. The New China News Agency's Hong Kong branch was asked to prepare a special report on public opinion in the territory – which earned a black mark for the Agency's local head, Wang Kuang, when it showed that most Hong Kong inhabitants rather liked things as they were. Fei Yiming, publisher of the Communist newspaper *Ta Kung Pao*, a slight, formal man who had nonetheless managed some blood-curdling rhetoric during the 1967 riots, led a Hong Kong delegation from the territory to the National People's Congress session which opened on 30 November, providing a further opportunity for the central government to test the opinions of its place-men in Hong Kong before committing itself finally and publicly to resumption.

The decision in principle to proceed with the resumption of Hong Kong was probably then taken around Christmas 1981, in time for it to be transmitted during a special fortnight-long United Front national work meeting, convened in Beijing on 21 December 1981. This meeting brought together the early 'key players' who would refine and communicate the policy, including Hu Yaobang, the Communist Party general secretary; Liao Chengzhi; and Xi Zhongxun, the Party secretary of Guangdong Province.[9] Certainly, a decision on Hong Kong had been taken by the time the United Front work meeting concluded on 6 January – for it was on this same day that Humphrey Atkins, a visiting junior British foreign minister, was received by Zhao Ziyang, the Prime Minister. And, whereas previous visitors had found Chinese leaders uniformly unwilling to advance the Hong Kong question beyond Deng's reassurances of March 1979, Atkins discovered Zhao in a quite different mood.

Zhao was positively forthcoming, telling Atkins that China would 'safeguard' its sovereignty over Hong Kong, and that the 'prosperity of Hong Kong [would] be maintained'. Hong Kong would remain 'a free port, and a commercial and financial centre', said Zhao. China intended, moreover, to 'discuss the position with various circles in Hong Kong and take account of their views' in devising its plans. Atkins was relieved. He had come to prepare the way for Thatcher, who intended to visit Beijing that autumn, returning the visit paid to London in November 1979 by Hua Guofeng. Hong Kong could scarcely not be on the agenda for that visit, yet, equally, Thatcher could scarcely be stonewalled in the way that Carrington had been. Now that Zhao was declaring that the Chinese were ready to talk business, the door on which the British had been pushing for almost two years had suddenly swung open. That same evening, 6 January, it was formally announced that Thatcher would indeed go to Beijing. And Hong Kong, it was understood, would be on the agenda.

Atkins continued on to Hong Kong where, encouraged by Zhao's response, he spoke unusually freely to journalists. He was quoted variously as saying that 'Come 1997, if nobody does anything at all, the government's powers over the New Territories cease', and that '[the Chinese] are very well aware that, if nothing is done, confidence will be endangered'.[10] Members of the Executive and Legislative Councils were briefed privately about the content of his talks with Zhao. A thrill of anticipation ran through the city. 'It was quite clear when Humphrey got back', recalled one Executive Council member, 'that this was the beginning of the negotiating process.'

IT WAS THE beginning, however, to an exercise into which British politics was also now injecting a note of change. When the Foreign Office had begun its groundwork for a negotiation of Hong Kong's future in 1978–9, it was motivated in part by a perceived need to capitalize on a perhaps brief period of relative stability in Beijing. It could scarcely have foreseen that, while the political climate in Beijing would in fact remain fairly constant, it would change so radically in London that, by the time talks on Hong Kong's future actually began, Britain would be represented by a prime minister more zealous for Empire than any since Churchill.

For the Labour government which had preceded Thatcher, and for its Foreign Secretary, David Owen, sovereignty over imperial relics had held no particular attraction or mystique. If China had offered to open talks on Hong Kong in 1979 on the understanding that some formal acknowledgement of China's sovereignty would be required, then neither Whitehall nor Westminster would have been particularly shocked or obdurate. Even under Thatcher in 1980–1, with Lord Carrington at the Foreign Office, a deal might have been done almost as easily. But then came the Falklands War, and with it a Falklands-factored Thatcher, for whom 'sovereignty' was live ammunition, and for whom the words 'negotiated settlement' were all but oxymoronic.

The Falklands War first appeared as a seemingly distant cloud on the political horizon on 3 March 1982, when a telegram from the British ambassador in Buenos Aires reported threats of unilateral Argentinian action against the islands. On 25 March, an Argentine party landed on the Falklands dependency of South Georgia; and on 2 April, taking Britain nonetheless by surprise, the Falklands themselves were invaded. From 3 April, when the House of Commons met for an emergency Saturday sitting, to 14 June, when the Argentine invading forces surrendered to the British, scarcely any other issue – least of all a lesser foreign-policy matter – could distract Thatcher from the conduct of her war.

The Falklands cast a long shadow. Months were lost during which Hong Kong, with the Beijing trip approaching, should have found an occasional space in the Prime Minister's briefing-papers. Lord Carrington, who had mastered the issues and met China's leaders, had resigned as Foreign Secretary, to be replaced by Francis Pym, who had done neither and who enjoyed much less of Thatcher's confidence. Then, with June, came the political imperatives of victory. A country which had just fought a war to hold one distant possession could scarcely yield another voluntarily, however different the context might be.

On 28 July 1982, two days after she had attended the service of thanksgiving for the Falklands victory at St Paul's Cathedral in the City of London, Thatcher finally convened a meeting in Downing Street to decide what she should say about Hong Kong. She was due in Beijing just eight weeks later. The fact that preparations had not been deferred even further was due mainly to Sir Edward Youde, Hong Kong's newly appointed Governor, who had taken it upon himself to cut through the non-communication between Pym and Thatcher and to deal directly with Downing Street. One Whitehall source recalls the events of that spring and early summer in these terms:

There had been the feeling, after Atkins, that we had to prepare for the Prime Minister's visit. There were a number of ideas floating around, including – this being a fairly standard preparation for important meetings – the possibility of informal feelers, to explore the position a little further without commitment, so that when the formal sessions began there might be a dotted-line picture of what could perhaps be agreed already in position. To do that, you would have needed some sort of early brainstorming session with the Prime Minister, to get some sort of steer from her about what sort of preparations she wanted and whether she wanted informal contacts. All of those thoughts were brought to a halt by the Falklands. It was virtually impossible to get any other file under the Prime Minister's nose.

Then, after the Falklands War, the thought of sticking a Hong

Kong file, you might as well have called it 'Proposal to Divest Sovereignty over Hong Kong to Foreigners', the idea of putting *that* under Mrs Thatcher's nose in her hour of triumph was more than any foreign secretary could bear. It was Teddy Youde who finally got things moving, going back to London and cranking the Prime Minister up.

The principal figures grouped around the Downing Street table that Wednesday afternoon were, in addition to Thatcher herself, Sir Percy Cradock, who had flown in from Beijing, Sir Edward Youde, from Hong Kong, and Alan Donald, the Foreign Office assistant under-secretary in charge of Asia and the Pacific. In addition to the record of Humphrey Atkins's meeting with Zhao Ziyang, the British had at their disposal an amplified account of China's intentions relayed through the agency of Edward Heath, who had been received by Deng Xiaoping in Beijing on 6 April. Deng had asked Heath whether Britain was likely to accept a settlement of Hong Kong's future based on the 'Nine Points' for Taiwan. Specifically, Deng explained, this would mean that sovereignty over Hong Kong would be reclaimed by China, and that Hong Kong would cease to be run by Britain. Instead, it would have its own government, run by Hong Kong people, and its social and economic systems would remain unchanged. It would remain a free port and a financial centre. The Chinese, in short, wanted a complete British withdrawal. Their position might or might not be negotiable, but at least it was now clear.

Thatcher's attitude was, according to one observer, 'obdurate in a lawyer-like way'. She began the Downing Street meeting by observing that Britain held title to Hong Kong by three treaties, only one of which was a lease. The other two treaties had ceded Hong Kong Island and the Kowloon peninsula to Britain in perpetuity. China denounced all three treaties as 'unequal', claiming that they were invalid because they had been imposed by force. But in the British view, supported by the British understanding of international law, all three were perfectly valid. Granted, the New Territories would revert to China in 1997 unless some action were taken; but if China wanted all of Hong Kong to be returned, as Deng was now indicating, then the only legal way of achieving this would be by obtaining Britain's agreement to an amendment of the terms of the two cessions. As to the New Territories, said Thatcher, concluding her summary, was it indeed necessary to accept the conventional wisdom that the rest of Hong Kong could not survive without them? Was it beyond the power of Britain and Hong Kong to arrange for the colony to fall back on its ceded portions?

Sir Edward Youde answered the last of these questions. He had foreseen the Prime Minister's line of attack, and had brought with him the materials to meet it. He produced photographs showing the notional border between the leased area of the New Territories and the ceded area of Kowloon. Along most of this line ran a main road, Boundary Street, which was just one more busy road in the sprawl of north Kowloon, crossed by tens of thousands of vehicles and pedestrians each day without a second thought. It was no more a natural frontier than, say, Euston Road in London. He had the statistics for traffic along and across Boundary Street, and he had the maps showing where in the New Territories lay the towns, villages, factories, roads, reservoirs and railways which were an integral part of Hong Kong. A division along Boundary Street, he explained, would be impossible. Not impractical. Impossible.

The discussion of Boundary Street took no more than ten minutes, and it was decisive. China's position was a strong one; stronger than the composition of the treaties themselves would suggest. Should Britain nonetheless try to stand on the cessions as a matter of international law? Here, Cradock set the tone. Simply to defy in absolute terms China's claims to sovereignty, he said, would look 'splendid and tough' for Britain in the short term. But it would rebound on the people of Hong Kong in the long term. China would enforce a handover, very possibly on much less amenable terms than it now seemed prepared to discuss.

Thatcher already knew the Foreign Office view; it was simply that she had difficulty in swallowing it whole. Cradock and Donald wanted her to work towards some form of compromise with China, not on the terms which Deng had outlined to Heath, but on the basis that Britain would relinquish its claim to formal sovereignty over Hong Kong in exchange for the right to continued British administration there under some revised form of treaty.

She resisted the notion of giving up sovereignty; but she had no alternative strategy of her own, and she was now obliged to agree that Hong Kong would stand or fall with the New Territories. There was, therefore, no real British 'strategy' for Hong Kong at this stage. Thatcher would go to China, and then she would see. For the meetings in Beijing, Cradock proposed a purely tactical objective. Britain and China had already made a joint commitment to Hong Kong's 'stability and prosperity', when Hua Guofeng visited London in 1979. Apart from that small piece of common ground, the subject was fraught with unknowns. Let the objective for Beijing, then, be a declaration in the name of both governments that formal negotiations were to begin with the aim of maintaining Hong Kong's 'stability and prosperity'. Nothing need be ruled out, and, equally importantly, no other preconditions need be written in. Then, when the negotiations began, the possibilities would become a little clearer. The proposal was adopted, and the meeting came briskly to its end.

IN BEIJING THAT summer, without a Falklands War to fight, and with a basic policy towards Hong Kong already established at the start of 1982, the detailed work was advancing rather more quickly. For eight months, beginning soon after the January visit of Humphrey Atkins, the Hong Kong and Macao Affairs Office organized a working group including representatives from the New China News Agency's Hong Kong branch, charged with reflecting upon the practical details of applying to Hong Kong the 'one country, two systems' concept – described, at this stage, by the slightly clumsier slogan of 'two social systems co-existing within one country'.

One early recommendation of the working party was that the concept of a 'special status' for Hong Kong would be better received if it were accompanied by a long-term guarantee which would not be capriciously withdrawn. This message, which would later be refined into a specific promise of 'no change for fifty years after 1997', was duly delivered in an early form when Gu Mu, a vice-premier of China, received Hong Kong's Financial Secretary, John Bremridge, on 10 March. Gu offered what he called a 'six-character constitution' for Hong Kong: '*Jin hau chang qi fan rong*', meaning 'lasting prosperity for a long time to come'.[11]

By 6 April, Deng was able to give the relatively specific version of China's plans to Edward Heath which was subsequently relayed to Downing Street. In that same month, a constitutional development was underway which, though conceived in the context of Taiwan, was also capable of accommodating Hong Kong. This development was the addition to China's national constitution of a new clause, Article 30 in early drafts, but later renumbered as Article 31, which supplied a legal basis for the implementation of 'one country, two systems' by empowering the state to set up 'special administrative regions' and endowing them with laws differing from those prevailing in the rest of the country.[12] A draft constitution including the new clause was approved by the Constitutional Revision Committee of the National People's Congress on 21 April and circulated to local congresses throughout China for explanation and comment.

The traffic of distinguished visitors from Hong Kong to Beijing continued, but still for China to gather impressions rather than to transmit information. On 21 May, Deng received Henry Fok, a billionaire property developer who had been a business partner of China for more than thirty years. The same day, Zhao Ziyang received Li Ka-shing, another property developer who was the most powerful figure in the Hong Kong stock market. On 26 May, Zhao received a group of industrialists led by Ann Tse-kai and Tang Hsiang-chien. A week later, Deng received Rayson Lisung Huang, vice-chancellor of the University of Hong Kong.

Finally, on 15 June, Deng decided that it was time to bring China's thinking into the open. He received, at the Great Hall of the People, a group of twelve Hong Kong and Macao personalities, led by Fei Yiming, the publisher of *Ta Kung Pao*, most of them delegates to the National People's Congress.[13] Deng made brief introductory remarks about China's intention of regaining sovereignty over Hong Kong while preserving its prosperity. He then invited the group to respond. According to the political fortnightly, *Pai Shing*, in its issue of 1 July: 'During the meeting, Deng Xiaoping put forward one principle. It was that shortly before or after 1997, China will regain sovereignty over Hong Kong and will devise a workable method for maintaining stability and prosperity in Hong Kong, enabling the free port to continue to give full play to its role'.

In saying that China would 'regain sovereignty', glossed *Pai Shing*, Deng was implying that:

Although the Beijing authorities do not recognize the unequal treaties, they are obliged squarely to face the question of Hong Kong, a question left over from history. Not only the people of Hong Kong brood about the time-limit of 1997; the PRC leaders also take it to heart. At the very least, a line has to be drawn at this date . . . According to the cardinal principle of the honour of

73

the Chinese nation, it is impossible to maintain the status quo in Hong Kong after 1997. That is to say, China must regain sovereignty, even though this may be only a symbolic action.

Participants in the meeting briefed correspondents of Hong Kong's political press, whose articles gave the territory its first authentic indications of the process now taking shape. The 1 July issue of *Cheng Ming*, a rival magazine, was pithier than *Pai Shing*. Also drawing on the 15 June meeting with Deng, it listed what it described as the 'principles and policies of the Chinese authorities for solving the Hong Kong issue'. These were:

- Hong Kong, Kowloon and Macao are territories of China, and China has sovereignty over them. The treaties signed with the invaders in the past are unequal treaties. The Chinese authorities cannot recognize the legitimacy of these treaties.
- Regaining sovereignty over Hong Kong and Macao is not something in the remote future.
- The concept of 'one country, two systems' will be adopted to resolve the sovereignty of Hong Kong and Macao.
- The existing systems in Hong Kong will not be changed – that is, Hong Kong and Macao will be allowed to maintain their capitalist social systems. Capitalism will be allowed to remain and develop.
- Hong Kong will remain a free port.[14]

The channelling of accounts of the 15 June meeting to the Hong Kong press marked the start of a public relations campaign that China would conduct more or less without respite for the next two and a half years in Hong Kong, aimed at progressively manipulating Hong Kong public opinion into accepting China's plans for resumption as both patriotic and inevitable.

The public relations work continued with an invitation issued on 16 July by Peng Zhen, vice-chairman of the National People's Congress, for 'compatriots in Hong Kong, Macao and Taiwan' to study the new draft constitution, including Article 31. To transmit the Party's own guidance on the document, Li Jianzhen, 76-year-old chairman of the Guangdong Provincial People's Congress, arrived at the Hong Kong branch of the New China News Agency on 21 July, where she received most of the same group of National People's Congress delegates whom Deng had addressed on 15 June, together with Hong Kong delegates to the Chinese People's Political Consultative Conference, a more loosely knit mainland 'advisory' body. A handful of correspondents for leftist newspapers were also briefed.

Pai Shing, citing New China News Agency sources, said of the visit: '[Li] was not only coming here to call a meeting about China's constitution, she was also going to convey the instructions of the central authorities to some major leftists concerning the future of this city.'[15]

Li confirmed that Article 31 would be the basis of Hong Kong's future status. She may also have indicated that it was now appropriate to talk openly about the existence of the Hong Kong and Macao Affairs Office of the State Council, set up secretly in 1978, since it was after this visit that its existence became generally known in Hong Kong. Then Li relayed the current status of the blueprint for post-1997 Hong Kong, which had been under development by the working party in Beijing since January. This blueprint, which would eventually become informally known as the 'Twelve Points for Hong Kong', remained very little changed in essence – though much reworked and elaborated – from its first coherent draft in August 1982 to the point at which it was incorporated into the body of the Joint Declaration two years later.

The emerging blueprint was given its first detailed public airing in a pair of articles which appeared in the August issues of a Hong Kong pro-China monthly, *Wide Angle*, laying out the Chinese position – presumably as Li had described it – with extraordinary candour and authenticity. Presenting the articles as the product of a series of interviews with 'well-informed people in Beijing and Hong Kong', the *Wide Angle* correspondent reported:

I was told that after China has taken over Hong Kong, the present system will remain intact. Hong Kong's status as a free port and international financial centre, the foreign exchange value of the Hong Kong dollar in the international markets, the various international trade agreements to which Hong Kong is a party, such as the Multi-Fibre Arrangement, the current economic and legal systems and the people's way of life will all remain the same . . .

After Hong Kong has returned to China, there will be no

change other than a five-star flag and a Chinese governor . . .
Hong Kong will remain as it is, able to indulge in its speculations
on the gold, stock and property markets as well as in its colourful
night-life . . .

People from mainland China will be subject to the same travel
restrictions . . . Laws will remain intact except for minor modifications. Hong Kong itself, not London or Beijing, will administer the judicial system. The highest Court of Appeal will also be
located in Hong Kong . . .

The future Governor can be chosen by election and then
endorsed by China. He need not be an advocate of socialism . . .
Anyone who agrees that China should take back Hong Kong,
and who has high qualifications and capabilities, is eligible for
that post. As for the rest of the governing machinery, there will
be no reshuffle.[16]

This, then, was the stage which China's policy-making had reached
by the end of July 1982: a 'one country, two systems' prescription so
categorical in form that it even had clauses covering the property
market and the national flag. While Mrs Thatcher was just now looking at photographs of Boundary Street, and bristling over British
sovereignty, the Chinese had already discounted its demise.

5

Mrs Thatcher
Makes a Stand

IT was long customary, in Hong Kong, to talk about 1997 as little
as possible in public. Civil servants never did so, this being one of
their fiercest unwritten rules of conduct. Businessmen offered
bland platitudes when pressed. Privately, there were the 'expressions
of concern' recorded by the government in the late 1970s,[1] and there
would undoubtedly have been many more in 1980-1 had specific
knowledge of the diplomatic impasse in Beijing not been restricted to a
very small circle of business and political figures in Hong Kong.

Some commentators broke the silence – notably Jimmy McGregor
of the Hong Kong General Chamber of Commerce, with his warnings
about investor confidence; and Louis Cha, the editor of *Ming Pao*,
who in a series of editorials echoed with uncanny precision the British
analysis which had been developed in 1978-9, and which had led to the
MacLehose initiative on land leases. In February 1980, Cha wrote
that:

the year 1997 has been haunting the people of Hong Kong,
and with each passing day the deadline draws closer. The time
will eventually come when an answer to the big question mark
hanging overhead cannot be further delayed . . . Trouble will
surface long before the arrival of the year 1997, and those having
the means at their disposal will not wait until 1997 to make any
move . . . Many people hold the view that Beijing should come to

a precise decision on Hong Kong's future in the next three years.[2]

And, a year later, in February 1981, Cha remarked that:

> Anyone with a moderate degree of sensitivity about their security would be reluctant to remain in Hong Kong when the New Territories [lease] has just ten years before expiry, unless a new arrangement has been made by then . . . If the issue is not resolved in the next one to two years, Hong Kong will certainly not remain a stable society . . .
>
> The Chinese authorities [cannot] expect to take back Hong Kong by serving one year's or half a year's notice on Britain. If this is allowed, sensitive people with means at their disposal will have left Hong Kong . . . Nor can the people of Hong Kong expect the Chinese and British authorities to guarantee jointly that the status quo in Hong Kong will remain unchanged forever. The status will change, [but] the change will be orderly and little harm done if people have fifteen years' notice that it will occur.[3]

But though such arguments were in the public domain, it was only in the early months of 1982 that the question of 1997 began finally to take its grip upon the popular mood. It did so partly because the prospect of the Thatcher visit had emerged as a focus for speculation, and partly because visitors to Beijing were returning with news of a heightened interest in Hong Kong affairs. But a much more important reason was that the Hong Kong stock and property markets had come to the end of their 1979–81 boom, and the mood of the city was growing generally darker.

Hong Kong tended to measure its happiness in dollars; and never had it felt so rich as when the stock market's Hang Seng Index peaked at 1,810 on 17 July 1981. But by the end of 1981, the index had declined to 1,470, while the property boom was simultaneously deflating and would be dead by the Chinese New Year holiday season of February 1982. It was then, in the spring of 1982, that hopes of another 'leg' to the bull market finally receded, to be succeeded by a new mood of fragility and uncertainty, a fertile soil in which anxiety about the future could flourish. Conventional wisdom quickly deemed that there could be no recovery in the financial markets without a satisfactory settlement of the lease question; and this view, as it achieved general acceptance, became a self-fulfilling prophecy.

The prohibition on civil servants speaking publicly about 1997 was matched by a similar if less perfect discretion on the part of members of the Executive Council, the Governor's 'cabinet'. But again, as anticipation of the Thatcher visit grew, and as the public mood became ever more fixated by the future, even the reserve of the 'unofficial' – non-governmental – members of the Executive Council began to crumble. It was a sign of the times that, when Sir Edward Youde was sworn in as Governor of Hong Kong in succession to Sir Murray MacLehose on 20 May 1982, the senior member of the Executive Council, Sir Sze-yuen Chung, gave a brief welcoming speech which, though seemingly bland enough in its general tenor, had been the subject of some lively discussion between Chung and his fellow unofficials. For Chung was a bluff man, less subtle and less dissembling than most of his colleagues, and his feeling was that the great taboo subject could and should no longer be suppressed. He told Youde:

> The first priority must be the question of the future of Hong Kong . . . Our continuing economic prosperity and social stability are very much dependent on the confidence which we the people of Hong Kong, and our overseas trading partners, have in the long-term future of Hong Kong. To maintain that confidence, it is necessary that the future of Hong Kong be resolved as soon as possible. It is inevitable that you, Sir, as Governor of Hong Kong, will play an important role in such a resolution.

Though the Hong Kong government declined to follow Chung's lead, continuing to treat 1997 as a subject which should not be discussed *devant les enfants*, succeeding months were to prove the accuracy of his analysis. By late June, in the wake of Deng's meeting with Fei Yiming and his party of National People's Congress delegates, 1997 was dominating the pages of Hong Kong's Chinese-language media. By mid-July, the gathering political storm had chased the last of the optimists out of the stock market, which lost a third of its value in the space of three weeks. On 12 August 1982, the Hang Seng Index closed at 960 points, barely half its level of a year earlier. Investors were particularly unsettled by a curious deal between the Hong Kong government and the Bank of China, announced on 9 August but rumoured some days beforehand, whereby the Bank would buy a plot of land in Central District at an artificially low price for its new Hong Kong headquarters. Though Chinese investments in Hong Kong had been seen as good news a year or two earlier, and would again be seen as good news a few years later, the stock market was inclined at this juncture to look for the negative side of everything. Some analysts saw the low purchase price as the start of Danegeld payments to bribe China into keeping its distance; others saw the new building as a symbol of imminent Chinese dominance. It was also widely noted that China's final payment for the site would fall due in 1996, a date taken to mean that even the British and Chinese governments could not yet see beyond 1997.

Those investors who had not already sold by mid-August simply stayed away from the stock market. Turnover fell to a quarter of its level a year previously. The property market was in a still worse state, with very few private transactions recorded as prices seemed to lose their meaning against so intense a background of uncertainty. The Hong Kong dollar was weak, if not yet frighteningly so, depreciating by some 15 per cent against the United States dollar in the year to August 1982.

By September, the month of the Thatcher visit, Hong Kong was awash with Beijing-inspired rumours about a resumption of Chinese sovereignty, and the installation of a China-backed government to replace the British. Every China-watching and pro-China publication had its own version of the Chinese plan.[4] Britain made no attempt of its own to address public opinion directly but instead invited the unofficial members of the Executive Council to London, ostensibly to give a Hong Kong perspective to Mrs Thatcher on 6 September before she left for the Far East.

The unofficial members' advice was modest enough. A British source recalls it in these terms:

> The main thing they said was that she should take care to listen to what the Chinese had to say. Because, although large chunks of it would be predictable, and although you could predict that there were not going to be any concessions at this opening stage, it was still very important to listen in case there were something there which might be a disguised hint or invitation. They said that

Chinese negotiating tactics could be extremely devious, particularly at the propaganda level, but that when you were sitting there in negotiation with them behind closed doors, actually setting out your starting positions, then it was of the utmost importance to listen. On that they were at one.

But it was not, in fact, primarily for their advice that Thatcher had invited the unofficial members to London. The trip was a well-publicized one, and its main purpose was to signal to Hong Kong that Hong Kong's own interests and views were being given a high priority in the formulation of British policy. To quote the same British source: 'The visit to London was very much part of the process of cementing the role of the unofficials, giving them a role which was not just confined to smoke-filled rooms and articulated in private telegrams, but which was a very visible role, and which was designed very much to be played back to an audience in Hong Kong.'

The British were thus not entirely insensitive to the propaganda battle ahead. But the inbred discretion of the Foreign Office, its distaste not merely for propaganda but for the mass media and even for public opinion in general, left it some distance behind its more loquacious Chinese counterpart. China, moreover, had a story to sell; and its campaign to 'soften up' Hong Kong opinion reached a climax on 20–21 September, the two days immediately before Thatcher was due to arrive in Beijing, when, with a magnificent contempt for the conventions of diplomacy, Beijing simply briefed selected Hong Kong newspapers with the full Chinese negotiating position. The *Hong Kong Daily News*, a non-Communist daily, reported the briefing in these terms in its issue of 21 September:

The stand taken by the Chinese government includes the following two main points:

i. The Chinese leaders will officially inform British Prime Minister Mrs Thatcher during their talks that China is determined to regain complete sovereignty over the New Territories, Kowloon and Hong Kong Island in 1997 when the lease on the New Territories expires. The entire area . . . will become once more a part of Chinese territory, thus concluding British rule over Hong Kong, which has lasted for more than a century, since 1842.

ii. It is hoped that both China and Britain will make common efforts to maintain and promote Hong Kong's prosperity before China officially regains its sovereignty over Hong Kong . . .

The Chinese government has taken a firm stand towards regaining sovereignty. This time, Beijing is going to notify Britain about the Chinese decision and is not going to put anything forward for bargaining purposes during the talks . . . The deadline has been set at 1997 to 'respect history'. Hong Kong and Kowloon are actually under British rule at present, and the lease over the New Territories expires in 1997. The Chinese side thinks that it will be more conducive and convenient to both parties if the change-over comes in that year, but this does not mean recognition of the lease . . .

Some outside rumours hold that Britain will retain the right of administration in exchange for yielding the right of sovereignty. This is absolutely impossible. Regaining the right of sovereignty includes regaining the exercise of sovereign rights which include the right of administration. Nonetheless, because Sino-British relations are good, and Britain has governed Hong Kong for years and is still governing it, China hopes that both China and Britain will make efforts to maintain and promote Hong Kong's prosperity in the fifteen years to come.

Before long, China will make a public statement about Hong Kong's status.

Though this was clearly an important declaration of intent originating with the Chinese government, it was a measure of the distance to be covered that the British and the Hong Kong governments were reduced to reading it in the newspapers just like everybody else. The same had been true of all the other 'leaks' throughout the summer by which China's position on Hong Kong had been progressively revealed: Thatcher's visit was to be the commencement of a diplomatic dialogue, not – as was more usual with summits – the climax, and very little had proved possible in terms of preparatory dialogue. As one British source recalls:

There were endless meetings about the programme. But I can recall no substantive communication about what [Thatcher and her hosts] were going to say about the Hong Kong issue. Obviously it was agreed that Hong Kong would be an important part of the programme, but for formality's sake it could not be the only thing. They had to have a session discussing the great issues of the day. But I can recall no exchange of ideas of substance about Hong Kong at all, in the immediate run-up.[5]

Of course, even if the British Prime Minister had been informed of China's plans for Hong Kong in some more official way before her visit, she would probably have been obliged to regard them as a negotiating ploy rather than – as the Chinese themselves seemed to expect – a revealed truth. Given the force of personality, the strong sense of nationalism and the disinclination to be contradicted which characterized both Margaret Thatcher and Deng Xiaoping, collision was perhaps inevitable.

In any case, it came.

MARGARET THATCHER'S PLANE landed in Beijing at half past one on the afternoon of 22 September 1982. It was the Prime Minister's second visit to China, the first having been when she was Leader of the Opposition in 1977. According to one civil servant:

She did not find China very attractive. She was a great exception to the general rule among political and business leaders, that having reached Beijing and had their tummies tickled, they are captivated by the place, seeing themselves as latter-day Marco Polo figures. When she went as Leader of the Opposition, she found it a rather unpleasant place governed by rather unpleasant people.

The coolness was mutual. The Chinese powers-that-be deemed that the arrival of the British Prime Minister should rank fourth on Beijing's main radio news programme that evening, being of lesser importance than a commentary on the Communist Party's recent national congress, a report on reactions to the congress among miners in Henan Province, and a short item on the arrival in Xi'an of another foreign leader, Kim Il-sung of North Korea.

Mrs Thatcher was accompanied by Sir Edward Youde, the Governor of Hong Kong; Robin Butler, her principal private secretary;

Bernard Ingham, her press secretary; John Coles, seconded from the Foreign Office as her private secretary; R.W. Gray, deputy under-secretary at the Department of Trade; and Alan Donald, assistant under-secretary at the Foreign Office. It was an unusual entourage for a prime minister's overseas visit in that it failed to include the Foreign Secretary. Hugo Young, in the press party, recorded that this was because, 'as the leader's aides casually suggested, she found it hard to be in the same room, let alone the same aircraft, as Francis Pym'.[6]

The strained nature of relations with Pym, who had proved insufficiently bellicose for Mrs Thatcher's purposes during the Falklands War, meant that the conduct of this first phase of negotiations with Beijing was being left more completely to the Prime Minister's instincts than would have been the case had Lord Carrington or Sir Geoffrey Howe been in place to guide her.

Her target remained the opening of negotiations without preconditions. She had listened to Sir Percy Cradock, Sir Edward Youde and Alan Donald, and she understood well enough the dangers not only for Hong Kong but also for Britain if a failure to reach early agreement on the 1997 question should create instability in Hong Kong, or, worse still, if China moved unilaterally towards the enforcement of a handover on oppressive terms. She knew that the central issue was continued British administration of Hong Kong, rather than sovereignty. Yet her heart was not quite with her head. However much political sense it might make to embark on a process which could scarcely end other than with a transfer of sovereignty over Hong Kong to China, she still felt instinctively that title to Hong Kong was rightly Britain's, and that some sort of stand should be made.

One British source gave this estimate of Thatcher's state of mind, as she prepared for her crucial meetings in Beijing:

Her strength as a politician was that she could see quickly the key issues that were important from her own point of view. Hong Kong was no exception. She did not for a moment think that Hong Kong was in any way comparable with the Falklands, despite the paranoia in the Foreign Office [that she might do so]. There were many important differences, number one among them from her point of view being that if Britain had had to welcome every last islander and every last sheep from the Falkland Islands into Britain, then there would have been no political consequences for the person who had opened the door to them. If Britain had to accept even a fraction of the population of Hong Kong, it would be political suicide.

That may sound like a cynical view, but I think what was in her mind was that a solution had to be found which would have the effect of substantially preserving what Hong Kong people valued about Hong Kong, so that the bulk of the population would want to stay there. She also wanted to protect Hong Kong from coming under the direct control of a Communist politburo, and that was a factor which pulled in the same direction.

I don't think she had a preconceived idea, at this stage, of what had to be done in order to achieve these objectives. She just knew that you did not start by playing the only card of significance in your hand [the willingness to co-operate in a transfer of sovereignty]. She thought you always had to be reasonably tough if you were going to achieve your objectives. So there were moral factors at work, and practical ones. They marched in the same direction, which was the direction of not allowing Hong Kong to become a political disaster for a British prime minister.

From the airport, Thatcher was driven to the Diaoyutai State Guest House on the western side of the city for a brief rest and a change of clothes, then on to a ceremonial welcome at the Great Hall of the People and a first meeting with her Chinese counterpart, Zhao Ziyang. This was the session on 'world affairs' which had been blocked into the programme to provide a slightly broader formal focus to the trip than that of Hong Kong alone. Zhao gave an exposition of the general tenets of China's foreign policy, to which Thatcher replied with observations on Afghanistan, Cambodia and the Lebanon, areas of foreign policy on which Britain and China had certain views in common.

It was not until that evening's banquet, at which Zhao Ziyang was host, that the main topic of the visit was first mentioned. Between toasts in *mao-tai* – the Chinese sorghum liquor, of which Clive James, also in the press party, observed: 'It has the same effect as inserting your head in a cupboard and asking a large male friend to slam the door' – Zhao made an obliquely phrased speech, saying: 'In our bilateral relations, there are problems left over from history that need to be solved through consultations. However, I believe that problems of this kind are not difficult to solve so long as both sides approach and develop Sino-British relations in a long-term strategic perspective.'

Thatcher, in her reply, cut through Zhao's polite circumlocution. 'We have not yet begun our discussions on Hong Kong,' she said. 'I look forward to pursuing this important matter with you tomorrow.'

Zhao, too, was looking forward to the next day; and he was on home ground. When morning came, it was he, not Thatcher, who seized the initiative. In a corridor at the Great Hall of the People, outside the room in which Thatcher awaited him for their second session of talks, he turned to a waiting clutch of Hong Kong journalists and made an impromptu declaration.

'China', he said, 'will certainly take back its sovereignty over Hong Kong.'

A rustle of surprise rippled through the audience.

'However, in my opinion,' Zhao continued, 'the problem of sovereignty will not affect Hong Kong's stability and prosperity. Hong Kong should not worry about its future.'

'Why not?' called a voice from the press.

'Why should they worry?' replied Zhao. 'China will certainly take a series of policies and measures to guarantee Hong Kong's prosperity and stability.'

With that, Zhao broke away to give Mrs Thatcher and Sir Edward Youde the same message in more detail, supplying a resumé of China's plans for Hong Kong similar in its essentials to that offered Edward Heath in April but elaborated now into a more structured list of key points.

The main purpose of Zhao's seemingly casual disclosure to the Hong Kong journalists, prior to his meeting with Thatcher, was to put China's position on public record and so to emphasize China's belief that this position would not and could not be altered. By so brazenly pre-empting Thatcher, Zhao was also showing that China did not regard Britain's participation as a necessary factor in China's development of future policies for Hong Kong. Finally, by choosing the Hong Kong press as his audience, he was demonstrating that China felt free to appeal directly to Hong Kong public opinion when it chose to do so. As a departure from diplomatic etiquette, it was economical and eloquent, and it also had the virtue of unsettling expectations. The British had regarded confidentiality as an essential element of the talks; their nerves were now on edge.

Nor were Thatcher's own nerves helped by the onset of a cold, aggravated by a punishing schedule which had begun with four days in Japan even before she arrived in China. Though her energy was waning, she insisted on carrying out relatively trivial engagements. On the Thursday, after her meeting with Zhao, she 'had to fight to stay awake' at a late-afternoon concert of Beethoven by student musicians at the Beijing Conservatory. She then continued with a tour of the Central Academy of Fine Arts, an appearance at a British Council book display and a dinner for British businessmen at the Jianguo Hotel before retiring for the night.[7]

The next morning, Friday, 24 September, was set aside for the most important meeting of Thatcher's stay: the session with Deng Xiaoping. Though Deng did not condescend to hold any formal job corresponding to his overall power, his main official post being that of chairman of the Communist Party's Central Military Commission, he was at the zenith of his reign, the strong-man of his country, and his sergeant-major's bark was the decisive voice on any issue of importance. Short-tempered, bossy, spitting and chain-smoking, he was no more inclined to self-doubt than Thatcher herself, and much less fond of argument. The stage was set for a two-hour meeting which was acknowledged, even in the coded language of British diplomacy, to have been 'abrasive'.

At the Great Hall of the People that morning, Deng was flanked by Huang Hua, his foreign minister, Zhang Wenjin, vice-minister of foreign affairs, and Ke Hua, ambassador to London. Liao Chengzhi was absent from this meeting, and throughout the Thatcher tour, because, it was said, he had 'broken his leg'. He was chronically ill, and was to die nine months later.

Arrayed to Deng's right were Mrs Thatcher, Sir Percy Cradock, Sir Edward Youde and Robin Butler; in the foreground, an intensively used spittoon. 'There has been a lively debate going on for years', reflected one diplomat, 'about whether Deng's habit of spitting into spittoons while receiving visitors is done for effect, or whether he really is a vulgar old bugger who cannot kick the habit.'

Deng was blunt. China, he said in his opening statement,

cannot but resume the exercise of sovereignty over the whole of the Hong Kong area in 1997. Upon such resumption, the Chinese government will take into full consideration the territory's special circumstances and adopt special policies in order to maintain the prosperity of Hong Kong.

In this regard, China's basic guideline is to resume the exercise of sovereignty over Hong Kong while maintaining its prosperity. These are two parts of an inseparable whole. In preserving Hong Kong's prosperity, China hopes to enjoy Britain's co-operation. Fundamentally speaking, the territory's ability to maintain its prosperity depends upon the adoption of policies suited to Hong Kong's circumstances upon China's resuming the exercise of sovereignty over, and administration of, Hong Kong.[8]

Mrs Thatcher retorted that, in Britain's eyes, Hong Kong was British by virtue of three treaties which were valid in international law, two of which were cessions. The only way in which China could legally resume Hong Kong would be through a variation of the treaties by mutual agreement. At this, Deng's mood shifted from assertiveness to genuine anger. His immediate comments were lost to the British record, but appear to have included the remark that Mrs Thatcher should be 'bombarded' out of her obstinacy.

The Prime Minister proceeded, nonetheless, with her brief. Britain, she said, understood the importance to China of 'the issue of sovereignty' over Hong Kong. But it was even more important in British eyes that arrangements should be made for the future administration of Hong Kong which would guarantee the maintenance of its stability and prosperity; and these questions would have to be resolved first, before sovereignty could be addressed, she said.

She could not accept that the Chinese proposals, for Hong Kong to function as a 'special' part of China, would provide the necessary guarantees of its stability and prosperity. Only continued British administration – British 'control', she said at one point – could provide that guarantee. Then, measuring her words carefully, she delivered as much of a hint on the eventual yielding of sovereignty as she was yet willing to give. If, she said, a 'satisfactory' agreement could be reached on issues of administration, then she would 'consider making recommendations to the British Parliament' on the issue of sovereignty over Hong Kong. But at this stage, she concluded, the two countries should pursue discussions at diplomatic level in order to see whether such a 'satisfactory' agreement could be reached.

Deng was categorical in his rejection. If he agreed to a further phase of British rule, he said, he would be no better than Li Hongzhang and the traitors of the Qing dynasty who had first yielded Chinese soil to Britain under treaties which were illegal and invalid. He could not do it. China would resume sovereignty, and sovereignty included administration. The British flag would have to go. The British governor would have to go. And it would be China alone which had the right to decide what policies were 'suitable' for Hong Kong in the future.

China hoped that Britain would 'co-operate' in the transition, Deng said, and was prepared to enter into 'discussions' to that end. But it would not be bound by their results. If they failed to produce an agreement acceptable to China within two years, then China would announce its own policies for Hong Kong unilaterally.

The British had not foreseen that the Chinese might choose to fix a deadline to negotiations; and Deng's pre-emptive rejection of both British sovereignty and continued British administration had been delivered in stronger terms than they had expected. But the agreement to negotiate had been reached, and as the principals prepared to adjourn for lunch, Cradock, the British ambassador, and Zhang Wenjin, the Chinese vice-foreign minister, drafted a communiqué for their approval. The brief statement showed only slight traces of the cracks over which it had been papered. It said: The leaders of the two countries held far-reaching talks in a friendly atmosphere on the future of Hong Kong. Both leaders made clear their respective positions on the subject. They agreed to enter talks through diplomatic channels following the visit with the common aim of maintaining the stability and prosperity of Hong Kong.'

The communiqué pleased the British by virtue of its omissions. Though both Deng and Zhao had treated China's sovereignty over Hong Kong as a premise of any further discussion, the communiqué drafted by Zhang and Cradock spoke only of 'respective positions' on the 'future' of Hong Kong. And, since the communiqué summarized for the record the basis on which negotiations were to begin, the British could now assert that both sides were approaching the negotiating table without any formal preconditions having been acknowledged – and, in particular, with the British claim to sovereignty over Hong Kong intact if not unchallenged.

A similar thought struck Zhang Wenjin at the last minute. As he and Cradock left for their separate lunches, Zhang remarked to the

British ambassador that the communiqué had, of course, been drafted 'on the understanding of the Chinese precondition'. Cradock replied that it had not.

The disagreement was not allowed to rest. At three o'clock that afternoon, as Thatcher began her main press conference of the visit, the text of the communiqué came chattering off the wires of the official New China News Agency. It proved to have acquired a coda, added unilaterally by China, which said: 'The Chinese government's position on the recovery of the whole region of Hong Kong is unequivocal and known to all.'

Thatcher was, at this very moment, insisting upon the secrecy of her talks with Zhao and Deng, and telling the impatient press: 'I think Hong Kong will recognize that, to maintain confidence, you must also maintain confidentiality.' When a journalist, fresh telex-tape in hand, asked her to comment on China's commitment to 'recovery of the whole region of Hong Kong', Thatcher said that she had not yet seen the statement, and was unable to respond to it as such. She was, however, roused to give an indirect answer by publicly repeating Britain's own claim to Hong Kong, saying: There are three treaties in existence. We stick by our treaties unless we decide on something else. At the moment, we stick by our treaties.'

This was a dangerous gambit, to repeat in public the line of argument which had caused such obvious anger to China's leaders in private. But Thatcher, like Deng, had clearly had enough.

Hong Kong reporters were subsequently briefed that a senior Chinese leader, though not necessarily Deng himself, had been moved by the treaty dispute to refer to the Prime Minister as a 'stinking woman'. In more measured terms, the *South China Morning Post* reported, citing 'Chinese sources', that Mrs Thatcher was 'probably the first British statesman in the past decade to dispute China's sovereignty over Hong Kong', and that her position was 'a step backwards'. Even then, Thatcher's words in Beijing were relatively mild, compared to those which would follow in Hong Kong.

By now, Mrs Thatcher's cold was plainly evident. Her voice, husky at the start of the press conference, was reduced to a croak by the end. The most dramatic evidence of her physical frailty had come as she was emerging from her talks with Deng at lunch-time, when, distracted by a question from the BBC's Beijing radio correspondent, Stephen Jessel, she had lost her footing on the steps leading down into

Tiananmen Square, and had tumbled to her knees. For Hong Kong, the image which dominated the evening's television news was rich in portent: a British prime minister seeming to kow-tow towards the mausoleum of Chairman Mao, at the centre of Tiananmen Square.

That night, Thatcher gave her farewell banquet at the Great Hall of the People, with Zhao taking his turn as guest of honour. It was a curiously subdued affair, with Zhao the only senior leader to attend. The next most senior ministers present were Chen Muhua, minister of foreign trade; and Huang Hua, foreign minister.

The protocol of such occasions was always obscure, since the older leaders, like Deng, who possessed power in their personal capacities rather than by the holding of particular jobs, could appear for foreign visitors or not, as they wished. But the British would undoubtedly have been more sensitive to the snub they were receiving had they been aware that Deng and all the other Communist grandees had chosen to pass up Thatcher's banquet in favour of another one taking place on the same night and in the same building, hosted by Kim Il-sung.

If Kim's visit had not been devised from the outset by the Chinese leadership primarily in order to provide a 'spoiler' to Thatcher, then that was certainly the use to which it was now being put. Having failed to secure from Thatcher any concessions over Hong Kong for which they might now fête her, Deng and the elders defected *en masse*. While Zhao was left to exchange politely pointed speeches with Thatcher about their 'valuable and stimulating' talks, Kim was down the corridor, singing the praises of a 'militant friendship . . . forged in the raging flames of war against common enemies' to an audience led by Deng Xiaoping, Hu Yaobang, Peng Zhen and a roll-call of the Politburo.

The Thatcher banquet ended soberly and early, the Prime Minister appearing not merely tired but also just a shade chastened. Her meetings with Deng and Zhao had 'brought home to her', in the words of one British diplomat, 'the force of the Chinese view, the readiness of the Chinese to talk, but their determination to recover sovereignty'. She now appreciated, perhaps for the first time, just how difficult and time-consuming the Hong Kong question would prove. In her speech that night, arch and conciliatory, she said: 'Our conversations have enabled me to attain a clearer insight into China's affairs, and a close personal understanding of the Chinese government's point of view. This complies with an old Chinese saying, which goes: "Seeing for one's self is a hundred times better than hearing from others".'

From Beijing, the Prime Minister's party went on to launch a ship in Shanghai, a visit memorable mainly for her introduction by an interpreter as 'The Quite Honourable Margaret Thatcher', and for the refusal of the champagne bottle to break on the bows of the *World Goodwill*, which she was christening as a favour to its owner, the ubiquitous Hong Kong magnate Sir Yue-kong Pao. At Guangzhou, Thatcher lent her support to the efforts of GEC and Cable and Wireless to land export orders in the province. Finally, on the afternoon of Sunday, 26 September, she arrived in Hong Kong.

THE TERRITORY, HUNGRY for news, already had a flavour of Thatcher's mood from the re-transmission there of the interview which she had given to Jim Biddulph, the BBC's Far East correspondent, in transit through China the previous day. In it, she had amplified precisely the insistence on the legality of Britain's claim to Hong Kong which had so angered China's leaders when she first made it privately and then publicly in Beijing. She had evidently taken a sharp, almost personal, offence at the way in which Deng and Zhao had simply dismissed her assertion of Britain's rights under international law, and, though she said little else publicly about her talks with Deng, she could not stop herself returning to the treaty question in terms increasingly disparaging of the Chinese. In her BBC interview, she told Biddulph: 'If one party to a treaty or a contract says "I cannot agree to it, I am going to break it," you cannot really have a great deal of confidence that any new treaty they make will be honoured . . . If you abrogate one, why should anybody believe that you are serious about another?'

Her stay in Hong Kong was a brief and breathless affair. The evening of her arrival she spent quietly at Government House. On Monday she was scheduled to meet soldiers of the British garrison, address businessmen and give a press conference. On Tuesday she was due to open a power station, visit the container port and a new town, ride the new underground railway and then fly out for Delhi.

The Monday lunch-time speech, to Hong Kong's assembled chambers of commerce, was an opportunity for Thatcher to close ranks with Hong Kong, saying that: 'Above all, I give you this assurance. In conducting those talks [with China], I shall speak not only for Britain, but for Britain's moral responsibility and duty to Hong Kong.'

For the general public, the main event was the Monday afternoon

press conference at which, though she had nothing further of substance to say about her talks in Beijing, her criticisms of the Chinese
attitude towards the treaties became fiercer still.

Answering a question which touched on the New Territories lease,
almost at the end of the press conference, she added a lengthy – and,
in respect of the question which had actually been asked, quite
unnecessary – closing point:

> One point about the treaties. I believe they are valid in
> international law. And if countries try to abrogate treaties like
> that, it is very serious indeed. Because if a country will not stand
> by one treaty, it will not stand by another treaty. And that is why
> you enter into talks. Because it is better, if you have got differ-
> ences between two sides, to agree to vary [treaties] in a way satis-
> factory to all, than for any one [side] to consider unilateral
> action.

One Hong Kong official later recalled his own surprise at hearing
this answer:

> It was a pity she embellished what she had to say . . . If I had
> had the chance to advise her, I would have said: 'Prime Minister,
> stick to stating what is a fact. Which is that the treaties are valid.
> That in itself is unpalatable enough to the Chinese, though that is
> no reason for not saying it, particularly in these circumstances.
> We cannot avoid saying it now. But stick to the facts, which are
> that the treaties are valid under international law, while the
> Chinese position, that they are invalid because unequal, is incor-
> rect . . .'
> But going on to talk about questions of trustworthiness was to
> add a gratuitous statement of opinion. It may be one with which
> 99.5 per cent of the world would agree, but it was unhelpful to
> the people we were trying to help.

Hong Kong speedily reached much the same conclusion. The media
and financial markets, which had given a positive initial response to
the news from Beijing that negotiations would begin, now perceived
that the differences between the two sides were far greater than the
common ground, and that there appeared every prospect of those

differences being exacerbated. Thatcher left Hong Kong the day after her press conference. Within a week, the Hong Kong stock market had fallen by 25 per cent; within a month the Hong Kong dollar had depreciated by 12 per cent. Thatcher had been and gone, wrote David Bonavia, 'Somewhat like one of those typhoons which roar in from the western Pacific, leaving a trail of destruction behind them. Seldom in British colonial history was so much damage done to the interests of so many people in such a short space of time by a single person.'

Such was the exaggerated emotional climate of those days: the sense which pervaded Hong Kong was that its future now rested in the hands of a few distant politicians through whose fingers it might easily slip and shatter by clumsiness alone. Yet in concrete terms, all that Thatcher had done was to refuse to make any immediate concessions to China in respect of Britain's claim to Hong Kong. She had been tactless in her public insistence on the treaties; but, China, too, had shown little inclination to be bound by the rules of protocol or confidentiality. In theory at least, there was nothing here to prejudice the start of the formal diplomatic negotiations, to which Thatcher and Deng had already committed their governments.

In practice, however, as Zhang Wenjin had indicated to Sir Percy Cradock just after the drafting of the communiqué, China wanted Britain to acknowledge Chinese sovereignty over Hong Kong before the negotiations began, as a precondition for further discussion. Sovereignty was not, in China's view, open to negotiation, since it had always belonged to China; and Thatcher's public disputation of that claim was an insult which China was now determined to avenge.

China's chosen weapon was propaganda, the tone of which modulated between argument, harangue and outright threat, but the general theme of which remained consistent: Britain could not speak for Hong Kong, or make any claim to Hong Kong, because Hong Kong people were Chinese, not British, and their motherland was China, not Britain. To reject British colonialism would be not merely a 'political' act on Hong Kong's part, but also a 'patriotic' one. It was not a choice, but a duty.

The New China News Agency began its criticism of Thatcher on a relatively mild note, with a commentary published in its Chinese-language service on 30 September, entitled 'Our solemn and just position on the Hong Kong issue', which said:

Hong Kong is a part of Chinese territory. The relevant treaties regarding the Hong Kong area as concluded and signed by the British government and China's Qing dynasty are unequal treaties and have never been accepted by the Chinese people . . .

The British people of the past and today are in no way responsible for the great British Empire's acts of aggression of a century ago. If today some people still adhere to these unequal treaties, this can only remind the Chinese people, the British people and the people of the whole world of the history of British imperialism's aggression against China.

Mrs Thatcher . . . said that Britain has a 'moral responsibility' for the residents of Hong Kong. We maintain that the matter of Hong Kong is a matter of primary importance to the state sovereignty and national interests of the thousand million Chinese people, including Chinese residents of Hong Kong. It is only the government of the People's Republic of China which has the right to say that, as a sovereign state, it has responsibility for the Chinese residents of Hong Kong.

But this was, by comparison with the polemics which would follow, a mere clearing of the throat. *Wen Wei Po*, the Hong Kong Communist newspaper, turned the volume up a notch with its editorial of 6 October, 'Regaining sovereignty has a legal basis', in which it said:

On Chinese soil, British Prime Minister Mrs Thatcher repeatedly declared that the 'Treaty of Nanjing' and the other two treaties 'must be respected' and 'cannot be abrogated'. Naturally this fallacy imbued with colonialism has aroused the indignation of Hong Kong compatriots and has once again recalled to the one billion Chinese people the history of aggression against China by the British Empire . . .

The fight to interfere in China's customs tariffs, the right to question China's sovereignty over foreign trade, consular jurisdiction, foreigners' rights to enter and leave Chinese cities freely, and the right to open Chinese ports to trade, as stipulated in the 'Treaty of Nanjing', the 'Treaty of Beijing' and other unequal treaties have all been dropped into the Pacific Ocean by the Chinese people since the five-star flag was first hoisted in 1949. And yet Mrs Thatcher wants the Chinese government to abide by those treaties today. Is it not, then, that she wishes to enjoy once more the aggressions of the past?

These polemics were then echoed within China's domestic press. On 9 October, *China Youth News* published a long article on 'The origins of the Hong Kong issue'; an army periodical, *Jiefangjun Huabao*, gave over four pages of its October issue to a picture-story on the Opium Wars of the nineteenth century; and *Workers' Daily* of 26 October published a feature describing the Nanjing treaty as 'a treaty signed at the muzzle of a gun'.

The unsettling effect of this propaganda on Hong Kong, acutely conscious of its physical vulnerability *vis à vis* China, was exacerbated by further ominous developments in the financial markets, where rumours were circulating about the imminent collapse of a diversified investment group, Carrian, which had been the 'glamour stock' of the 1979–81 property boom. The rumours were accurate, and Carrian's announcement of 'liquidity problems' in late October marked the start of a slide into bankruptcy which was to cost its bankers and shareholders more than US$2 billion.

On 6 October, Sir Edward Youde made a brave attempt to stimulate some optimism by telling a meeting of the Legislative Council, Hong Kong's rubber-stamp legislature, that: 'Meetings in Beijing to follow up Mrs Thatcher's visit have begun. The contents of the talks must necessarily remain confidential. The aim will be to complete them as soon as possible.' But Youde's suggestion of bustling diplomatic activity was, if accurate in fact, certainly misleading in spirit. He was referring to nothing more elaborate than a single contact between Sir Percy Cradock and Zhang Wenjin, at which Sir Percy had made a formal re-submission of the British proposals for Hong Kong already outlined verbally by Thatcher. This formal submission yielded no new ground to China on sovereignty, but merely recommended that a new agreement be reached between Britain and China which preserved British administration over Hong Kong beyond 1997. This administration could, if China wished, be characterized as 'transitional' in nature; and if these arrangements appeared acceptable to Hong Kong, then the British government would support a treaty containing a form of words recognizing China's sovereignty over the whole territory.[9]

As nothing more was heard about these 'meetings in Beijing', Hong Kong sank back into its gloom. The Hang Seng Index, which had stood in July at 1,300 points, fell by the end of October to just 772. The Hong Kong dollar stood at HK$6.83 to the US dollar, down from HK$5.83 a year earlier, its weakest rate in more than twenty-five years, and enough for the currency-market professionals to worry about the psychological effects which would follow when the dollar fell, as it surely now would, below a rate of HK$7 to the US dollar.

'Hong Kong's summer of frayed nerves', reported the *Financial Times* on 28 October, 'has given way to an autumn of depression and uncertainty.' Hong Kong's own *Wah Kiu Yat Po* had a more vivid image for the long, painful wait for news. It reflected that: 'The cruellest form of death in China is death by a thousand cuts, in which the victim's skin is slowly peeled off, scrap by scrap. After a time, the victim comes to crave that he may die instantly, so that his slow and painful torture may be ended.'[10]

6

The Negotiations
Begin

HE deadlock on sovereignty was sustained, from the British
side, because the British saw the proposed negotiations strictly
in terms of a bargaining process. The Foreign Office accepted,
and it believed that Mrs Thatcher privately accepted, that the dialogue
which she had opened in Beijing was fated to end in a concession of
sovereignty to China, whatever else it produced along the way. But the
Foreign Office still affected to hope, however faintly, that continued
British administration of Hong Kong could be achieved; and it took
the view that a British concession on sovereignty should be made only
in exchange for a Chinese concession on administration.

The alternative view would have been to say that Britain stood
to gain more of what it wanted for Hong Kong by taking a non-
adversarial approach, offering voluntarily the concession on sovereignty which China sought, in order to engender an atmosphere of
goodwill and to encourage voluntary concessions from China on matters of administration. This was more the sequence of events which
China purported to have in mind, and for which it continued to press
in the aftermath of the Thatcher visit.

But the British were not prepared to gamble on China's goodwill. In
the words of one participant: 'We did not accept that we should give
the game away in one go. Whatever our private thoughts might have
been about what was to happen at the end of the day, there was no
prospect of our saying to China "We will give up". Simply to have

given in to their diktat would have been politically intolerable.'

This was not just an extension of post-Falklands bravura. It was also a recognition that to surrender sovereignty without a fight, and then to find China still intractable, would be a terrible political blunder. Better for Britain to fight and lose than not to fight at all. There was also the effect on Hong Kong to consider. Britain would not be able to argue that an eventual settlement was the 'best possible' deal that could ever have been achieved with China unless a modicum of blood had been – metaphorically – spilt in the negotiating of it. There was, then, a sense in which the British needed a fight; and the Chinese were happy to oblige. Their scatter-gun salvoes against Thatcher having inflicted relatively little damage in October, they turned in November to more precise weaponry.

On 1 November 1982, Xi Zhongxun, now vice-chairman of the National People's Congress, made the first public allusion to the two-year deadline which Deng Xiaoping had fixed for the proposed Sino-British negotiations. He told a visiting Hong Kong delegation that: 'We want to solve this issue through diplomatic channels. A plan on how to solve this issue should be worked out within one or two years.'

Though this was, in itself, no more than a casual aside, it declared China's willingness to play more openly upon the deadline in more categorical form, and so to show Hong Kong how tightly Britain's hands were already tied.

A further important intervention came on 20 November, when Liao Chengzhi received a delegation from the Hong Kong Factory Owners' Association at the Great Hall of the People, and gave a presentation on China's plans for Hong Kong at which the slogan 'Hong Kong people rule Hong Kong' – *Gang ren zhi gang* – was used for the first time on record by a high government official. According to various accounts of the meeting, Liao told the group that China would recover sovereignty over Hong Kong by 1997 at the latest; that Hong Kong would then be ruled by Hong Kong people; judicial and legal systems would remain unchanged, though with the court of final appeal located in Hong Kong; the Hong Kong dollar would be retained; passports would say 'China-Hong Kong'; and the Royal Hong Kong Jockey Club would stay in business, but with the 'Royal' tag deleted.[1]

Liao's briefing was to be among many which mocked the 'confidentiality' which was supposed to attach to the Sino-British talks on Hong Kong. The Chinese defended such behaviour by saying that they were simply stating China's own policies, which was not something for which they required Britain's permission.[2] But it was more than confidentiality which was being ignored. Liao, in his presentation to the Factory Owners' Association, was showing China's willingness to bypass the British and their 'negotiations' altogether, and to sell its policies directly to the people of Hong Kong. The slogan under which this campaign was being launched, 'Hong Kong people rule Hong Kong', cleverly celebrated the removal of British colonialism while ignoring its replacement by authority from Beijing.

The New China News Agency began to step up its local propaganda work in Hong Kong, taking a similarly relaxed attitude towards 'confidentiality' and, indeed, towards the negotiations themselves. A businessman who emerged from a briefing-session reported:

> We asked them why, if Beijing had made up its mind what to do about Hong Kong, Sino-British negotiations were being held at all. The official said that China recognized the role the British had played in building up Hong Kong to what it is now. The object of the talks was therefore to draw up a suitably ceremonious departure for the Governor. And he wasn't joking.[3]

China's place-men in Hong Kong began to make extravagant claims for China's capacity to run the territory without Britain. Fei Yiming told the China News Service: 'Did some people not say that the Chinese could not rule Shanghai well? Facts have shown that the Chinese are completely capable of ruling Shanghai well. Since they can rule Shanghai well, they can also rule Hong Kong well.'[4]

Wang Kuancheng, chairman of the Hong Kong Chinese Chamber of Commerce, drew attention to the oil fields then believed – erroneously – to be on the brink of development in the South China Sea. He told the National People's Congress in Beijing on 30 November, in remarks intended for Hong Kong consumption: 'Can the Hong Kong economy not prosper, with an immense oil field under exploration in its neighbourhood? Hong Kong is merely a small place, like a little bird. How many grains of rice can such a little bird eat? The oil projects will surely be able to feed Hong Kong.'

Finally, just to make sure that the British were receiving the message loud and clear, the Chinese briefed British newspaper correspondents as to their position: they wanted a public concession on sovereignty, to match the public snub which they felt Thatcher had dealt them. The *Daily Telegraph* reported: 'Teng Hsiao-ping [Deng Xiaoping], China's leader, is insisting that Britain publicly agrees to relinquish sovereignty over Hong Kong Island and Kowloon in 1997, when the lease on the New Territories expires, before talks on the future of the colony are opened.'

Yet the Foreign Office, as 1982 drew to a close, was still philosophical. The view of the time was, in one recollection: 'Basically, the Chinese were stone-walling while their propaganda barrage hit full steam. Then there were the efforts to appeal directly to the populace of Hong Kong, which were also hitting full steam. Really, it was all in order to see whether they could get the solution which they wanted without actually having to negotiate with us much at all.'

THE START OF 1983 brought a number of changes to the diplomatic landscape. In Beijing, Zhang Wenjin, Sir Percy Cradock's interlocutor, moved on to become China's ambassador to Washington, and was replaced at the Ministry of Foreign Affairs by Yao Guang, who had been ambassador in Paris. Zhang was outwardly similar in personality to Cradock himself – scholarly, dry, and with an old-fashioned courtesy. Yao was a much less intellectual, much more dogmatic figure – so much so that, among the marginalia of later British files, would come a note recording the view that arguing with Yao was 'like a hard day on the Western Front, trudging through the mud'. He was a much less satisfying adversary than Zhang, but perhaps for that reason a more effective one.

China had still not replied formally to Cradock's proposal of October; the replacement of Zhang by Yao was later given as the reason for this hiatus. It was only at the end of January that Yao and Cradock held a first meeting. There, Yao repeated that China saw no place for negotiation on the sovereignty issue, nor would it allow British rule of any kind in Hong Kong after 1997. Discussions between Britain and China would have to be conducted on the basis that Britain recognized China's sovereignty over Hong Kong, and that the agenda would be limited to the maintenance of Hong Kong's 'stability and prosperity' in the years *before* 1997. Cradock's scope for response was limited. All he could say was that the communiqué of 24 September had proposed the opening of negotiations without setting any preconditions, and that Britain wished merely to proceed on this basis.

What Britain did not, at this stage, fully appreciate was that while Yao was engaging Cradock, Liao Chengzhi's Hong Kong and Macao Affairs Office was in the process of turning its blueprint for Hong Kong, as unveiled successively to Heath and Thatcher in 1982, into a final text suitable for presentation to the annual plenary session of the National People's Congress in June.

The fact of the work was in no sense secret. Liao had told a group of New Territories villagers, whom he received in January 1983, that: 'China is working on a draft formula which has yet to be presented to Britain . . . The format of Hong Kong people administering Hong Kong can only be implemented after it has been presented and recorded by the National People's Congress. That is the only requirement.'[5]

However, it was only in late February, when the British were told that the formal text was near to completion, that they digested the implications. At worst, the adoption of a Hong Kong blueprint by the NPC could set the stage for China to abandon the planned negotiations with Britain, citing the sovereignty deadlock. At best, adoption would make China's negotiating position almost completely inflexible. Cradock and Youde were sufficiently worried to arrange a post-haste return to London on 5 March for a meeting with Thatcher on 7 March, at which they would try to secure her agreement to a means of drawing the Chinese back towards the negotiating table.

Thatcher was not at first particularly tractable. She went so far as to suggest that a United Nations-sponsored referendum in Hong Kong might be one way of proving to China that 'continued British administration' was the preference not only of Britain but also of Hong Kong. Cradock suggested something less dramatic. He favoured a letter from Thatcher to her Chinese counterpart, Zhao Ziyang, repeating with a slightly stronger emphasis the phrase she had used in private conversation with Deng about her willingness to 'consider making recommendations' to the British Parliament on the sovereignty issue, once an agreement had been reached on administration. Thatcher suggested that Cradock draft such a letter, and fixed a second meeting for 9 March.

At the 9 March meeting, Cradock produced his draft. It said that if the negotiations yielded 'arrangements acceptable to the people of Hong Kong', then the Prime Minister 'would be *prepared* to

102

recommend' to Parliament the transfer of sovereignty.[6] Thatcher accepted the formula, putting in motion what the British later came to call the 'first finesse' of the negotiations.

It was a finesse, in that the letter to Zhao was designed, by Cradock if not by Thatcher herself, to draw the Chinese out, by conveying in gesture more than it actually said in words. Its real message was: the British did not want to concede sovereignty at this juncture, but nor did they want to argue about it.

China took the hint, although a response was slow in coming. Yao Guang passed the letter on to Zhao Ziyang, whose reply was finally returned to Cradock in May, and almost as quickly leaked by China to the Hong Kong press. In China's view, a new atmosphere had been created, and formal talks could begin. It was agreed that two rounds of purely procedural talks could take place in late May and early June, so that an agenda and the negotiating teams would be in place for the commencement of substantive talks in July, after China had disposed of its National People's Congress and Britain its general election in June.

WHEN BEIJING LEAKED details of the Thatcher letter, it encouraged the press to conclude that a 'concession' of sovereignty had now obliquely been made. A first report, in the Hong Kong Communist newspaper *New Evening Post* of 13 May, said that the British had 'adopted a compliant attitude on the issue of Hong Kong's sovereignty' and were preparing 'to make a political withdrawal'.

This form of propaganda, not without a germ of truth, was not in itself unduly distressing to the Foreign Office, which would have been far more worried had the letter not worked at all. It was, however, much more disturbing to the members of the Executive Council who, against the wishes of the Foreign Office, but in a victory for Sir Edward Youde, had been admitted at the New Year into the charmed circle of confidentiality surrounding the Sino-British diplomacy, and were beginning to make their presence felt.

The Executive Council comprised, at the start of 1983, six official and nine unofficial members. The lifting of the veil of secrecy in favour of the official members of the Executive Council was of no real significance: they were obliged, whatever happened, to toe the government line. It was the unofficials about whom the Foreign Office – and particularly Sir Percy Cradock in Beijing – were apprehensive.

The unofficials would be handling top-secret information, though they were not positively vetted; they had no professional experience of diplomacy or politics; their participation greatly increased the likelihood of disagreements within the British camp; and, if they were deemed to speak for Hong Kong, then any final agreement with China would be hostage to their approval.[7]

Unusually, Cradock failed here to carry Thatcher with him. Youde argued that it would be almost impossible for him to govern Hong Kong effectively if he were obliged to exclude even his Executive Council, supposedly his most trusted advisers, from informed discussion of the most important issue of the day. Already, he observed, the members of the Executive and Legislative Councils were growing restive, feeling that they should be able to work in a more informed way for Hong Kong's interests; their discontent would quickly be echoed throughout Hong Kong, if its representatives were seen to be shut out of the negotiations altogether. And, if Britain's aim was an agreement 'acceptable to the people of Hong Kong', then the people of Hong Kong would be far more likely to accept an agreement which they felt their representatives had been able to shape.

Thatcher ruled that the Executive Council should see and comment on all the British papers relating to the Hong Kong dialogue as they flowed between London, Beijing and Hong Kong, and that its views should be taken into account by the British side. This understanding was probably affirmed to the Executive Council by Lord Belstead, the junior Foreign Office minister, when he visited Hong Kong on 9–11 December 1982 and spoke publicly about the need for Hong Kong to play a part in the talks, comparing an eventual settlement to a 'three-legged stool' which would depend for its stability on the support of Britain, China and Hong Kong.

The unofficials were, initially, enthusiastic about their participation. But as the months wore on, and they realized the limitations within which they were working, they came to take a somewhat jaundiced view. In the words of one:

We were in an anomalous position. We were informed of the progress. We gave our advice, such as it was, through Teddy [Youde]. But we never took part in the process directly.

I have no doubt we were a pain in the arse to a lot of people. I am sure the British thought, 'These blokes, they sit in their large air-conditioned offices in Hong Kong and give us advice and then go to a large lunch at the Hong Kong Club and they have no idea how difficult it all is.' And they were probably right.

The Chinese did not want to know what our thoughts were. But it enabled the pro-government press in Hong Kong to say that Hong Kong was being consulted. This was a gross exaggeration. We were being consulted in our personal capacities. We were absolutely forbidden to take soundings, so sometimes our views might have been wrong.

Thatcher's March letter to Zhao came at a time when the Executive Council members were unaccustomed to the Byzantine nature of the diplomatic process, and felt their moral responsibility for Hong Kong weighing heavily on their shoulders. As they interpreted events, a letter-drafting exercise carried out in Downing Street, of which they had been informed, but no more than that, was being claimed by China as a turning point in the negotiations, and one which was now being deemed to predicate a British surrender. The unofficials suspected that they were being outpaced by some level of private collusion between the Foreign Office and China, and they were not pleased.

Though they could do nothing about the letter itself, their displeasure found a quite separate focus when they learned of a lunch which had taken place in London on 5 March, just as Cradock and Youde were flying back for their Downing Street meeting. The host was Sir Edwin Bramall, Britain's Chief of Defence Staff, who had been the Commander, British Forces, in Hong Kong in the mid-1970s, and who retained an interest in Hong Kong and China relations. The guest of honour was Ke Hua, the Chinese ambassador to London, who was due to depart in April. The other guests included Lord Chalfont; Alan Donald, assistant under-secretary for Asian and Pacific affairs at the Foreign Office; and Sir Jack Cater, Hong Kong's Commissioner in London.

Whatever was said at that lunch – recollections vary widely – Cater came away convinced that Bramall and Donald had been signalling to Ke Hua that Thatcher's position on sovereignty was now more flexible. He conveyed his concern about this event to Hong Kong. The Executive Council's response was to complain by telegram to the Foreign Office about what it understood to be Donald's comments, and to request that Donald be denied the posting which he might otherwise have expected, as ambassador to Beijing in succession to Sir Percy Cradock. Donald became, in effect, the scapegoat for Hong Kong's frustrations. As Derek Davies, editor of the *Far Eastern Economic Review*, wrote later that year, when it became known that Donald would not, after all, be going to Beijing: 'Donald is one of the FCO officials identified in the minds of [unofficials] as an advocate of "honourable withdrawal" by Britain . . . Exco demonstrated its power by helping deny Donald the ambassadorship.'[8]

THE EFFECT OF Thatcher's letter was thus to raise tensions within the British camp, but at the same time to lower them between Britain and China. Beijing began a 'charm offensive', to show Britain how much easier the dialogue could be if conducted on China's terms, and the name-calling which had followed Thatcher's visit to Beijing the previous September was replaced by measured praise. Xi Zhongxun, vice-chairman of the National People's Congress, told a delegation of 'young people' from Hong Kong on 19 May: 'Mrs Thatcher is a wise woman, and we think highly of her. However, to liken it to a game of chess, her first move was wrong. Then she changed her mind, and her second step was correct.'

The next stage for Britain and China was to fix an agenda. Both sides were now agreed that 'sovereignty' had a place on it, but they disagreed as to whether that place should be first or last. As one British source explained:

The Chinese had accepted by now that they needed input from us on what might and might not work [for Hong Kong]. So, though they would not necessarily have admitted it in quite that form, it was accepted that post-1997 arrangements would be on the agenda. But the Chinese desire was obviously to deal with the arrangements for the transfer of sovereignty first, and then talk about the rest later – since, if sovereignty was not going to be a precondition of the negotiations, as they had originally wanted, then it was logical that they should want it to be the number one item on the agenda instead.

Eventually, it was China which chose to give ground. As Deng Xiaoping later told Hong Kong deputies to the National People's

Congress: 'We must let the British out of an embarrassing situation. It is possible that the negotiations will not begin with "regaining sovereignty", but with the second question, namely, "What do we do after 1997?" After we have finished discussing this second question, there will be nothing left in the first question worth discussing.'[9]

The agenda which was finally agreed in late May consisted of just three lines:

1. Arrangements for the maintenance of stability and prosperity after 1997;
2. Arrangements in Hong Kong between now and 1997;
3. Matters relating to transfer of sovereignty.[10]

In a further token of China's renewed interest in the negotiations, the Hong Kong blueprint was not presented, as Britain had feared, at the National People's Congress in June. Instead, after the NPC and Britain's general election had passed without repercussion, the Chinese Ministry of Foreign Affairs announced on 1 July that the formal negotiations would begin in Beijing on 12 July. To mark the break with the procedural skirmishing, it referred to this as the 'second phase of talks on the future of Hong Kong'.

Matters now began to move more quickly. Youde and the Executive Council unofficials made another short visit to London on 4–5 July to shake hands with the new Foreign Secretary there, Sir Geoffrey Howe, and the new junior minister responsible for Hong Kong, Richard Luce. They reviewed the position papers on which the British negotiators would base their presentations to China, and received assurances once again from Thatcher that no deal would be done which was not 'acceptable to the people of Hong Kong'.

As the Hong Kong party prepared to leave London, the Chinese Ministry of Foreign Affairs announced the principal members of both countries' negotiating teams. The Chinese team-leader would be Yao Guang, previously China's ambassador to Paris, supported by Li Jusheng, second director of the Hong Kong branch of the New China News Agency, and Lu Ping, adviser to the western European department of the Ministry of Foreign Affairs. The British team-leader would be Sir Percy Cradock, the British ambassador in Beijing, supported by Sir Edward Youde, Governor of Hong Kong, and Robin McLaren, Political Adviser.[11]

The British line-up had been agreed only after more wrangling in Beijing. Youde had wanted it to include the Hong Kong Attorney-General, Michael Thomas; but China baulked at a line-up which appeared to represent Hong Kong rather than Britain. It was a matter of principle to China that the structure of the negotiations should not imply any separate identity for Hong Kong. Having waited 140 years to retake the colony, it was highly sensitive to any hint of self-determination.

Youde was acceptable at the negotiating table because China was able to maintain that he was a representative of the British, not the Hong Kong, government. When, in an uncharacteristic moment of jet-lagged impatience, Youde insisted to reporters waiting for him at Kai Tak airport on 6 July that he would 'represent the people of Hong Kong' in the negotiations, China very firmly slapped him down. A spokesman for the Chinese foreign ministry said in Beijing: 'The Sino-British talks on the Hong Kong issue are bilateral . . . Mr Youde will take part in the talks as a member of the British government delegation. Therefore, he can only represent the British government in the talks.'

The fiction that Youde held no special brief for Hong Kong was made the more transparent by China's decision to appoint Li Jusheng to its own team, to 'mark' the Hong Kong Governor. But it was a fiction which Britain accepted, and China's rebuke to Youde was not contested by the Foreign Office. It was, indeed, all but amplified a week later by an un-named British diplomat at the Beijing embassy, who told the *Los Angeles Times*: 'The people of Hong Kong will not have a direct voice in the negotiations. We will seek their advice, and so, I imagine, will the Chinese. Nor will they vote on the results. That is just the way it is.'

To further mark their displeasure at Youde's claim, Beijing then refused a visa to Peter Tsao, the civil servant whom Youde had proposed should accompany him as a press aide. Though the refusal was ostensibly based on a passport technicality, the intention was to underline China's opposition to any Hong Kong 'voice' at the talks. As the Communist *New Evening Post* remarked in an editorial: 'One is at a loss to know how [Tsao] could have been requisitioned for Youde's personal service . . . Even if there were news to be made public, this would be a matter for the representatives of Britain and China.'

ON THE MORNING of 12 July 1983, ten months after Thatcher and Deng had agreed that negotiations on the Hong Kong question should begin, the British and Chinese teams met one another in what had, a century earlier, been the Austro-Hungarian legation building in the Taijichang quarter of Beijing. It was now a state guest-house belonging to the Ministry of Foreign Affairs, and had doubtless been chosen as much for its historical echoes as for its convenience. The agreed modalities were simple ones, recalls one official:

> Talks were to be held in the morning only, at the Chinese insistence. They said the afternoons were too hot. We thought it was really because they had to consult the higher-ups. But it was convenient, because we had a mass of our own reporting to do.
>
> They were to be two-day sessions. We would meet; begin with formal statements by the leaders of the delegations; get things on record. Then we would withdraw for coffee, come back and have a more impromptu session with statements and comments. Normally, only the leaders would speak. Occasionally, Teddy Youde would speak. If he did, then Li Jusheng would speak. Otherwise no one else spoke. Then, at the end of each session, there was a dinner for the delegations at which we could run over some of the things which had been said.

The first round ended, next day, with a brief communiqué which described the talks merely as 'useful and constructive', and recorded that a second round would be held on 25–26 July. This news was of little consolation to the sixty journalists who had stood for two hours in the Beijing rain on the morning of 13 July waiting for details, and who besieged the hapless Yao Guang with their unanswered questions as he made his way slowly to a waiting car.

It had, in fact, been a relatively uneventful meeting, and there was little more to say. There were no great breakthroughs or improvisations or flights of fancy on either side. The British position remained that Hong Kong should enjoy 'continued British administration' after 1997, while the Chinese held that sovereignty and administration were 'inseparable'. The British had brought with them a series of papers in which the workings of Hong Kong were analysed in such a way as to highlight the seemingly indispensable nature of the administrative 'link' with Britain. With China's agreement, the British used the papers as the basis for a presentation which occupied the first round of talks and would continue into the second and third rounds.

The papers were the product of a department of the Hong Kong government called, with splendid obfuscation, General Duties Branch, which had been set up in 1982 to oversee the territory's contribution to the negotiations. Other Hong Kong government departments lent a hand in their areas of expertise, as did the Political Adviser's Office, the Foreign Office in London and the British Embassy in Beijing. There were papers on health and welfare, education, the civil service, the legal system, taxation, trade and other topics: the information in them was drawn from the public domain, and presented in a flat, analytical fashion. One source familiar with the papers says: 'They were basically quite boring, but factual, trying to make things intelligible to Chinese officials who would not necessarily be coming to it from the basis of understanding. If you put them all together, you would have a rather boring civics textbook applicable to Hong Kong in 1983.'

The British motive for presenting this material at the negotiating sessions was not exclusively, and not even primarily, that of influencing the negotiators across the table. The considerations were part formal, part tactical. As the same source explains:

> You had to start somewhere. There are some formal aspects to negotiations which you cannot afford to ignore, particularly since the Chinese are extremely punctilious. Getting on to the record of the discussion a clear exposition of what we saw as the most important features of Hong Kong was a formal step that had to be taken. Otherwise we would have been talking about ephemeral issues, bouncing around all the time.
>
> We [also] had to prepare for the possibility that the talks might break down, and that the only way of helping to retrieve the situation would be to demonstrate publicly, especially in Hong Kong, that we had been actively seeking to achieve the stated objective of preserving Hong Kong's stability and prosperity. That would have meant, in those very difficult circumstances, throwing the books open to inspection. That was not the objective . . . [but] it was a sort of insurance-cover against the worst-case scenario, a total breakdown of the talks, the Chinese making a sham of it and imposing their own solution.
>
> Then, on the more positive side, we were conscious of the people who were standing behind the people doing the nego-

tiating. It is clear that Deng [Xiaoping] took a personal interest, and he and the other senior leaders were very patchily informed about Hong Kong. There were some surprising points of understanding, and some surprising points of total ignorance. And while they would no doubt have applied a discount factor to whatever we said, the presence on the record of a factually accurate description might be useful from their point of view as well. If we were going to build something together, then we needed a foundation.

The second session of formal negotiations took place on 25–26 July, the third on 2–3 August. In all, the British presentations occupied twelve hours. China's comments were relatively brief, and were characterized more by repetitions of its general stand than by arguments with the points which the British were making. According to one source:

Whenever the Chinese had an opportunity to say something, as they did each round, they banged away on the same old theme, that sovereignty and administration were indivisible. It was not a comment, it was not really a response, it was simply a restatement of a position.

It is a Chinese negotiating strength that they never get tired of saying the same thing. And they see the people on the other side of the table approaching a nervous breakdown at the thought of hearing the same thing all over again. Very, very effective. Yao Guang was one of the most uninteresting people you could hope to meet, and he did a very good job.

Another source concedes, with hindsight, that the British may have been over-confident: 'It was very easy for us to score what were essentially debating points. We were glib. They were slow and uncouth. But it was all a bit illusory. It helped morale, but it didn't affect the real course of discussion.'

What was taking place was in no sense a 'negotiation'; it was more of a *tableau*, with the Chinese listening to a long exposition in which they had no real interest, and occasionally protesting their boredom and disagreement. At the end of the second round, two-thirds of the way through their 'civics' course, the Chinese decided publicly to

111

register their impatience. Whereas the previous communiqué had described the first round of talks as 'useful and constructive', the Chinese insisted that 'constructive' now be dropped, leaving the second round to be described merely as 'useful'.

Then, on 29 July, in the interlude between the second and third rounds, the Chinese dropped a small bombshell. A group of Hong Kong secondary school students returned from Beijing to announce that they had been presented, by unnamed Chinese officials, with a detailed plan for Hong Kong's future. This was, to all intents and purposes, the Hong Kong and Macao Affairs Office blueprint in its final form. The text declared: 'Sovereignty and administrative power cannot be separated, otherwise sovereignty becomes meaningless', and promised that, after 1997, the Hong Kong 'special region' would:

- Keep its capitalist system
- Remain a free port and a financial centre
- Retain a convertible currency
- Not be run by emissaries from Beijing
- Have a 'mayor' elected by local inhabitants, who should be a 'patriot'
- Run its own affairs without central government interference, except in matters of defence and foreign affairs
- Have 'considerable' freedom to take part in international activities
- Issue its own travel documents
- Keep its present legal system, so long as this did not conflict with Chinese sovereignty, and have its own final local court of appeal
- Be responsible for its own law and order, to be maintained by the police force
- Tolerate political activities, even of the Nationalists, so long as these did not constitute sabotage
- Conduct its own 'social reforms' without impositions from Beijing.

By publishing the so-called 'Twelve-Point' plan in full, China was treating the formal negotiations as all but irrelevant; it was saying, in effect, that if the British negotiators insisted on talking about a British administration of Hong Kong after 1997, then the Chinese would simply open their own dialogue, about a Chinese administration of Hong Kong after 1997, directly with Hong Kong itself. Deng had said that China reserved the right to act unilaterally, and China was now doing exactly that.

This gesture of contempt for, as much as impatience with, the formal negotiations brought a new sharpness to the third round. The British concluded their presentation and gave copies of their papers to the Chinese delegation; Yao Guang formally rejected the British proposal for 'continued British administration' and delivered another homily on the indivisibility of sovereignty. The Chinese then proposed that the communiqué describe the third round as 'frank', the diplomatic code-word for 'bad-tempered', which the British resisted. In the end, the communiqué recorded simply that talks had taken place, with no adjectives at all. With little to show for their work, and high summer upon them, the two sides parted until September to allow a pause for rest and reflection.

HONG KONG, HOWEVER, was in no mood for rest or reflection. On 4 August, the day after the third-round communiqué, the Hang Seng Index fell 36 points, or almost 5 per cent, merely on the omission of the adjectives 'useful and constructive' from the communiqué, which had reinforced perceptions that the talks were not going well. The Hong Kong dollar had fallen below HK$7.50 to the United States dollar on 5 August, and the city was depressed and jumpy.

Xu Jiatun, a former Party secretary of Jiangsu Province, had been appointed director of the New China News Agency with effect from 30 June 1983, and was now the man charged with the uphill task of reassuring Hong Kong about Beijing's good intentions. As a serving member of the Central Committee, Xu was a senior figure in the Party at a national level, and certainly the most senior ever to have represented it in Hong Kong. Nobody could properly have called him urbane, particularly in his early weeks in Hong Kong when he sported the regulation mainland wardrobe of nylon shirts, white socks and thick black sunglasses. But he was warm, sincere in a Communist way, and – by the standards of the Central Committee – open-minded about Hong Kong's virtues and vices.

Xu cultivated the Chinese constituencies in Hong Kong. His deputy, who arrived with him, Li Chuwen, looked after the foreigners. Li, an austere intellectual and a one-time priest, spoke the English of a university professor. He had previously been director of the Shanghai municipal government's foreign affairs office, a visiting lecturer at the city's foreign languages college, and a senior adviser to the Shanghai Research Institute of International Economic Affairs. Though Xu and Li's contrasting styles soon caused them to grate upon one another, they functioned for the world outside as a formidable and usually effective double-act.

On his first full day in Hong Kong, 1 July, Xu visited *Ta Kung Pao* and *Wen Wei Po*, the newspapers which would serve as his principal propaganda organs in the territory. In the days which followed, he toured the China-controlled schools, banks and corporations in the territory, and began accepting dozens of invitations to banquets, sports events and cocktail parties. By 25 August, the *Far Eastern Economic Review* was reporting that:

> Xu dines out nearly every night with bankers and businessmen (he does not touch alcohol) relaying Beijing's message that there is no need to worry, that there will be only minimal changes after China recovers sovereignty . . . When told that there is a need for an official British presence, Xu replies that this is not possible. Whether or not his guests believe that capitalism will continue, they depart believing that the British will not be able to remain.

With Xu in place, and with the first three rounds of formal talks failing to produce any breakthroughs, Beijing resumed its attempts to secure through propaganda in Hong Kong the concessions which Britain had declined to give through negotiations in Beijing. In Beijing's view, the sovereignty question was now resolved, however fussily the British might insist that it still remained subject to an overall agreement. The next prize which China sought was a public disavowal by Britain of any intention to administer Hong Kong after 1997, as it was presently arguing that it should.

Hu Yaobang, the General Secretary of the Chinese Communist Party, gave fresh impetus to China's demands by telling a visiting Japanese delegation on 15 August:

> We consider the so-called three Hong Kong treaties to be unequal. But it is a fact that the treaties exist. Moreover, it is

114

clearly written into the [New Territories] treaty that the date of expiry is 30 June 1997. Therefore, we do not intend to bring forward or postpone this date. We will recover Hong Kong on 1 July 1997. As far as China is concerned, our attitude is one of respect for history.

The talks we are having with the British side are concerned with the question of how to maintain Hong Kong's prosperity after 1997 as well as the problem of how to proceed during the transitional period from now until 1997. China has a set of systematic policies for maintaining Hong Kong's prosperity.[12]

This was the first formal commitment by China to retake Hong Kong on a specific date. Had any date other than 1 July 1997 been given, it would, of course, have been extraordinary. But merely by confirming the obvious, Hu was encouraging Hong Kong to come to terms with the prospect of a British withdrawal and to plan accordingly. On 17 August, his remarks were echoed and applauded in Hong Kong at a seminar for officials of left-wing trades unions. The Communist newspaper, *New Evening Post*, reported:

The atmosphere was fervent. Participants unanimously pledged full support for the Chinese government's policy statements on recovering sovereignty over Hong Kong. Now that the Chinese government has explicitly stated that recovery of sovereignty will not come later than 1 July 1997, this generation of workers feels very excited and inspired to be able to experience personally this uncommon change in Hong Kong and to see with its own eyes the imminent removal of a century of national shame.

A long and seductive editorial in *Wen Wei Po* on 23 August buttressed China's case for a British withdrawal by arguing that Britain's contribution to Hong Kong's economic success was in any case greatly overstated, and by claiming that Hong Kong Chinese who resisted the formula, 'Hong Kong people rule Hong Kong', were 'self-abased and lacked confidence in themselves'. The only cloud over Hong Kong's future, it concluded, was 'the morbid state of mind, whereby we worship foreigners and despise ourselves'.

To anybody who was reading the newspapers that summer in Hong Kong, the sense that some kind of crunch was coming was inescapable

– the more so when, on 30 August, a 'high-ranking official' of the New China News Agency, perhaps Xu himself, gave an over-ambitious briefing to the local press which, in trying to show that China understood the practical complexities of running Hong Kong, ended up by proving rather the reverse. Highlighting the position of Hong Kong's foreign-exchange reserves, a desperately sensitive topic as the local currency continued to sag, the 'official' declared: 'After 1 July 1997, when China regains sovereignty over Hong Kong, the British government will have to return unconditionally to the new government under the control of the Hong Kong people all of the HK$30 billion reserves that the Hong Kong government currently has deposited abroad.'[13] The combination of naïvety and covetousness displayed in such remarks chilled Hong Kong business circles. From that 30 August briefing onwards, the decline of confidence became almost tangible.

The British, certainly, began at this point to prepare for a bumpy ride. Another meeting was convened at 10 Downing Street for 5 September, with Youde, Cradock, Luce and also the defence minister, Michael Heseltine. As the Hong Kong dollar grew daily weaker and China's propaganda fiercer, Youde worried about the fragility of public order. Nonetheless, he was obliged to report his Executive Council's insistence that no ground should be given, and no compromise offered to China, at the fourth round of talks.

The British camp was now dividing. In simple terms, the Foreign Office was in favour of giving ground on administration, while the Executive Council was against it. Yet, that having been said, at least some unofficial members of the Executive Council doubted that anything would in fact be gained by holding out any longer against China. They advised Youde as they did, nevertheless, because they felt that Hong Kong public opinion would not easily forgive them for endorsing a deal on China's terms, at least until it had been shown that such a deal was unavoidable. The Foreign Office, in turn, could not risk advocating a deal without the Executive Council's support, because the unofficials could probably, if they exerted themselves, make or break the 'acceptability' of that deal to public opinion in Hong Kong. So the Foreign Office, too, was obliged to agree to hold the line, if only so that the unofficials, and through them, Hong Kong, might see the futility of doing so.

Thatcher sided readily enough with the unofficials. If Hong Kong

1. Hong Kong, *c.* 1898: An unidentified colonial official encamps at the border of the recently acquired 'New Territories'. The fence in the background was erected by Chinese officials in 1861 after the ceding of Kowloon, to mark what remained until 1898 the northern limit of the British colony.

2. Hong Kong, 1900: Li Hongzhang (with cane), the doyen of China's diplomats and signatory of the New Territories lease, is received in Hong Kong by the Governor, Sir Henry Blake (seated). Li, who travelled extensively overseas in his later years, brought China its first railway and telegraph systems, co-founded its largest shipping line and cotton mill, and was reputedly its richest private citizen.

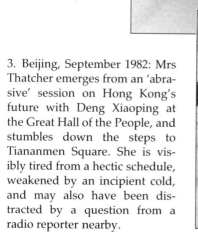

3. Beijing, September 1982: Mrs Thatcher emerges from an 'abrasive' session on Hong Kong's future with Deng Xiaoping at the Great Hall of the People, and stumbles down the steps to Tiananmen Square. She is visibly tired from a hectic schedule, weakened by an incipient cold, and may also have been distracted by a question from a radio reporter nearby.

4. Hong Kong, September 1982: 'So far, so good', Mrs Thatcher replies at a press conference in Hong Kong, when asked about her talks in Beijing. At her side are (*left*) Sir Edward Youde, the Governor of Hong Kong, and (*right*) Bernard Ingham, her press secretary.

5. Hong Kong, September 1982: 'Sofa, so good'. Mrs Thatcher takes tea with a Hong Kong family in a public housing estate, in an imperfectly conceived public relations exercise.

6. Hong Kong, September 1983: Youde emerges from Government House with Xu Jiatun, head of the New China News Agency's Hong Kong branch. Behind them can be seen (*centre*) Sir Philip Haddon-Cave, Chief Secretary of Hong Kong, and (*left*) Robin McLaren, the Governor's Political Adviser. Since arriving in Hong Kong, Xu has abandoned his cadre's wardrobe of nylon shirts and white socks in favour of local tailoring.

7 Hong Kong, September 1983: Richard Luce, Foreign Office minister responsible for Hong Kong, addresses reporters at Kai Tak airport, with Youde at his side. In the midst of the Hong Kong dollar crisis, Luce attempts to calm the charged atmosphere by warning against 'megaphone diplomacy', but merely provokes Beijing into a further fury of propaganda.

8. Hong Kong, April 1984: Sir Geoffrey Howe (*right*), Foreign Secretary, arrives for a dinner with members of the Executive and Legislative Councils, at which he will say that a British withdrawal from Hong Kong in 1997 has become inevitable. He is greeted by (*centre*) Sir S.Y. Chung, senior member of 'Exco', and (*left*) Roger Lobo, senior member of 'Legco'.

9. Hong Kong, July 1984: The Foreign Office mandarins emerge from a meeting with the Executive Council. Sir Percy Cradock (*right*), the Prime Minister's foreign policy adviser, oversees the negotiations from London, while Sir Richard Evans (*left*) heads the British team in Beijing. Dr David Wilson (*centre*) leads the British half of the working group delegated to draft the main text of the Joint Declaration, and will later be appointed Governor of Hong Kong in succession to Youde.

10. Beijing, August 1984: The opening of the twenty-first and penultimate round of formal negotiations at the Diaoyutai State Guest House, when a brief photo-call is permitted. Zhou Nan, leader of the Chinese delegation, smiles across the centre of the table at Evans. Land leases dominate the agenda.

11. Hong Kong, September 1984: Hong Kong VIPs leave for Beijing to watch the initialling of the draft text of the Joint Declaration. Sir Michael Sandberg (*centre*), chairman of the Hongkong and Shanghai Banking Corporation, is seen off by Xu Jiatun (in glasses), and Xu's deputy, Li Chuwen.

12. Beijing, September 1984: The initialling of the Joint Declaration at the Great Hall of the People. Evans and Zhou Nan are at the table. Behind the flags, Youde banters with Ji Pengfei, director of the Hong Kong and Macao Affairs Office. To the left of Youde are Wilson and McLaren.

13. Beijing, September 1984: Toasts after the initialling ceremony. In the foreground are (*left to right*) Wu Xueqian, China's foreign minister, Ji Pengfei and Evans.

14. Beijing, December 1984: Mrs Thatcher, Deng Xiaoping and Zhao Ziyang celebrate the signing of the Joint Declaration, watched by contingents of British and Chinese diplomats. Deng's head partially obscures the face of Sir Geoffrey Howe.

15. Beijing, December 1984: Deng Xiaoping receives Mrs Thatcher at the Great Hall of the People for mutual congratulations. During the conversation, Thatcher describes China's blueprint for Hong Kong as 'an ingenious idea'. Deng replies that it blends 'dialectical Marxism and historical materialism'.

wanted an uncompromising stance from Britain in the fourth round, it could have it with her full backing. Cradock had little choice but to accept the situation. They would see what happened.

Deng Xiaoping himself also chose this time to make his own final attempt to win Britain over without a crisis. Receiving Edward Heath on 10 September, Heath's sixth visit to China since 1974, Deng spoke candidly about his frustration with – as he saw it – British intransigence. He told Heath that, if Britain would only agree now to withdraw from Hong Kong in 1997, then the whole business could be concluded in an atmosphere of goodwill, on terms with which Britain, Deng said, would certainly be satisfied.

Unfortunately for Heath, he was due to visit Hong Kong before returning to London. The highly strung territory, and in particular its Executive and Legislative Councils, were in a defensive mood, and were disinclined to listen to Heath putting China's side of the story. When Heath came to address a private dinner for members of the two councils on 12 September, disaster followed. A guest at the dinner tells the story:

> Heath had been up to Beijing as a sort of old friend. We thought he was pretty unsympathetic to Hong Kong. He came to lecture us about how we were being pig-headed, and should agree to this and that and the other. Near the end of the meeting, Sir S.Y. Chung, who was then senior member of the Executive Council, said in a very joking fashion, 'Well, I think it is time for dinner. We can carry on our discussion there. I must say, you seem to have been well brain-washed in Beijing.'
>
> At that, Heath leapt to his feet, said he had never been so insulted in all his life and that he wanted an apology. S.Y. was a good chap, and a very diplomatic sort of fellow, so he said, 'I did not mean to insult you. I offer an unreserved apology, so if I have given you any offence . . .'
>
> But Heath said, 'No, I am not eating with people like you,' and stormed out. Poor Teddy Youde, who had been looking forward to a quiet evening at Government House, suddenly found Heath rolling up there in a taxi because the Government House car had not been waiting for him when he walked out. It really was a most shocking evening. I felt extremely embarrassed by the whole thing.

The incident with Heath, trivial as it was, reflected the jittery mood of the city. There seemed no escape from China's embrace; no end to China's demands. Was it better to yield to the inevitable now, or to carry on behaving as though miraculous deliverance might intervene?

7

Crisis and Concession

A S the fourth round of talks approached, China published increasingly harsh and explicit condemnations of the British proposal to continue administering Hong Kong beyond 1997. On 15 September, the New China News Agency, quoting Hong Kong leftist journals, accused the Hong Kong government of manufacturing pro-British public opinion to use as an alibi for Britain's own imperialist ambitions. It linked this allegation to China's stand on administration over Hong Kong, saying:

If administrative powers remain in British hands, how can China be said to have recovered sovereignty? In what sovereign state in the world is administrative power in the hands of foreigners? This absolutely cannot be determined by 'public opinion' of any kind. No matter what 'public opinion' says, if there is separation of sovereignty and administrative power, there is no sovereignty.

Less predictably, the Chinese delivered much the same message via the British press, in the form of a rare on-the-record interview given to the *Financial Times* by Zhou Nan, the vice-foreign minister who was being groomed to succeed Yao Guang as China's chief negotiator. Zhou told the newspaper:

Some people suggest China and Britain could jointly administer Hong Kong. This is totally lacking both in jurisprudence and

119

reality. Sovereignty and administration are inseparable. To separate sovereignty from administration means to replace an old unequal treaty with a new one . . . China is determined to recover complete sovereignty and administration of Hong Kong. The position of China is unshakeable and firm.[1]

There was nothing new here for the readers of Hong Kong's Communist press, which included the British Foreign Office. But the *Financial Times* article sent a chill through expatriates in Hong Kong, who either could not read the Chinese newspapers, or regarded them as less reliable than the *FT*.

The effect of this political confrontation, combined with the slump in Hong Kong's stock and property markets which had been underway since the spring of 1982, was to encourage local and foreign investors to withdraw their capital from Hong Kong, and to push the Hong Kong dollar, which floated freely on the foreign exchanges, inexorably towards a currency crisis. Local banks had raised interest rates 1.5 percentage points, to 13 per cent, on 9 September, but still the Hong Kong dollar fell to new all-time lows, reaching HK$7.89 to the US dollar on 14 September. In the year since Mrs Thatcher's visit to Beijing, it had lost one-third of its value.

The effect of this depreciation was felt much more directly in Hong Kong than were, for example, the effects of the sterling depreciations of 1976 or 1985 in Britain. All of Hong Kong's fuel, almost all of its food and most of its consumer goods were imported; inventories were small. The falling dollar provoked immediate price rises for almost everything. Hong Kong was, moreover, a small and fragile place: it really might disappear, if only into China, and its currency really might collapse to nothing under such circumstances. This was not a depreciation caused solely or even primarily by economic factors, which could reasonably be expected to correct itself in time; this was a phenomenon born of justifiable fear, now flirting with despair.

On 16 September, Sir John Bremridge, Hong Kong's Financial Secretary, made a series of comments which, while they were intended to shock the financial markets into common sense, and China into a certain prudence, had the opposite effect. Asked whether the Hong Kong government could take any action to support the Hong Kong dollar, Bremridge said: 'It is not possible to fix the exchange rate of the Hong Kong dollar at any particular level. This must depend on the forces of the market place.' The Hong Kong dollar, he continued, was being weakened by the uncertainties associated with the 1997 negotiations. And among the biggest sellers of the currency, he added, in a sideswipe which particularly enraged China, was the Beijing-owned Bank of China itself, which daily exchanged the Hong Kong dollar revenues of Chinese corporations for the US dollars which Beijing preferred to hold in its reserves.

The Chinese had been arguing for some months now that the main cause of the Hong Kong dollar's weakness was in fact its neglect and mismanagement by the Hong Kong government.[2] They interpreted Bremridge's remarks as a counter-accusation that the Bank of China was responsible for the incipient crisis. The battle for the Hong Kong dollar thus moved into the open, and the Communist press lost any residual inhibitions about directly accusing the British of 'playing the economic card' – by which it meant allowing a crisis of confidence to push Hong Kong towards financial ruin in order to demonstrate the supposed necessity of British rule. *Wen Wei Po* editorialized:

> Mr Bremridge's purpose in playing the 'economic card' was obvious. On the one hand, he wanted to demonstrate that British administration was indispensable to the Hong Kong economy, in order to strengthen British bargaining power at the conference table and achieve the goal of the so-called 'extension of administrative power'. On the other hand, he wanted to shirk responsibility for the economic chaos, and shift the blame on to China.[3]

On 17 September, *Tin Tin Daily News*, a newspaper newly sympathetic to the Chinese cause, claimed that 'large quantities of Hong Kong dollars were being sold by British financial groups in London and even as far away as New York'. On 18 September, the *Hong Kong Daily News* said the British believed there to be 'no harm in having a certain amount of chaos, as this might strengthen the British bargaining position'. On 19 September, the same paper quoted a local academic, Hsueh Feng-hsuan, as saying: 'The current fall in the Hong Kong dollar has been deliberately provoked by the authorities, to cause contradictions in the hope of making the people of Hong Kong lose confidence in China.'

In the increasingly nervous world of Hong Kong business, many wholesalers were now denominating their invoices in US dollars, having lost confidence in the local currency. A few companies were paying wages in US dollars, leading other workers to demand similar treatment. On 18 September, following the announcement of higher electricity prices, 3,000 people gathered in Victoria Park on Hong Kong Island to protest about the cost of living. On 19 September, the Hong Kong dollar suddenly lurched down to HK$8.35 against the US dollar, before recovering slightly to close at HK$8.19. If the British had felt that a crisis of some sort was needed in order to justify a further negotiating concession, then it was arriving right on time: the fourth round of talks, the first since the summer recess, was set for 22–23 September.

TWO DAYS PRIOR to the opening of the fourth round, the Beijing *People's Daily*, the newspaper of the Communist Party Central Committee, published a long and learned article entitled 'The recovery of Hong Kong by China conforms to international law', which it described as an excerpt from a paper by the legal scholar, Jin Fu, to be published in the winter issue of the *Journal of International Affairs*. The article, disguised as a historical sketch of Hong Kong's annexation from China's perspective, was in reality a summary of and commentary on the positions adopted so far in the Hong Kong negotiations by the British and Chinese sides. The British, said Jin, were advocating 'the exchange of sovereignty for administrative power'. As to China's position: 'When China says it will recover its sovereignty over Hong Kong, it means regaining its sovereign rights including administrative power. It definitely does not mean regaining its hallowed sovereign rights only in nominal terms while yielding up its administrative power.'

It was, continued the *People's Daily*, 'a sheer lie, to say that Hong Kong's prosperity cannot be separated from British administration'. It was equally dismissive of Britain's claim to have a 'moral obligation to the Hong Kong people', saying:

> The whole world knows that most Hong Kong people are Chinese, and only the Chinese government can be their true representative. The British government has no right to represent them . . . The relationship between the British government and the Chinese residents in Hong Kong is like that between a colonial

ruler and its subjects. Therefore, in the present talks, Britain is not qualified to be their representative.

As the *Financial Times* commented in its annual survey of Hong Kong, published that month:

> Britain's proclaimed 'moral obligation' to Hong Kong appears to turn on a belief that the affinities which Hong Kong people value most deeply are not racial or territorial but affinities with liberal, social and economic values, with capitalism and personal freedom . . . [Whereas] in Beijing's eyes, to support reunification of Hong Kong with the motherland is to be a Chinese patriot. To oppose it is to be a traitor to the race. The question is one in which Britain has no *locus standi*.[4]

The positions were clear and irreconcilable, and they remained so at the opening of the fourth round, when Sir Percy Cradock, in line with the instructions which he had received at Downing Street on 5 September, offered no concession to China. He reiterated the British view that continued British administration was required to guarantee Hong Kong's stability and prosperity beyond 1997. Yao Guang offered, yet again, China's view of the indivisibility of sovereignty and administration. Perhaps the only surprising aspect of the first day's talks was that they were not conducted in an atmosphere of any very visible anger or irritation, merely with a sort of fatalism on both sides.

Tempers frayed, however, on the second day, as – in the absence of any possibility of progress – the discussion turned mainly on the nature of the communiqué. The British pressed the Chinese to permit the issue of a positive-sounding communiqué, in order not to upset further Hong Kong's financial markets. The Chinese declined, with Yao telling Cradock that the financial crisis was Britain's affair, and that Britain was capable of ending it if it so chose. Again, as after the third round, the communiqué emerged shorn of adjectives. It merely announced the intention of holding a fifth round of talks on 19–20 October.

The day of the communiqué, 23 September, was a Friday. On the Saturday morning, a working half-day in Hong Kong, anxiety finally spilled over into panic. The Hong Kong dollar lost 8 per cent of its value at opening, to be quoted at HK$9.50 to the US dollar. Queues formed at supermarkets as families bought up tinned and dried foods, household goods, anything that would keep. Newspapers reported that virtually all foreign merchants were refusing to accept Hong Kong dollars, and that Taiwanese suppliers of fresh fruit and vegetables were halting shipments to Hong Kong altogether. Local shops began posting signs saying that they would accept only US dollars. Though there were no outbreaks of violence, the mood of the city had grown volatile and more than a little frightening. It was a crisis to which nobody seemed to have an answer.

Nobody, that was, except a man called John Greenwood, the true hero of this dark hour for Hong Kong. Greenwood was an economist who specialized in monetary affairs, and was based in Hong Kong as the chief economist of the fund management group GT. He published, under GT's aegis, a bi-monthly journal called the *Asian Monetary Monitor*, to which he had contributed several essays over the years setting down his worries about the stability of the Hong Kong dollar. His general theme was that Hong Kong, which had its own currency but not its own central bank, would benefit from the availability of a mechanism to regulate either the money supply or the exchange rate of the Hong Kong dollar; but his ideas found no echo in the government, which was ideologically resistant to any institutional change which smacked of interference with the free markets on which Hong Kong prided itself. A 1981 paper called 'Time to Blow the Whistle', which concluded that the Hong Kong government would be unable as the system then stood to intervene effectively to influence the Hong Kong dollar's exchange rate if it should ever wish to do so, had earned Greenwood a summons to see Bremridge, then newly installed as Financial Secretary, who told him that the exchange rate was not a problem, the banking system was sound, the economy was growing strongly, 'and we wish you would shut up'.

Greenwood remained confident of his diagnosis, but appreciated that he was unlikely ever to convert Bremridge to the cause of active intervention. It was only in the summer of 1983, with the Hong Kong dollar crisis already visible on the horizon, that he finally came up with a scheme towards which he thought the Hong Kong government might soften:

It dawned on me that I could present an option which did not require the authorities to conduct intervention. You could fix the price of the currency by requiring the banks to pay foreign currency for the issue of new Hong Kong dollars. And that would, in a sense, not require intervention, because the authorities would not be intervening in the foreign exchange market to peg the rate.

. . . Essentially, it was a reconstruction of the old gold-standard system or the old silver-standard system which had prevailed in Hong Kong, and of the subsequent colonial form, the currency board. Currency boards in colonies would traditionally hold foreign currency against any issue of notes.

At the end of August 1983, Greenwood drafted a paper which he called 'How to Rescue the Hong Kong Dollar', and circulated it among the three most eminent monetary economists that he knew: Maxwell Fry, Milton Friedman and Alan Walters, the last of whom was still an economic adviser to Margaret Thatcher, though living in Washington. All three endorsed its thesis. In mid-September, he submitted the paper privately to the Hong Kong government.

For a few days there was silence, as the fourth round of negotiations came and went in Beijing. Greenwood remembers his own apprehension on the night of Friday, 23 September, after the failure of the Beijing talks: 'I told my staff that afternoon that if there were riots over the weekend and if they felt unsafe, they should not come into work on Monday morning. You could see the signs of tension in the streets that day. People standing around, looking at television screens, angry because their money was going down the drain.'

On the afternoon of Saturday, 24 September, after the terrifying plunge of the Hong Kong dollar that morning on the exchanges, Greenwood was invited to attend a meeting the next morning in the Hong Kong government's Monetary Affairs department, where he would be asked to present and discuss the ideas in his paper.

The lined faces around the table suggested that few people there, Greenwood included, had slept well. Facing him were the Secretary for Monetary Affairs, Douglas Blye, and his deputy, Anthony Latter; the Banking Commissioner, Colin Martin; two government economists; and two representatives of the territory's leading banks, the Hongkong and Shanghai and the Standard Chartered. The discussion ran for some five hours. Greenwood sketched his proposal. An exchange rate would be fixed and published at which the Hong Kong government would undertake to buy or sell Hong Kong dollar banknotes. So long as the government always stood willing and able to deal in banknotes in either direction at the stated rate, all other Hong Kong dollar transactions would follow that rate, since no buyer or seller would accept from any third party a rate significantly inferior to that which could be obtained from the government.

The consequence of pegging the exchange rate in this way would, however, be to leave interest rates to take the strain of any surges in supply or demand. And what Greenwood could not have known, as he was making his presentation that Sunday morning, was that the Hong Kong dollar crisis was only one of the items on the government's agenda. A local bank, Hang Lung, was on the verge of default, in circumstances tainted with fraud. The collapsing stock and property markets, aggravated by a wave of white-collar crime, had left several other banks looking unsteady. The issue was not merely to decide whether Greenwood's mechanism could stabilize the Hong Kong dollar, but also whether in doing so it might, by squeezing interest rates, accelerate a banking crisis.

Greenwood thought, when he left that afternoon, that the mood of the meeting had been against him. It was not until late that evening that he learned his proposal was being hesitantly endorsed. An unsigned statement, issued by the government as a press release, said that the government was 'actively developing' a scheme to give it 'a more significant role in the exchange rate determination mechanism'. This would mean, said the press release, 'a substantial revision of the mechanics' of banknote-issuing, 'in such a way as to produce an exchange rate which would more accurately reflect the fundamental strength of the economy'.

The statement was a holding action, designed to reassure the market without committing the Hong Kong government to anything too specific. Its effect on market professionals was more one of bafflement than of reassurance – not because it was too technical, but simply because it omitted too many important details, hinting at a managed exchange rate without saying how this would be achieved or at what level. The effect was satisfactory in the circumstances, all the same: trading in the Hong Kong dollar all but halted, with dealers quoting spreads so huge as to deter all but the most desperate customers while they tried to discover what the government planned.[5] The run had been stalled.

Bremridge, who had been attending the annual meeting of the

International Monetary Fund in Washington, rushed back overnight to arrive groggily at Kai Tak airport on the Monday. Seemingly unaware of the holding statement, he added a further layer of confusion by saying that he had no intention of fixing the exchange rate. But even with Bremridge back, fundamental changes to Hong Kong's monetary system could not be decided by Hong Kong alone. The Chancellor of the Exchequer, together with senior officials of the Bank of England, were in Washington; and Thatcher herself was on a North American tour. The only answer seemed to be to fix a meeting for Thatcher, the Chancellor and the Bank of England at the British Embassy in Washington, which Alan Walters could also attend.

The meeting took place on Thursday, 29 September. The main question, the one to which the Treasury and the Bank of England required an answer, was whether a fixing of the Hong Kong dollar might put Britain's own reserves at risk. They worried that if the Hong Kong government, backed by the British government, imposed an exchange rate which then produced a run on the Hong Kong dollar, then a draining of Hong Kong's own reserves would create a strong political obligation for Britain to cover the deficit. A Bank of England official, Charles Goodhart, and a Treasury official, David Peretz, were instructed to make an immediate trip to Hong Kong to assess whether the 'peg' would hold. The two spent a week talking their way around the government and the banking sector, eventually persuading not only themselves but also Bremridge, who had remained sceptical, of the virtues of the Greenwood plan.

With Peretz and Goodhart convinced, London's approval was given to the peg, and documentation was prepared. For simplicity's sake, and to inspire public confidence, the US dollar was chosen as the currency against which the Hong Kong dollar would be fixed; the only question now being, at what rate. The 'peg', it was thought, should be slightly above the recent market rate in order to recoup at least some of the currency's speculative losses, but not so high as to provoke a rush to convert and so push up interest rates. The decision was taken on the evening of 14 October by a group which included Youde, Bremridge and Sandberg. Since the market rate had lately been around HK$8.50 to the US dollar, there was an initial inclination to set the rate at HK$8, a number which had the additional advantage of being considered auspicious in Hong Kong, because it supplied, in Cantonese, a near-homophone for 'prosperity'. But Bremridge felt that HK$8 was too simple a number, lacking an appropriate air of scientific calcula-tion. A slightly stronger rate, HK$7.80, was arbitrarily fixed and then published. The peg was in place. And, as the weeks passed, it held. Greenwood had been absolutely right.

THE HONG KONG dollar crisis was a public event which defined for those who lived through it the point at which the tensions of the negotiations threatened finally to snap those threads which held Hong Kong together. But entwined with it was a much more private political crisis, the consequences of which were still more enduring.

The British had held their ground in the fourth round to see if the Chinese would yield. The Chinese had not done so, nor had they flinched when the Hong Kong dollar crisis ensued. It was time for Britain and Hong Kong to think about yielding. The job of concentrating minds fell to Richard Luce, the Foreign Office minister responsible for Hong Kong, who arrived in the territory on 24 September.

Luce was returning from Brunei. It had been pencilled in some weeks previously that, if by any chance the fourth round had gone well, and China had hinted at concessions, then Luce would have been able to divert to Beijing and carry forward the momentum. But that, clearly, was not to be; and on 27 September, Luce found himself attending an enlarged meeting of the Executive Council, with Cradock also present, to discuss Britain's own retreat.

The mood of some unofficials, led by Sir S.Y. Chung, was to 'tough it out'. There was still, they thought, the possibility that the Chinese might be bluffing, and that the Hong Kong dollar crisis might be bringing them even now to their senses. And if not, then there would be at worst a stand-off, which was to be preferred to conceding Hong Kong irrevocably to China. But Cradock differed. It was an illusion, he said, that the Chinese might 'agree to disagree'. The unofficials simply did not understand the politics of the people with whom they were dealing. If necessary, he said, the Chinese would take Hong Kong as a wasteland. The next round of talks might well be the last, unless Britain brought something new to the table. China would simply prepare for a takeover on its own crude terms. It would be very rough indeed.

Sir Philip Haddon-Cave, Hong Kong's Chief Secretary, was in favour of holding out. Bremridge, carrying the dollar crisis and the banking crisis on his shoulders, said he doubted that the situation in the financial markets could be 'held' were the talks to break down. Though Luce was there to listen, rather than to hand down a decision at this stage, his own mood appeared to be in tune with that of Cradock: Britain had agreed to hang on for one more round, and it had done so. The risks of hanging on any longer were now too great.

Ironically – since his Hong Kong trip foreshadowed the major breakthrough of the talks – Luce was to provoke a spectacular display of Chinese anger by his own mild attempts to calm the situation in Hong Kong. In a press conference before leaving, he ducked questions about the progress of the talks, emphasizing the need for confidentiality, but added: 'You cannot indulge in what I would call megaphone diplomacy. You cannot negotiate in public . . . If we start engaging in a counter-argumentative campaign with the Chinese government, that will not help anybody.'

Though Luce had not accused the Chinese directly of 'megaphone diplomacy', this was how his statement was interpreted in the Communist press, which responded with some of the rudest personal invective of the talks. In an editorial entitled, 'Forget It, Mr Luce', no less an authority than the *People's Daily* accused the minister of 'babbling', and declared:

> Look here, Mr Luce, do you not acknowledge that erroneous arguments carried in the British press are the position maintained by the British government in the talks? Is this not breaking the confidentiality of the talks through a megaphone? . . . The British government alone will be responsible for all the consequences arising from any unfortunate failure of the talks caused by Britain's clinging to its colonialist position.

This editorial, and similar ones in the Hong Kong press, were read in the British camp as confirmation that the Chinese were now close to breaking with the negotiating process altogether. In one official assessment: 'These were positively rabid statements, with Beijing calling Luce a liar. It was in the middle of a howling gale of propaganda, admittedly. But we were obviously now in a different ball-game.'

Cradock returned to London once again, this time to propose to Mrs Thatcher that the time had come to amend Britain's negotiating position on administration, much as it had amended its position on sovereignty in March. The new keyword would be 'conditionality'. Cradock recommended that Britain should state formally that its own basic position remained unchanged, and that it believed that only continued British administration after 1997 could guarantee Hong Kong's stability and prosperity. However, it should say that it was prepared 'on an entirely conditional basis' to 'explore' whatever other arrangements China might have in mind for Hong Kong after 1997. Then, if a solution could be devised on the basis of that Chinese plan, in which Britain had confidence, Britain would back it.

Though Thatcher accepted Cradock's formula, it still had to be 'sold' to Hong Kong. Youde and the Executive Council unofficials made a further trip to Downing Street for two days of meetings with Howe and Thatcher on 7–8 October, where they agreed, after some initial reluctance, to endorse this 'second finesse'.[6]

It was not the happiest of meetings, but it was the great watershed of the negotiations. From now on, Britain would cease to insist upon its own view of Hong Kong's optimal future and co-operate instead in 'exploring' China's view. 'Conditionality' or no, in practical terms the argument was over. For if Britain was to spend the remaining months of negotiations discussing China's plan, then there would be very little choice as to the final outcome. Either Britain would endorse China's plan, or it would decline to endorse it, in which case the plan would be implemented nonetheless.

A formal message was drafted, for Cradock to relay to the Chinese government. It said Britain was prepared 'to see whether Britain and China could together construct on the basis of proposals put forward by China, arrangements of lasting value for the people of Hong Kong'. If this could be achieved, then 'the British Government would be prepared to recommend to Parliament a treaty enshrining them, and to do its utmost to assist their implementation'.

The message was given first to Zhou Nan at the Ministry of Foreign Affairs, then again at the fifth round of negotiations when they opened on 19 October. Not unreasonably, its nuances seemed at first to puzzle the Chinese. They recognized it as a significant concession. But they were not quite sure whether Britain was proposing to explore China's proposals in addition to asserting the desirability of continued British administration; or whether the British were now saying, in a roundabout way, that continued British administration was truly being dropped from the agenda.

130

At the negotiating table, Cradock emphasized the conciliatory mood. Britain, he said, saw itself only as a 'caretaker' of Hong Kong. To underline Britain's desire to 'explore' the Chinese proposals, he suggested that smaller working groups be set up to address concrete issues. Yao Guang responded with a gesture of goodwill: China would agree to restore the words 'useful and constructive' to the communiqué describing the talks.

Yet China was not quite convinced; and its scepticism about Britain's intentions returned in the weeks that followed. The event which most disturbed China's composure was the participation of the Prime Minister in a BBC World Service radio phone-in, during which she responded to a question posed – perhaps somewhat disingenuously – by a reporter from a Hong Kong television station. Asked whether Britain still wished to maintain a presence in Hong Kong after 1997, Thatcher replied:

Well, these kind of things are exactly what we are now negotiating about. And obviously, we think that the British link is very important indeed, because it is partly responsible for the kind of success we have had in Hong Kong. Now, when you have said that, you don't have to go into to say, well now, precisely what is the nature of this link and the nature of the law and so on. Because you want continuity of the system as far as you can possibly have them. But these are matters for the negotiating table and what goes on at the negotiating table must remain confidential.

Whatever else China might have made of Thatcher's rambling syntax, this did not sound like the 'change of heart' which they had understood Cradock to have been conveying to them in Thatcher's name just a fortnight earlier. The notion of a British 'link', they suspected, was administration by another name. *Wen Wei Po* accused Thatcher of 'using an ambiguous phrase to cover up and confuse the issue'.[7]

What China read as a second danger signal came a few days later from a non-governmental source, the *Financial Times* newspaper, in its issue of 11 November. This contained a story reporting the changed British position, but with a strong emphasis on the 'conditionality' of the stand. Though Britain, it said, had 'shelved' its insistence on 'continued British administration after 1997':

131

This revised approach, it is understood, does not amount to an irrevocable concession, but is a conditional move to enable the talks to move forward . . . Officials in London and Hong Kong were at pains to stress that neither side has made any irrevocable concessions . . . and that, in spite of the optimism generated last month, there were likely to be 'rough times ahead'.

Again, there was nothing here which contradicted the message delivered at the fifth round. But if – as China certainly assumed – the story had been 'inspired' by British officials, then it might be taken to indicate a certain half-heartedness on Britain's part.

To allay China's suspicions, Cradock secured authorization to deliver an additional oral message at the sixth round of talks, on 14–15 November, amplifying the concession offered at the fifth round. He reaffirmed Britain's 'genuine' wish to 'explore the Chinese proposals' for Hong Kong, and gave a formal reassurance that Britain would seek 'no links of authority' with Hong Kong after 1997, if other arrangements were agreed. This appeared to be the categorical statement for which China had been waiting. They were now ready, they said, to discuss what China's own proposals 'meant in practice'.

The shift was reflected immediately in China's public statements. On 16 November, the day after the sixth round, a spokesman for the Ministry of Foreign Affairs said that relations between Britain and China were 'normal'. Communist publications ceased their attacks on the former British position, and began instead to focus on expositions of the Chinese plan for 'one country, two systems'.

The new campaign was supervised by Ji Pengfei, a retired foreign minister who had succeeded Liao Chengzhi as head of the Hong Kong and Macao Affairs Office after Liao's death in June. On 22 November, Ji received a delegation of Hong Kong and Macao industrialists, led by Wang Kuancheng of the Hong Kong Chinese Chamber of Commerce, at the Great Hall of the People, and told them that China was now confident that the Sino-British talks would reach a 'satisfactory' solution by September 1984, the deadline which Deng had first fixed. Ji talked about 'Hong Kong people ruling Hong Kong', and told the industrialists that Hong Kong's separate status after 1997 would be protected, not only by the new clause in the constitution providing for the establishment of 'special regions' of China, but also by a 'mini-constitution' which would be drafted for Hong Kong alone. This last remark was an early glimpse of the 'Basic Law' which China planned to draft in its own name for Hong Kong, once a Sino-British agreement had been reached.[8]

A fuller statement of China's plans appeared in *Ta Kung Pao* on 5 December, two days before the seventh round of talks was due to begin in Beijing. The article, entitled 'Cannot two systems co-exist for a long time?', contained a fair summary of the position which China then presented to the British during that seventh round. It emphasized China's intention to keep Hong Kong's social and economic systems separate from those of the mainland for at least fifty years, and to leave them substantially unchanged from their present forms. It singled out Hong Kong's status as a free port and an international financial centre, together with the legal system and the freely convertible currency, as aspects of the territory which China was particularly determined to preserve. It concluded:

What warrants our special attention is that China has not only formulated a set of feasible procedures and principles for Hong Kong, but is also regularizing them through legislative procedures. Article 31 of the new constitution, adopted last year, stipulates the establishment in Hong Kong of a special administrative region administered by a government organized by the local people . . . The State Council is drafting the Basic Law, or mini-constitution, for the Hong Kong special region. This law will be announced in September 1984, to solicit opinions comprehensively. After that, it will be submitted to the NPC for approval.

The seventh round of talks duly came and went. For the British it was an interesting but also a slightly dispiriting occasion. Finally, they were relieved of the obligation to persist in battering their own proposals for continued British administration against the brick wall of China's monotone rejection. Instead, it was the Chinese proposals which were on the table, and which the British were testing and questioning.

The dispiriting factor came, not in the addition of any new material from the Chinese side, but in the *absence* of any new material. The Chinese plan for Hong Kong, as its representatives now made formally clear, amounted to nothing more than the twelve-point scheme which had been publicly released to the secondary school students in June. China wanted the British to endorse simple declarations of intent that Hong Kong should remain, for example, 'a free port' and 'an international financial centre', without any technical detail as to how this would be achieved. Once Britain had put its name to a short document of general principles, China alone would supply the necessary detail during its writing of the 'Basic Law'.

This scarcely conformed with the British idea of a 'satisfactory agreement', or of 'arrangements of lasting value' to Hong Kong, the phrases which Thatcher had used in setting out the circumstances in which she would recommend a new treaty to Parliament. The seventh round thus put an end to one set of tensions within the Sino-British negotiations, only to replace it with another. The first set, relating to the end which was in view, had now been resolved in China's favour. The fig-leaf of conditionality aside, it was clear enough that the settlement would provide for a British withdrawal from Hong Kong and a Chinese administration. The new set of arguments, which began with the seventh round, concerned the means to that end, the form of settlement: in essence, whether it was to be the short statement of principle which China wanted, or the long, detailed agreement which Britain wanted.

It was, in many ways, back to square one. The British resigned themselves to the prospect that the only way in which they might ever hope to shoehorn the requisite quantity of detail into the eventual agreement would be by supplying it themselves. The Hong Kong government's General Duties Branch, which had spent the previous autumn drafting papers to show how British administration was indispensable to the everyday workings of Hong Kong, had begun, after the fifth round of talks and the change in British tactics, to draft a second set of papers showing how Hong Kong might survive on its own. Where the previous set of papers had anatomized Hong Kong in structural terms, highlighting the ubiquity of the British 'link', the new papers anatomized it in functional terms, looking at the internal workings of the various systems and institutions, and isolating those aspects of them which would have to be made self-sufficient of both Britain and China, if Hong Kong really were to survive a British withdrawal and regroup its resources under a local government.

Two of the new British papers were tabled at the seventh round, including one on Hong Kong's legal system which suggested that, if

Hong Kong were to sever its ties with the British Privy Council, then it would benefit from allowing foreign judges from common-law jurisdictions to sit in its own appeal court as a reinforcement of its expertise. For the first time, something approaching lively debate sparked into life around the table, as the Chinese defended their 'principles' and the British their 'details'. But both sides were tired by now, and ready for a seasonal break. The fundamental breakthroughs had been made, and both team-leaders, Sir Percy Cradock for Britain and Yao Guang for China, were preparing to stand down. Their achievements were saluted by an unusually loquacious communiqué. 'The two sides', it said, 'reviewed the course of the talks and the progress made so far.'

8

A Matter of
Form

D
ESPITE the tension and uncertainty surrounding the early
negotiations, and even during the currency crisis of September 1983, there had been no violent manifestations of
public unrest in Hong Kong. But the strain was cumulative, and by the
turn of 1984 the mood of the city was a dark blend of exhaustion,
sullenness and impatience. The negotiations were mainly to blame,
but not solely: the economy was weak, the collapse of the stock and
property markets had eroded the savings of thousands of families, and
the government was too preoccupied with 1997 to give its full attention
to everyday municipal problems.

The event which finally brought to the surface the undercurrents of
the public mood was small enough in itself: a strike by local taxi-
drivers, angry at a government proposal to increase sharply their vehi-
cle registration and licensing fees. Had these been less pressured times,
the government would probably have proceeded more cautiously,
investing the time needed to win public opinion over to the belief that
the increases were necessary. Instead, the enabling legislation was
brusquely gazetted at midnight on 11 January – and, by the taxi-
drivers, still more brusquely denounced the next day.

The drivers' first tactic was, in a nicely judged political gesture, to
announce that they would ask the New China News Agency to take up
their case. The NCNA declined to do so.[1] Next, the drivers took to the
streets with an effective form of direct action, using their cabs to

blockade junctions throughout the urban areas of Hong Kong, bringing traffic to a halt. Police and drivers exchanged angry words and gestures; crowds gathered; the few cabs which defied the strike were attacked, and some drivers beaten.

On the second day of the blockade, 13 January, the taxi-drivers prevailed. Twenty members of the Legislative Council said that they would oppose the proposed taxi bill, a level of resistance sufficient to make it all but certain that the bill would be withdrawn by the government. On Hong Kong Island, the taxis began once more to circulate, and the streets to return to what passed in those days for normality. But across the harbour in Mongkok, the densely populated working-class sprawl on the western side of Kowloon, the tension failed to dissipate as evening approached. Long after the taxi-drivers had moved on, gangs of youths were still gathered at street corners, taunting the police. At six o'clock, when police attempted to end one such episode by arresting a group of youths, the party was pursued back to the Mongkok police station by a crowd which swelled within minutes from dozens to hundreds. A crude fire-bomb, hurled from the crowd against the door of a nearby bank, signalled the onset of a full-scale riot.

By midnight, the police estimated that about 10,000 people were engaged in the fighting, burning and looting. No deaths were reported; but by the time the violence died away at 2.30 a.m., more than 30 people had been seriously injured. Of the 172 people subsequently arrested, 117 were charged with robbery, burglary, arson and possession of offensive weapons. The lawlessness was confined to that single night, with no regrouping of the crowd on the following day.

In discussing the causes of the riot, officials noted that Mongkok was a heartland of the triads, the big, loose-knit criminal gangs of Hong Kong, and they attributed leadership of the crowds to criminal and hooligan elements. But privately, they conceded that the political background could not be excluded from the analysis: this was, after all, the worst unrest that Hong Kong had experienced since the Cultural Revolution, and there was, indisputably, a degree to which the rioters had been encouraged by the vulnerability of order and authority in Hong Kong. The public declarations by China of its intention to oust Britain from Hong Kong, and its denunciations of the legitimacy of British rule, had the natural consequence of making the colonial government appear both weak and transient. When, in 1967, Hong

Kong's Communist rioters had taunted the local police by shouting, 'Do you think the British will take you with them when they go?', the threat had still seemed a distant one, and the police had held the line. Now, the threat was more immediate, and, certainly, one which would crystallize within the working lifetime of any young police officer or, for that matter, civil servant. Would the line hold again, under comparable strain?

Thus, the real lesson of the Kowloon riot, for those who cared to think about it, was that the consequences of any 1997 settlement would be felt a long time before that date. Already, the Hong Kong government was in danger of being perceived as a lame-duck government; and, the closer 1997 approached, the more it would have to depend for its authority upon the support of China as well as Britain. But that would in turn beg the question of how Britain could secure China's support for the Hong Kong government prior to 1997, without at the same time inviting its interference in Hong Kong's affairs. The problems of the transitional period were raising themselves on the streets of Kowloon, well before they had been directly addressed by the negotiators in Beijing.

For Youde and his Executive Council, the Kowloon riot was, at the very least, a warning that some sort of positive statement about the negotiations needed to be made in Hong Kong very soon, which would lower the tension there by emphasizing the common interest of Britain and China in a satisfactory settlement and offering some indication that such a settlement was in prospect. Youde had the opportunity to deliver that message during a trip to London with Executive Council members on 16–17 January for sessions with Howe, Luce, Cradock and Thatcher, meetings which had been planned mainly to discuss how the Chinese blueprint, presented at the negotiations in December and now being publicly aired in interviews by Ji Pengfei, might be elaborated in ways acceptable to Hong Kong.[2] When Youde told Thatcher that Hong Kong was becoming 'restless', and that some form of reassurance was acutely needed, Thatcher appeared sympathetic enough for Sir S.Y. Chung, the senior member of the Executive Council, as he left Downing Street, to tell waiting reporters that Hong Kong would 'soon know what the future held', though he could give no date for this revelation.

IT WAS AT the January meeting, also, that the Executive Council first encountered Sir Percy Cradock in his new incarnation as foreign policy adviser to the Prime Minister. He had, in deference to Thatcher's wish that he should lead the British team through the path-finding stages of the negotiations, postponed by several months his retirement as British ambassador to China. He had finally returned to London at the end of 1983 where, with the rank of Foreign Office deputy under-secretary, he was based in 10 Downing Street, and continued to oversee the negotiations on Thatcher's behalf.

Cradock's replacement in Beijing would, ordinarily, have been Alan Donald who, as assistant under-secretary for Asia and the Pacific at the Foreign Office, had been closely involved in the negotiations since their inception. But with the Executive Council's intervention to block Donald's appointment to Beijing (he was made ambassador to Indonesia instead), the post went to Sir Richard Evans, deputy under-secretary in charge of economic affairs, who spoke Chinese and who had served previously in China in 1955–7 and 1962–4, but who was a newcomer to the Hong Kong negotiations.

China mirrored the British move by changing its own team leader. Yao Guang gave way to Zhou Nan who, as an assistant foreign minister in Beijing, had been growing steadily more visible in the margins of the negotiations. One British source offered this private assessment of Yao:

> People are generally not very great admirers of Yao's style, but in terms of getting what the Chinese needed, he got it. He just waited there like soggy mud, and he would never offer the sort of firm ground you needed for a logical argument. All of Cradock's brilliant logic just sank into this mud, while Yao himself just waited for the Chinese position to take effect . . . He was a slow and ponderous man, but he achieved China's goal, and he is the man to whom it should be credited at the junior level.

Zhou Nan, a career diplomat, had served at China's mission to the United Nations in New York throughout the 1970s, and spoke fluent English. The Foreign Office, initially pleased by the appointment, looked forward to a more sophisticated and pragmatic interlocutor. As one observer viewed the change: 'Zhou Nan was bright, and he was certainly a relief – even if he turned out in the end to be not very nice.'

The eighth round of talks, the first under Evans and Zhou, was set for 25–26 January. As it approached, the Foreign Office elected for an outward show of optimism, putting the best possible face on the negotiations, both for Hong Kong's sake and its own. With China's terms now all but certain to form the basis of any settlement, it was time to stop focusing on the inadequacy of those terms, and instead to build up some confidence in them. A new, positive tone infused the briefings given to diplomatic correspondents in London before the eighth round began, and this was quickly echoed in their copy. Under the headline, 'Hong Kong Optimism', *The Times* said in its main leader of 24 January that China was to be commended for the 'subtlety and discretion' of its Hong Kong policy-making. Historically, commented the newspaper, China had 'shown great respect for the sort of written international agreements that Britain is now working towards'.

The eighth round continued the discussion, begun at the seventh round, of the post-1997 Hong Kong legal system, and of aspects of constitutional arrangements. The topic of military forces in Hong Kong was also raised, the central question – for Britain – being that of whether Chinese troops would be stationed in Hong Kong after 1997. As to the routine of the talks at this stage, according to one source:

They were rather boring and formal. Typically, in January, February and March, [the British] would start the session by tabling one or two papers, then make quite a long statement of introduction spelling out what was in the papers, and the implications. That would take thirty to fifty minutes, following which it would be interpreted.

Then, Zhou Nan would usually make a general statement about the need for the British to get a move on, or for the British to show more flexibility. Or he might make a start immediately on the papers from the previous meeting. This would also be a very formal set-piece. At the end of the second day's session, we would discuss the date for the next meeting.

There was no formal meeting-by-meeting agenda. The day before the meeting, somebody from the British side would go to the foreign ministry. The Chinese would then say if there was something they particularly wanted to discuss.

The papers which the British were presenting, their second set, quite distinct from those which had been presented at the first three rounds of the negotiations, were characterized by the same source in these terms:

> They were a whole series about how Hong Kong operated, the systems of administration, justice, shipping, economic management, ostensibly to tell the Chinese what it was all about, but in fact to get them to take account of this view of things in reworking and greatly expanding their own prescriptions. The papers were prepared in Hong Kong, by General Duties Branch. They contained nothing which could not have been picked up in Hong Kong by diligent inquiry.
>
> The Chinese professed, Zhou Nan in particular, to be rather bored by the papers. But he would always comment on them – 'We will do this', or 'We will not do that'.

According to a Hong Kong official, it was in their analysis, rather than in their raw material, that the papers being presented at the start of 1984 differed from those which had been presented at the first three rounds of talks in July and August 1983:

> There were strong similarities [between the two sets]. There was a formal aspect to all this, which was that the earlier papers had led to the conclusion that the British administrative link was necessary. We were now operating on a different premise, and in order to reintroduce the same basic material into the record, you had to go through the process again.
>
> The papers were now looking at, not just how to preserve the status quo, but how to achieve that objective while making as few changes as possible, consistent with the resumption of sovereign and administrative rights by China. But a lot of the basic work, the descriptive work, the analysis of what was essential, was reproduced, in effect [from the first set of papers] in a different framework.

But in pronouncing himself 'bored' with the British papers, and with detailed arguments about post-1997 arrangements, Zhou Nan was not merely speaking for effect. Under his stewardship, the Chinese approach to the negotiations quickly gained an additional dimension, focusing as much on the form and the timing, as on the content, of an eventual treaty. In effect, though informally, Zhou was forcing the talks forward from the first to the second and third agenda items; from discussion of arrangements beyond 1997 to a discussion of the pre-1997 period and of the transition itself.

On the matter of timing, though China had been working from the outset towards its unilateral deadline of September 1984, [3] it did not appear to have given much thought to the formal stages of the treaty-making process, and to the time which each of these phases would consume. Zhou was sceptical when, in the course of February, the British warned that the process would be a lengthy one. According to one diplomat:

> It was very difficult to get the Chinese to accept that there had to be three stages. The first was initialling. The second was signature, prior to which the treaty had to be published, discussed, debated. The third was ratification, prior to which the treaty had to be laid before Parliament for forty days, so that questions could be asked and so that the government or opposition could call for a debate.

Having digested this information, the Chinese response was to bring forward to July the point at which they wished a draft agreement to be ready, in order that the various procedures outlined by the British could also be concluded before Deng's September deadline. Chinese officials began publicly to endorse this new timetable, taking their cue from a comment made after the eighth round of talks by Li Jusheng, a member of the negotiating team. Enlarging on the comment in an interview with *Ta Kung Pao* published on 22 February, Li said: 'It is hoped that the talks can be completed in July. The Hong Kong people are anxious to know.'

As to the form of an agreement, Zhou Nan observed that problems of drafting were sure to occur when the British and Chinese governments were approaching the Hong Kong question from such different premises on sovereignty. It might be easier for both parties, he suggested, if 'parallel declarations' were made, the course followed a decade earlier by China and the United States, under Henry Kissinger's guidance, during the early stages of their *rapprochement*. This device, said Zhou, would permit Britain and China to make statements about common objectives, while differing on aspects of the political background. Both countries could support China's plans and policies for Hong Kong after 1997, but Britain would not be required to endorse China's views of the sovereignty question and the nineteenth-century treaties.

The idea of 'parallel declarations' was an unattractive one to the British government, which felt that neither Parliament nor Hong Kong would be satisfied with anything less than a treaty subscribed equally by Britain and China. By one recollection: 'London and Hong Kong reacted rather sharply. They wanted an agreement that was entirely binding on the Chinese in international law. They thought that sort of agreement was best achieved by sticking to something more conventional.'

But even these reservations were minor ones, measured against those provoked by China's next revelation. In the words of one diplomat: 'Suddenly, they dumped the protocol on us.'

The protocol, also unveiled in February, was a Chinese-drafted document, intended to supplement the main treaty on post-1997 arrangements and covering the management of Hong Kong in the period prior to 1997. To the British surprise and dismay, its central element was the creation of a Sino-British joint commission to oversee all major aspects of Hong Kong's administration in the final years of British rule, including civil service appointments, fiscal and monetary policy, land sales and constitutional development. It would exercise, in the Chinese phrase, a 'high degree of surveillance' over the territory, intensifying in the four years immediately before the transition.

The British decided that the new Chinese proposals raised issues which could not be dealt with by the negotiators alone. Instead, they suggested that China invite the Foreign Secretary, Sir Geoffrey Howe, to Beijing to raise talks to a ministerial level. With China's agreement, and following discussion at the ninth round of formal talks on 22–23 February, the Howe visit was formally announced.

THE CLOSER BRITAIN moved towards China's deadline, and towards its basic terms for a settlement, the more frustrated Hong Kong's Executive Council members became. They had been informed of the progress of the negotiations, as Thatcher had promised; and they had been allotted generous amounts of ministerial time to express their views directly. But never, it seemed, had they managed to change anything. At each turning-point in the negotiations they were obliged to approve a course of action to which, they were told, there was no real alternative. Now, they were being drawn towards a resolution which, with its acceptance of a withdrawal of British administration, was diametrically the opposite of the arrangements which Hong Kong had appeared to favour when the talks began. Most troubling of all, because of the constraints of confidentiality, there was no way in which the members of the Executive Council could measure their own views and instincts against public opinion, since they themselves were bound by confidentiality, and the rest of Hong Kong lacked access to the facts of the situation.

That the Executive Council had continued nonetheless to work constructively with the Foreign Office until now, and that a usually cordial dialogue had been maintained, was due almost entirely to the diplomatic and personal skills of Sir Edward Youde. As one participant recalled: 'Youde was holding everything together. He was very patient, he was carrying an immense strain, he was facing crises almost daily, and he had a bad-tempered embassy in Beijing.'

Probably never before in Hong Kong had a Governor and an Executive Council worked so closely together, and with such mutual trust.[4] At first, Youde's quiet, dogged style of work had jarred with unofficials who had grown used to Sir Murray MacLehose's grander ways. In the words of one: 'Youde was the committee man. MacLehose had the gambler's charm, the statesman's sweep.' According to a civil servant: '[Youde] was viewed with enormous suspicion in Hong Kong when he first came here. He was regarded as a bureaucrat – his previous job title had been Chief Clerk, and he had very much the aspect to go with it. I remember extraordinary hostility towards him in the corridors of power, particularly among the expatriates.'

The watershed in Youde's relations with the Executive Council had come in the winter of 1982, when he had secured their admission into the charmed circle of confidentiality surrounding the negotiations against the opposition of his Foreign Office colleagues. Then, as the negotiations dragged on, and the frequency of Executive Council meetings rose from one to two or three a week, Youde's bureaucratic skills came to be valued rather than disparaged. As one Executive Council member recalled: 'He was a master of committee work. Whatever was said, he could always find a consensus.'

But by 1984, though Youde could still hold the Executive Council together, the divergences between the London and Hong Kong camps were reaching the point at which disagreements could no longer be smothered. Forced to choose a side, Youde gravitated towards Hong Kong.

Such a collision loomed in February, when the British had to decide how to respond to China's tightening of the deadline. Youde and the Executive Council had in any case been inclined to view Deng's deadline as a bargaining-chip by which Britain should not volunteer to be bound; and they opposed the more so the foreshortening which China now proposed. They suggested that if a compromise were needed, then some form of interim announcement only might be made in September, whereby China would make certain unilateral commitments regarding Hong Kong without any corresponding commitments from Britain.

London took a different view, with Cradock arguing that it would be foolhardy to treat China's deadline as though it contained any element of bluff. Hong Kong's interest, he said, lay with securing from China a detailed and definitive agreement on future policies, and a deadline was not necessarily inimical to this. Providing it were a reasonable deadline binding both sides, then China, too, could be compelled to accept concessions and compromises in order to deliver the agreement on time.

Cradock's agruments prevailed. It fell to Richard Luce, again making a stop-over in Hong Kong on his way back from Brunei, to tell the Executive Council on 26 February that Britain would try to reach a compromise with China over the deadline, but that, in principle, a deadline might have to be accepted. He explained that Sir Geoffrey Howe would attempt during his visit to Beijing to secure China's agreement that the September deadline could apply, after all, only to the initialling of the agreement, and that signature and ratification could follow later.

Luce also tested the Council's views on China's pre-1997 protocol, and received a brusque response. So strongly were the Council members opposed to anything which smacked of interference by China before 1997, that they were not satisfied merely with the opportunity of relaying their views to Howe via Luce, but said that they wanted Howe himself to come to Hong Kong before proceeding to Beijing, so that they might stiffen his sinews in person. The reply to this request from Howe's office was that he had no time to do so, but that they might, if they wished, visit London the following week and see the Foreign Secretary there.

The Executive Council's increasingly fractious mood was a manifestation of the battle fatigue now beginning generally to infect the

Hong Kong business and political establishment which, despite its outward show of tight-lipped confidence, was tiring of the slow progress towards an increasingly dubious-looking agreement. Two public events underlined the growing impatience. The first was an announcement on 24 February by Rogerio Lobo (later Sir Roger Lobo), senior member of the Legislative Council, that he would be proposing a motion at the next Council session, declaring that: 'This Council deems it essential that any proposals for the future of Hong Kong should be debated in this Council before agreement is reached.'

The second event was a statement by Jardine Matheson, the territory's oldest and most famous trading house, on 28 March, that it was going to move its legal domicile from Hong Kong to Bermuda. A century and a half earlier, William Jardine and James Matheson had all but founded Hong Kong, persuading Lord Palmerston to fight the first Opium War and building the first warehouses on the Hong Kong shoreline. Now, William Jardine's great-great-great-great-nephew, Simon Keswick, made his announcement of the firm's relocation with the family's characteristic candour, saying: 'We want to ensure that, in future, our holding company is able to operate under English law, and to have access to the Privy Council in Britain . . . It is a free world, and we are doing things on behalf of our shareholders.'

There was an angry reaction in Beijing to both of these announcements, with Zhou Nan, on behalf of the foreign ministry, refusing to accept Evans's protestations that the British government had not connived in either the Lobo motion or the Jardine move.

In the case of the Lobo motion, the Chinese scepticism was understandable enough: Lobo was himself a member of Youde's Executive Council and, when the motion was debated on 14 March (it was passed unanimously), senior members of the Hong Kong government spoke in support of it. Lobo subsequently insisted that the initiative had not been inspired by the British or Hong Kong governments. But wherever it originated, the motion was a modest act of defiance, challenging China's insistence that the settlement of Hong Kong's future was a matter between Britain and China in which Hong Kong itself could have no independent voice or interest.

As to the Jardine Matheson move, Evans and other British officials insisted that they had had no foreknowledge of Keswick's statement and that relocation to Bermuda was, in any case, a purely commercial decision which Jardines was free to take.[5] They were, nonetheless, privately dismayed by the timing of the Jardine move, coming as it did just before Howe was due to tackle the Chinese leaders on the subject of their pre-1997 protocol. For, while Keswick was correct in arguing that the company belonged to shareholders who could move it wherever they chose, the Chinese would doubtless be inclined to take a less legalistic view of events. They would instead see Jardine Matheson, with its fortunes founded in the nineteenth-century opium trade, putting its billions into a swag-bag and carrying them off to Bermuda, leaving Hong Kong the poorer for the loss. Such things could only reinforce China in its view that some sort of joint commission was needed in the transitional period, if British interests, under the protection of a British flag, were not to strip Hong Kong bare before departing.

Against this unpromising background, three further rounds of formal talks – the tenth on 16–17 March, the eleventh on 26–27 March and the twelfth on 11–12 April – took place, overshadowed by anticipation of the Foreign Secretary's visit. The main text on the table was still the Chinese 'Twelve-Point Plan', which China was now proposing to preface with a declaration on the matter of sovereignty, and follow with the protocol establishing the pre-1997 Sino-British joint commission.

The British, for their part, were concentrating their efforts on arguing that China's 'basic points' could not plausibly stand alone, and that substantial supporting detail would be necessary, probably in the form of an annex. When the exchange of drafts and counter-drafts yielded a block of text acceptable to both parties, then this was put to one side as possible material for such an annex, were it to be included in an agreement. According to one participant:

There was a lot of discussion about the 'building blocks' for what became Annex I of the Joint Declaration, but no agreement. The arguments tended to be about detail versus simplicity, with the Chinese always pulling to keep it simple, and us pulling in the direction of detail. The Chinese were very keen to have our working papers; the focus was on trying to distil the essentials out of them, to make them concentrated but still effective, and then to avoid further hacking and pruning by the Chinese.

According to another:

> The Chinese technique was to look at what we had written, to take the parts of it which they liked, and then to come back and say to us: 'Thank you, you have put a number of questions to us, let us now explain our plan in more detail.' And then they would read back to us from our own paper, but leaving out the bits they did not like. Then they would say, 'And this is the Chinese plan.' They could not have said, 'Yes, this is something which we can agree with you,' because [Hong Kong] was Chinese territory, and it was for them to tell us what they were going to do with it . . .
>
> What was surprising to us was the percentage – sometimes 60 or 70 per cent [of the agreed text] which *did* come from our papers. Often much more than we would have expected.

But with the discussion still not yet anchored in any certainty as to what form the eventual agreement would take, nor by when it would have to be completed, the 'building blocks' were being shaped without knowing whether there would be a place for them in the eventual structure. That, it was hoped, would become clearer with the Howe visit to Beijing, arranged for 15–18 April.

FOR THE CHINESE, Sir Geoffrey Howe's willingness to come to Beijing was in itself a positive sign, a reassurance that the British did genuinely want to move forward towards an agreed solution despite having been forced into concessions on the key issues of sovereignty and administration. Accordingly, they received him with every show of cordiality, and warmed to his even-tempered, low-key style of discussion. The contrast with Thatcher, their last ministerial-level interlocutor, was obvious if unspoken.

In meetings with Wu Xueqian, his Chinese counterpart, on 16 April, and Zhao Ziyang on the following day, Howe outlined his ideas for moving the talks forward. He wanted China to accept September as a target for initialling, not ratifying, the agreement; he wanted the agreement to be a detailed one, not merely a statement of principles; he wanted China's reassurance that the final document would be a legally binding treaty; and he wanted to begin tackling the problems raised for Britain by the protocol on pre-1997 arrangements.

At a session with Deng Xiaoping on 18 April which lasted for nearly two hours, Howe concluded the discussions which he had begun with Wu and Zhao. On timing and form, Deng was willing to show some flexibility. He accepted Howe's proposal that the September deadline should apply to initialling only, with signature and ratification to follow. He would allow that, so long as China's 'Twelve Points' formed the centre-piece of the main text of the agreement, then a 'certain amount' of detail about post-1997 arrangements for Hong Kong might also be appended, in an annex equal in legal status to the main text. He also agreed with Howe that it would be useful in the near future to establish a working group, separate from the main negotiating teams, which could concentrate on the actual line-by-line drafting of the text of an agreement, leaving the main negotiating teams to continue their arguments over policies and principles.

On some important points, however, the meeting was inconclusive: while Deng agreed that the final document should be binding, rather than merely a statement of intent, he still favoured parallel declarations rather than a simple treaty. He was also vigorously attached to the joint commission described in the protocol, an idea which appeared to be largely his own, and evidently nursed some very lively convictions about the willingness of the British to enrich themselves at Hong Kong's expense. 'Some parties', he said, in what was taken by the British to be a reference to Jardines, 'are working to leave Hong Kong in a mess.' He warned, too, that the Hong Kong government should not dissipate its wealth before 1997, whether by selling off large quantities of Crown land or drawing down the government's fiscal and monetary reserves, or committing itself to expensive new spending programmes.

Finally, Deng raised another matter over which the negotiators had reached a deadlock: the role of the People's Liberation Army in Hong Kong after 1997. In the eighth and later rounds of negotiations, Britain had tried to persuade China that there would be no need to replace the British garrison with a Chinese one; Deng wished it to be known that he thought otherwise. The right to station troops was, he said, part of the substance of sovereignty. Howe replied that it was an important right, but one which he hoped China would consider carefully before exercising. On that note, the meeting drew to a close.[6]

The next day, 19 April, Howe arrived in Hong Kong and briefed the Executive Council privately about his talks. In one member's view: 'He hadn't come to say much which was positive. It was negative,

149

and he had come to clean up. But at least it was good news that we had someone who could go up to Beijing and get on with the boss.'

Howe spent the late evening at Government House with Youde and a small party of civil servants, meditating on his press conference, set for the following day. Youde had urged in January that a statement be made about the talks which would clear the air in Hong Kong; Howe, while in Beijing, had secured China's acquiescence to make one. The only real question was that of Hong Kong's likely reaction. According to one Hong Kong official: 'The question was: should it be said now? Should Howe say that there would not be a British administration after 1997? There was not much debate. Everybody advised him to come clean at that stage.'

That evening, Howe rehearsed half a dozen times with his entourage the questions and answers which were likely to follow his statement. How could Britain trust China to honour the agreement which it reached? How could Hong Kong's freedoms be respected by a country which was not itself free? How would Hong Kong be able to register its own approval or disapproval of the agreement? The prepared answers to these and other likely questions were designed to be soothing rather than scientific. For in truth, nobody knew.

On the afternoon of 20 April, Howe stood up in the Legislative Council Chamber, borrowed for his press conference, and delivered to Hong Kong the most momentous news about 1997 ever to have been spoken by a British minister, saying: 'It would not be realistic to think in terms of an agreement that provides for continued British administration in Hong Kong after 1997.'

He went on to outline the various pledges already made by China to leave Hong Kong substantially unchanged, and said that Britain and China 'share [a] . . . desire to see the continuation of Hong Kong as a society which enjoys its own economic and social systems and distinct way of life'.

He carefully side-stepped the various areas of the negotiations in which serious problems still lurked – notably, the form which the final agreement would take; the absence of external guarantees that China would do what it said; Deng's insistence on the joint commission; and the likelihood of a PLA garrison in Hong Kong after 1997. Only in the most general of ways did he finally allude to these and other uncertainties which remained, saying:

We are still negotiating. Several points of substance remain to be resolved. I cannot anticipate the details of an eventual agreement. We are working to a programme which takes account both of the Chinese wishes and of all our own requirements . . . These are complex and difficult negotiations. We are still some way from an agreement. But a good deal of progress has been made, and there is [the] will on both sides to bring our work to fruition in an agreement which will ensure the stability and prosperity of Hong Kong.

There was, strictly, nothing in Howe's statement, or his subsequent answers to journalists' questions, which might not have been deduced weeks earlier by any regular reader of the Chinese press; the only 'news' was the willingness of the British themselves to articulate what was already generally discounted, to cast aside the fig-leaf of 'conditionality' and admit that they were not going to be in Hong Kong after 1997 whatever the talks in Beijing might yield. The effect, nonetheless, of hearing the British Foreign Secretary say these things in his own solemn way was to give the news a sudden, piercing finality which overpowered many of his listeners. Tears were shed widely that afternoon, including some by Hong Kong government officials watching just feet away from where Howe spoke.

So now Hong Kong knew. And there had been a desire for candour, but also a measure of strategy, in Howe's decision to 'lift the veil' over 1997 that day. For the British were beginning to focus on how they would, when the time came, secure some visible show of approval from Hong Kong for whatever agreement they eventually proposed, and in preparation for that day they would need to test the evolution of public opinion, to discover what sort of deal the public was expecting, and to isolate the issues which were likely to cause the most acute concern. To assess and prepare public opinion, it was first necessary to inform the public.

The impact of Howe's press conference was satisfactory in that it was uneventful. It appeared, after the initial shock, that the public mood in Hong Kong had discounted accurately enough the drift of the negotiations, even if it had been ignorant of the underlying detail. As Louis Cha, editor of *Ming Pao*, analysed the response in his column of 21 April: 'People here have realized that there cannot possibly be any other arrangement to that which Sir Geoffrey described. It would have been quite another matter, had the British government made the announcement two years ago.'

What the British had not, however, foreseen was the effect that the new climate of *glasnost* would have on those Executive Council members who had been fretting since the preceding September about their role in an agreement to hand Hong Kong back to China. Free at last to speak out within the limits set by Howe, they began to draft a manifesto listing their own concerns about the probable agreement, and planned a lobbying mission to London to express those concerns to whoever in the political and media establishments there would listen to them.

The scheduling of a House of Commons debate on Hong Kong for 16 May supplied a focus for their plans. On 9 May, a delegation of ten Executive and Legislative Council members, led by Sir S.Y. Chung, set off for London, publishing as they left a 1,000-word statement raising a series of highly sensitive questions about the achievements and the shortcomings of the negotiations so far – including, from the British government's own perspective, the most sensitive subject of all, that of Britain's obligations to the holders of British Dependent Territory Citizenship in Hong Kong. The statement, noting that half Hong Kong's population held BDTC passports, asked:

What . . . will be the fate of Hong Kong's British Dependent Territory Citizens? How will their rights and status be preserved? How will BDTCs continue to enjoy British protection? Will they, and other Hong Kong belongers who cannot accept the idea of living under Communist authority, have a right to settlement in the United Kingdom? And should not the British Government negotiate settlement places for them?

As to the eventual Sino-British agreement, the delegation declared, its 'acceptability' to Hong Kong would depend upon its:

Containing full details of the proposed administrative, legal, social and economic systems applicable after 1997; *providing* adequate and workable assurances that the terms of the Agreement will be honoured; *stating* that the provisions of the Basic

Law will incorporate the provisions of the agreement; and *guaranteeing* that the rights of British nationals will be safeguarded.[7]

Finally, the Hong Kong group posed two troubling questions which, as its members knew perfectly well, the British could not answer: 'How is it proposed that the "acceptability" [of a Sino-British agreement] will be put to a test? What will be Her Majesty's Government's reaction if Hong Kong people do not accept the Agreement or parts of it?'

This was, for the Executive and Legislative Council members, unused to conducting their business in the public arena, a very muscular and even courageous stand to take; the response to it was predictably frigid. Though the delegation was received by Thatcher and Howe, its members were treated cruelly by Conservative MPs during the Commons debate. Edward Heath, who had clashed so embarrassingly with Chung the previous autumn in Hong Kong, urged the government 'not to pay undue attention' to the delegation which, he said, 'did not represent the views of the people of Hong Kong'. Thatcher's government was, for once, pleased to take Heath's advice. Nor was there any comfort from the Opposition where Denis Healey, Labour's foreign affairs spokesman, praised the 'realism' being shown by Howe and the Foreign Office in accepting the inevitability of a British withdrawal.

To complete the misery of the Hong Kong delegation, the House of Commons debate coincided with a session of the National People's Congress in Beijing, enabling the lobbyists to be denounced by the British and Chinese Parliaments simultaneously. They were, they discovered, colliding with a new geometry of power created by the approaching Sino-British agreement – a geometry which moved them from the centre to the margins. Now, it was for Britain and China to make Hong Kong policy in tandem, and for Hong Kong to accept it.

9

The Joint
Declaration

T HE hope had fluttered briefly in Foreign Office hearts that Sir
Geoffrey Howe's visit to Beijing in April might have supplied
the impetus needed to send the talks rolling forward under
their own momentum, gathering speed towards an agreement as they
went. But it was not to be. Despite Deng's seemingly accommodating
mood, too much had been left inconclusive about the form of the
agreement, and too little headway made on the joint commission.
The fifteenth round of talks, on 30–31 May, was unproductive, with
the protocol still on the table, and Zhou Nan's team still not, in one
British diplomat's words, 'really accepting the need to get into detail'.

But the Howe visit had, at least, cemented a friendly relationship
between the Foreign Secretary and his Chinese counterpart, Wu
Xueqian, a mutual trust which quickly proved a valuable asset when
Chinese officials began fulminating against the Hong Kong lobbying
mission to London in May, and suggesting that the mission might have
been encouraged by the British government in order to complicate and
frustrate the negotiations. Howe was able to send a strong private
message to Wu, assuring him that this was not the case and that the
manifesto was the work of the Council members alone. This message,
according to a British official, 'significantly helped the [Chinese] to
understand the position, so that they backed away from what would
have been a rather ugly outburst at that time'.

After the fifteenth round of talks, Howe sent a further message to

Wu: he was anxious that the commitment to an agreement, which had been so evident on both sides during his trip to Beijing, should be translated as quickly as possible into substance at the negotiating table. He and Wu agreed that the working group, blessed in principle by Deng, should be launched in tandem with the main negotiations, and should concentrate on finalizing the text of the main agreement, based on China's 'Twelve Points', while the Evans and Zhou teams continued their wrangling over the supporting material.

The announcement of the working group was duly made after the sixteenth round of formal talks, which took place on 12–13 June. The Foreign Office appointed David Wilson, who had succeeded Alan Donald as assistant under-secretary responsible for Asia and the Pacific, as the leader of its new team; China appointed Ke Zaishuo, a diplomat of similar rank. The brief for the working group stated that it would 'meet full-time between the rounds of formal talks', and that the team-leaders, Wilson and Ke, would report to the leaders of the formal talks, Evans and Zhou. On 18 June, Wilson arrived in Hong Kong together with Fred Burrows, the Foreign Office legal adviser, to join the other members of the team, Robin McLaren and Gerry Nazareth, the Hong Kong government's law draftsman. After talks with Youde, they proceeded to Beijing for their first meeting with Ke on 21 June.

The point was now drawing near at which the Sino-British talks, after twenty-one months of deadlock, recrimination and fruitless wrangling, would finally break through into the three months of frantic productivity from which the Joint Declaration essentially emerged. But one further catalyst was needed: it was supplied by the tireless Sir S.Y. Chung who, in conjunction with two other Executive Council members, Lydia Dunn and Lee Quo-Wei, decided to launch a second lobbying mission, this time to Beijing.

In Chung's view, it was the duty of the unofficial members of the Executive Council to relay the views and the interests of the people of Hong Kong to those in power over them. Since China was now on the point of publishing the blueprint by which Hong Kong would be ruled for generations to come, Chung felt, in the words of an Executive Council colleague, that 'he should make one last effort to show that we were representing and looking after the interests of Hong Kong. It was really a rather ill-conceived visit, to be honest, but Sir S.Y. was the leader of Exco, and he worked like a Trojan.'

Chung arranged an invitation from Beijing for his group to be received by Deng, and prepared a presentation, warning that the Hong Kong public was sceptical about China's ability to make 'one country, two systems' work in practice, and that it feared being overrun by Communist bureaucrats whose influence would quickly erode the liberal social and economic systems which China was ostensibly committed to preserving.

This was a reasonable and honest point of view; but it was not what Deng expected or wanted to hear, having become accustomed to awed and sycophantic visitors from Hong Kong, who – prodded when necessary by the New China News Agency – busied themselves telling him how much Hong Kong was looking forward to 1997 and Chinese rule. When on 23 June at the Great Hall of the People, Chung and his colleagues began telling Deng their somewhat different story, Deng responded with anger and sarcasm, treating the visitors as though they had been 'turned' by the British for propaganda purposes. Deng told Chung:

> What you have said can be reduced to a single sentence. You have no trust in the policies adopted by the People's Republic of China and the government here. You have said only that you trust me, but those are empty words. This is not the proper attitude . . . If there is no trust, there is little that we can say . . . Frankly, you do not believe that the Chinese are capable of ruling Hong Kong.

From London, the Foreign Office viewed and analysed the meeting with profound dismay. A fortnight earlier, on 25 May, Deng had already dealt one severe blow to Hong Kong's fragile confidence by declaring in front of television cameras that China firmly intended to station PLA troops in Hong Kong after 1997, and that it was 'bullshit' to imagine otherwise. Now, in the course of discomfiting his Executive Council visitors, Deng flung his proposals for pre-1997 Hong Kong power-sharing into the public domain, saying to Chung, 'On the 13-year transition . . . We are no less worried than you. We therefore suggest the setting up of a joint working group in Hong Kong.'[1]

It was this spectacle, of the formal talks and their supposed confidentiality being thus supplanted by a harangue in the Great Hall of the People, which persuaded Howe that the only way of rescuing the situation was for him to make a second visit to Beijing and attempt there to finish the discussions which he had begun in April. The protocol had to be dealt with, and some agreement on the joint commission reached. Youde and Evans were invited back for talks at Downing Street on 4 July, to decide how best to proceed.

Youde arrived to report the view of his Executive Council: Howe should not go to Beijing. Britain had given enough ground. By going to Beijing, Howe would simply be advertising a desire to reach an agreement at almost any cost in further concessions. Instead, in the Hong Kong view, the British should reject Deng's joint commission and risk a new phase of brinkmanship. Again, Cradock and Youde found themselves on different sides of the argument. Cradock maintained that, unless Howe made a visit to Beijing quickly and unblocked the negotiations. there would be no time to reach an agreement by September whatever else might occur. The correct formula, Cradock said, was for Howe to go, but to make at the same time a firm statement that Britain would not sign an agreement on Hong Kong unless the terms were right.

London prevailed over Hong Kong, and an invitation was arranged for Howe to visit Beijing on 27–31 July. In preparation, Richard Luce flew to Hong Kong on 12 July, the closing day of the eighteenth round of formal talks, again to collect views from the Executive Council. The meeting was a stony one, with Luce defending the London position that an agreement of some form had to be reached by September, if China was not to announce its own plans for Hong Kong unilaterally, and that compromises would probably have to be made, even on the joint commission, to achieve this. The Executive Council should accept such compromises, he said, and should also be prepared to accept that the eventual agreement, whatever its shortcomings, would be the best one possible in the circumstances.

The Council members, supported by Youde, focused their arguments on an insistence that a joint commission should not be allowed to erode the authority of the Hong Kong government before 1997. They suggested various ways of reducing its influence: by delaying its creation until 1990, rather than convening it immediately as the Chinese wished, or by convening it as an *ad hoc* rather than a standing body. It was Sir S.Y. Chung and Maria Tam, a Hong Kong barrister, who put forward the idea of 'mirror-imaging', which would prove central to the compromise eventually reached by Howe in Beijing. Since China, they argued, would use the joint commission as a conduit into Hong Kong affairs prior to 1997, then Britain should seek a continuation of the commission beyond 1997 so that Britain, too, would be able to oversee both sides of the transition.

As Howe's departure for Beijing drew closer, the Foreign Office sent a carefully balanced series of public signals to China highlighting both its desire to reach a mutually acceptable agreement in September, and its continuing resistance to the joint commission.

By means of a written answer to a parliamentary question, Howe revealed British plans to publish the eventual Sino-British agreement in the form of a white paper, immediately after it had been initialled. He also ruled out the possibility of a referendum on the agreement in Hong Kong, a device which China fiercely opposed. Instead, said Howe, the 'acceptability' of the agreement would be tested by an assessment office which would collect public opinion for collation into a published report. In a later London press briefing on 19 July, an unnamed Foreign Office official amplified the very limited role which Hong Kong would play in this stage of the process. The *Guardian's* diplomatic correspondent, Patrick Keatley, reported that, according to British sources, 'The draft agreement on the future of Hong Kong that is expected to emerge from the Peking negotiations in September will not be open to amendments . . . There is no question of returning to the bargaining table after the talks. The people of Hong Kong will be asked simply to accept or reject the deal.'

These were the positive signals, confirming Britain's willingness to ensure that the agreement, once reached with China, would move as uneventfully as possible towards ratification. At the same time, however, the Foreign Office began to diffuse the 'strong statement' which Cradock had recommended at the Downing Street meeting on 4 July, to the effect that the British would nonetheless refuse to sign a treaty which they did not feel able to recommend to Hong Kong. The *Financial Times* of 20 July reported, again on the basis of a Foreign Office briefing:

Intractable problems remain in the talks with China over the future of Hong Kong, senior British officials said yesterday. They raised for the first time the possibility that Britain might refuse to sign an agreement by the September deadline required by China . . . One important difference between Britain and China remains Peking's unwillingness to conclude a detailed agreement.

As to the joint commission, the newspaper continued:

> Whitehall also admitted yesterday for the first time that Britain is considering a Chinese demand for a joint Sino-British group to monitor the colony's transition to Chinese rule in 1997 . . . Officials said Britain had not ruled out this idea, which seems likely to dominate Sir Geoffrey's Peking discussions. It was emphasized, however, that there was no question of Britain giving up the right to govern Hong Kong until 1997.

The Times of 25 July, the day of Howe's departure, carried the Foreign Office's final salvo. Noting that the Howe visit was intended to 'give a good shove' to the talks, it reported that 'British officials do not rule out the possibility that, in the event of an impasse in the talks, they would publish details of the negotiations to date, to let the people of Hong Kong know the degree of rigidity they have encountered in the Chinese position.'

FOR MOST OF the flight to Beijing, Howe was huddled in the back of his Royal Air Force plane with Sir Percy Cradock and Anthony Galsworthy, a past member of Cradock's negotiating team who was now head of the Hong Kong desk at the Foreign Office in London. Working from a note prepared by Galsworthy, they finalized a British counter-draft to offer China as the basis for establishing a mutually acceptable and much-diminished version of Deng's joint commission.

The starting-point for the British draft was a phrase in the Chinese protocol which stated that the joint commission would not be 'an organ of power'. In fact, as the British saw it, the Chinese document then proceeded to assign very considerable powers to the joint commission, by providing that, particularly in the four years immediately preceding 1997, virtually no major decisions could be taken in Hong Kong against its wishes. Throwing out most of the specific powers which the Chinese wanted to attribute to the joint commission, and emphasizing the body's status as an 'organ of liaison' rather than an 'organ of power', Howe, Cradock and Galsworthy ran through four drafts of their own proposal, eventually arriving, as their plane crossed Colombo, at their own version of a second annex to the eventual treaty.

After spending the night of 26–27 July in Hong Kong for a meeting with the Executive Council, Howe's party continued on to Beijing where, on the morning of Monday, 28 July, he and Wu Xueqian began a day-long session of talks during which Howe began to rehearse in detail the British view of the protocol, the problems he foresaw with the joint commission, and the revisions proposed in the British draft. 'I do not believe', he said hopefully, 'that there is all that much difference between us as to what we feel we have to achieve, but only in the way that we ought to achieve it,' a sentiment to which Wu nodded his agreement.

It was a useful morning; but only with lunch, and a discreet proposal from Zhou Nan, did the British suddenly discover just how productive their visit might be. Zhou had issued a private invitation to Cradock and Galsworthy. To them, he made an unexpected and quite extraordinary series of remarks. China, he said, now viewed the Hong Kong question as having reached its most crucial phase. Important and final decisions were about to be taken on the Chinese side. In order to reach an agreement with Britain in time for the September deadline, China was prepared to make a series of offers which would accommodate Britain's main reservations. In particular, China would be willing to accept most of the proposals made by Britain to limit the powers and stature of the joint commission; and China would accept a form of words for the text of the overall Hong Kong agreement binding on both China and Britain. But if Howe chose not to seize this opportunity here and now, Zhou warned, then China would withdraw its offers, and the negotiations would, in effect, be over.

There was time for the British briefly to discuss Zhou's offer in the garden of the Diaoyutai State Guest House, where Cradock advised that there could be no doubt as to the seriousness of the offer, and that these were the best terms for which Britain could hope. As Howe returned to his talks with Wu, Cradock retreated to the Embassy, where he drafted a telegram to Thatcher outlining Zhou's offer and seeking her authority for Howe to negotiate on the basis of it. During the early evening, while Wu was hosting a banquet for Howe at the Diaoyutai, Thatcher's reply came, giving Howe a broad instruction to settle as best he could. The deal was on.

The next morning, Wu and Howe spent three hours negotiating a remit for the joint commission, largely on the basis of the British draft. It was to be renamed the Joint Liaison Group; it was to be, explicitly, 'an organ of liaison, not an organ of power'; it was to 'play no part in the administration of Hong Kong'; it would remain in existence until the year 2000, giving Britain the *droit de regard* after 1997 which Maria Tam and Sir S.Y. Chung had suggested; and it would establish its base in Hong Kong only in 1988, meeting until then on a rotating basis in London, Hong Kong and Beijing. The negotiating teams, under Evans and Zhou, were convened during the afternoon to fine-tune the text; and with that day's work, the Joint Liaison Group was conceived, and the rest of the protocol, which had weighed so heavily on the negotiators for so many months, was ready, with Deng's authorization, to be briskly and coolly discarded.

David Wilson and Fred Burrows had also been pursuing with Zhou Nan discussions about the wording of the main treaty document which continued into that evening's dinner. The next morning, 30 July, a provisional text was ready for Howe to review in his meeting with Zhao Ziyang.

Howe and Zhao worked through the proposed treaty, which now began by discarding the preamble originally tabled by China's negotiators denouncing British 'colonization' and 'extortion' of Hong Kong in damning terms, and substituting a much milder declaration by China that it intended to 'resume the exercise of sovereignty over Hong Kong with effect from 1 July 1997'; and a complementary declaration by Britain that it would 'restore Hong Kong to the People's Republic of China' on that same date. This formula, now called the 'joint' rather than 'parallel' declaration, allowed – as China had foreseen – the two parties to deal with the sovereignty question while preserving their conflicting positions.

The next material to be blocked into the emerging Joint Declaration was China's 'Twelve Points', as refined and revised by the Ke-Wilson working group. These points were deemed to embody 'the basic policies of the People's Republic of China regarding Hong Kong' and were presented, accordingly, as a declaration by China alone. The twelfth point, stating that China would draft a Basic Law for post-1997 Hong Kong, also specified that the Basic Law would incorporate the policies set down in the Joint Declaration, an important provision in British eyes, since it would in theory severely limit China's ability to diverge from the Joint Declaration after 1997 through local legislation.

The next clause contained the joint Sino-British commitment, by which the Executive Council had set so much store, that Britain alone would be 'responsible for the administration of Hong Kong' until 1997, and that China would 'give its co-operation in this connection'.

Next came the clause so important to Britain, that Britain and China would 'agree to implement the preceding declarations and the annexes to this Joint Declaration'; and that 'the Joint Declaration and its annexes should be equally binding'. These were the sentences which allowed Britain to present the Joint Declaration as an 'agreement', binding in its entirety equally upon Britain and China.

Other clauses, referring to arrangements for the Joint Liaison Group, land leases, and ratification of the agreement itself, remained to be finalized at a later stage. But already, after the session with Zhao, it was as if the two main working days of Howe's trip had achieved more concrete results than the preceding twenty-two months of negotiation. With the way ahead substantially cleared, Howe prepared for a meeting with Deng on the morning of 31 July, which was to be taken up as much with congratulation as with negotiation.

Deng had returned to Beijing from the Communist Party leadership's seaside retreat at Beidaihe, and was in an ebullient mood, displaying his suntan to Howe. 'You can see my skin has gone brown, like an African,' he said. 'I have changed my nationality.' Describing the agreement which was now at last in sight, Deng said it would have 'great impact internationally'. It was, he said, 'an example to the world, for settling questions between states, left over from the past'. Even Thatcher, with whom he had argued so fiercely, qualified for what was, by Deng's lights, high praise. He told Howe: 'In France, it was General de Gaulle who brought an end to French colonial rule. Now we can say that Prime Minister Margaret Thatcher will bring an end to British colonial rule.'

At Deng's side were Ji Pengfei, Zhou Nan and the Chinese ambassador to London, Chen Zaoyuan; next to Howe were Sir Richard Evans, Sir Edward Youde and Sir Percy Cradock. The delegations smiled with indulgence and relief at Deng's easy mood. Deng joked about the grandeur of the British team: he was impressed, he said, to be surrounded by so many knights of the realm. In reply, Howe distributed compliments towards Deng's seconds, saying that a negotiation without Zhou Nan would be like 'a banquet without *mao-tai*' – a turn of phrase which provoked Zhou, as he escorted Howe to the airport, to ask: 'But Sir Geoffrey, did you ever find *mao-tai* too *strong* for you?'

Deng gave his approval to the main points on which agreement in principle had now been reached: the Joint Liaison Group as the sole vestige of the protocol; the shape of the Joint Declaration; the main text; and the initialling in September. According to one official:

When it was clear that Deng thought all the main features had been covered, and that we had come substantially to agreement, he said, 'We have concluded that we can trust the British people and the British government. Please convey to your Prime Minister that we hope she will come to sign the agreement, and to your Queen our hope that she will come to visit China.' It was a package of benedictions. Touching. You really felt that you were in a very courtly atmosphere.

The invitation to the Queen was, for the British, an unforeseen bonus – a public gesture of goodwill far more powerful than any reassurances which might be given in private, since it all but locked the two countries into reaching a settlement on genuinely amicable terms. As one British source saw it: 'It was marvellous. We realized then that we really *had* made the breakthrough.'

Bidding Howe's party farewell later that day, Zhou Nan evoked the mood of the moment with a graceful fragment from a Sung dynasty poem: 'Just when the weary traveller despairs of finding a road, lo, a village appears, and shades of willow and riotous flowers beckon.'[2]

It now remained for Howe to present the deal to Hong Kong, and to discover whether Hong Kong, too, would see it in terms of 'shades of willow and riotous flowers'. The occasion was a particularly sensitive one because, unusually and deliberately, the Executive Council had not been kept up-to-the-minute on the final British proposals regarding the Joint Liaison Group, nor on the breakthrough in Beijing. According to one British source: 'Youde was very concerned that no hint of the possibility of a deal on the JLG should reach Hong Kong before the Foreign Secretary announced it himself . . . There would be a lot of turbulence if people were given only a partial picture.'

Ordinarily, the Executive Council members would doubtless have been angry at such treatment. But when Howe met them briefly and informally on 31 July to sketch out the deal, the dominant mood was one of relief. In one British recollection:

The Foreign Secretary's party came down from Beijing. Met
Exco that afternoon. Told them what we had got. They were
astounded. There was total silence. The next morning, Howe met
Exco again formally, and was told that they were very grateful.
The objectives of their May paper had been achieved. Sir S.Y.
Chung said he had 'high hopes that the agreement would be
acceptable to the people of Hong Kong'.

That afternoon, Howe broke the news publicly to Hong Kong. He
told a press conference:

> Very substantial progress has been made. We have agreed, first,
> [on] the framework and key clauses of an agreement which will
> preserve Hong Kong's unique economic system and way of life;
> second, that this agreement and its annexes will all be legally bind-
> ing; third, [on] satisfactory provisions for liaison and consulta-
> tion after the conclusion of the agreement . . . We aim to complete
> our work and initial an agreement before the end of September . . .
> Hong Kong's economic and social systems, its distinctive way
> of life and its position as a financial, trading and industrial centre
> will be secured. Though there is still a lot of work to be done, I
> am confident that we are on course for a conclusion that we shall
> be able to commend both to the people of Hong Kong and to the
> British Parliament.

He went on to outline the main points of the Joint Declaration
itself – points which China had first set down, and which in their
slightly more polished form were now the backbone of the emerging
Sino-British treaty. The document would, he said:

- Preserve Hong Kong's familiar legal system and the body
  of laws in force in Hong Kong . . . Judicial power, including
  the right of final appeal, will be vested in the courts of Hong
  Kong . . .
- Enable Hong Kong . . . to decide its own economic and trade
  policies, [and] maintain its status as a free port and a major
  manufacturing and trading economy . . .
- Provide for the continuation of Hong Kong's status as a separate customs territory . . . participating in international organizations and trade agreements, such as the Gatt . . .

- Provide for Hong Kong to manage its own financial affairs
  . . . and for the continuing convertibility of the Hong Kong
  dollar and the freedom to move capital . . .
- Continue arrangements for continuity of employment in
  public service, and the safeguarding of pension rights . . .
- Maintain Hong Kong's systems of port management [and]
  shipping . . .
- Enable Hong Kong residents to continue to enjoy the right to
  travel and move freely in and out of Hong Kong;
- Provide for the maintenance of Hong Kong's educational
  system;
- Provide for the preservation of all the rights and freedoms
  which the people of Hong Kong now enjoy.

It was not, as Howe acknowledged, an 'exhaustive' list, and it was
possible to deduce from his omissions the handful of specific points
about post-1997 arrangements where the negotiating teams still lacked
basic agreement. One was land, where China and Britain could still
not decide on a system for equitably reconciling land sales, leases and
revenues with the hiatus of 1997. Another was nationality, where
China was refusing to recognize British Dependent Territories Citizenship and passports, which roughly half Hong Kong's population
would be holding in 1997. A third was aviation, on which China's own
national airline wished to take over the valuable landing rights
attaching to Kai Tak airport, instead of devolving these to Hong
Kong. Howe was silent also on the question of China's plan to station
troops in Hong Kong, and on the movement of the territory towards
'representative government', to which he had referred in his previous,
April, visit.

But for Hong Kong, these omissions were almost invisible blemishes
on an unexpectedly detailed and generous presentation. The news that
the Joint Liaison Group would continue its work until 2000, taking –
as Hong Kong then saw it – just a fraction of the finality away from
1997 itself, proved a particularly potent psychological boost. The
stock market rose sharply, and the press was all but lyrical. The *Far
Eastern Economic Review* commented: 'Any doubts about the Joint
Liaison Group are not shared by the majority in Hong Kong, who see
it as a realistic response to the actualities of the next 13 years. They are
in no mood to look a gift horse in the mouth.'

WITH HOWE'S DEPARTURE from Beijing, and Deng's benediction, the weight of work fell squarely on the shoulders of the Wilson-Ke working group which, with the covering treaty now largely in place, was focusing on Annex I, the section which would elaborate the policies set down in brief in the main text. This was to be the detail for which Britain had argued so vigorously – although since the policies which it elaborated were China's policies, the detail, too, had to be set down in China's name.

The principle of detail having been fully accepted by China, there was often a high degree of congruence between the British and Chinese views as to what that detail should say. In most areas of fiscal, commercial and economic policy, there was little or no disagreement: both governments wanted Hong Kong to carry on exactly as it did at present, with a free port, a convertible currency, low tax rates and tightly controlled public spending. For Hong Kong's legal and judicial systems, China and Britain agreed on as little change as possible, but with a Court of Final Appeal located in Hong Kong. There was agreement, too, that Hong Kong should participate as a distinct if not independent entity in international forums and agreements, particularly those which affected its trading interests. In terms of a post-1997 political structure, though the negotiators had yet to fix a method for constituting the legislature, they agreed that the government should remain 'executive-led' after 1997, with a powerful chief executive. China was, finally, prepared to write into the Joint Declaration a series of undertakings to preserve the civil rights of Hong Kong people, including freedom of speech, assembly, religion and travel, providing that these freedoms were stated to be exercisable 'according to law'.

On these relatively less contentious areas, the Wilson-Ke working group began drafting Annex I, hauling into place the 'building blocks' which had been set aside from the earlier rounds of formal negotiations. Even then, some quantitative arguments continued. According to one source: '[The Chinese] tried always to keep it brief. They had a word-limit from Deng Xiaoping on the length of the Joint Declaration, which in the end we greatly exceeded. They never actually told us this, but we would hear it informally – somebody said it was ten thousand characters – so as to keep flexibility for China at a later stage.'

The Wilson-Ke working group started its sessions at the International Club, close to the British Embassy, and it was only with great reluctance that the members later accepted a transfer to the Diaoyutai State Guest House, venue for the formal talks, a bus ride away. When, during August, the volume of work, and the scale of particular technical problems, primarily those associated with land questions, threatened to overwhelm the Wilson-Ke group, a second group, led by Robin McLaren and Lu Ping,[3] was devolved from the first group to work on these problem areas. It was this group which drafted what became Annex III to the Joint Declaration, on land leases, as well as the memoranda on nationality, and the section of Annex I relating to aviation.

According to one participant:

The working groups began by working mornings and after-noons, but found it was not possible to carry out all the necessary consultation. So we met in the mornings, we reported the results in the afternoon, and made our recommendations to London and Hong Kong as to what we should do next.

London was just getting into work as our telegrams went off, and it was late in the day in Hong Kong. Hong Kong would carry on into the evening getting their views over to London. London would take the decisions and communicate them to Beijing, where we would receive them first thing the next morning, and prepare ourselves on the basis of those instructions, go into the morning session, and the process would repeat itself.

'London', in this case, meant mainly Cradock, who made most of the daily decisions about what Britain could or could not accept in the annexes. In Hong Kong, the pressure was all but intolerable, as the General Duties Branch, under Lewis Davies, spent the days consulting with officials in Hong Kong, and the nights exchanging traffic with the Foreign Office in London. But there was, for the British, some small measure of consolation in all this urgency: with China now committed publicly to an agreement, the deadline cut both ways. According to one Hong Kong official: 'It was quite clear this time that the Chinese were not going to call the whole thing off. And so the fact that the Chinese leaders had ruled that [the Joint Declaration] *did* have to be concluded by Day X actually worked in our favour. It was the Chinese negotiators who were under pressure, and the more so when *we* dug our heels in.'

While the working groups hacked their way through Annex I, the main negotiating teams tackled the big outstanding issues of principle, starting with nationality: the questions of what citizenship, and what passports, the people of Hong Kong would be deemed or allowed to hold after 1997.

Though the twentieth round of formal talks, on 8–9 August, touched upon nationality, resolution was only reached through informal meetings between Zhou Nan and Sir Richard Evans, away from the negotiating table. China regarded nationality as an issue too sensitive for compromise of any explicit and minuted kind; it was not, unlike Britain, in the habit of creating categories of citizenship according to geographical circumstance. But it was prepared, nonetheless, to sketch out an accommodation with Britain on the main practical questions, and to express that accommodation in an 'Exchange of Memoranda', associated with – but not an integral part of – the Joint Declaration.[4]

The Exchange of Memoranda, like the Joint Declaration itself, but in a more comprehensive way, allowed the two governments to make unilateral statements which were overlapping rather than interlocking. The British memorandum said that British Dependent Territories Citizens in Hong Kong, or some 2.5 million of the 6 million residents there as of 1984, would retain after 1997, when they came under China's sovereignty, 'an appropriate status which, without conferring on them the right of abode in the United Kingdom, will entitle them to continue to use passports issued by the Government of the United Kingdom'.[5]

The Chinese memorandum said that 'All Hong Kong Chinese compatriots, whether they are holders of the "British Dependent Territories Citizens' passport" or not, are Chinese nationals.' But it went on to say that holders of BDTC passports could nonetheless use these documents 'for the purpose of travelling to other states and regions', though they could not claim British consular protection in Hong Kong or in China. In effect, China was saying that BDTC passports would have no meaning as an indicator of nationality for 'Hong Kong Chinese' after 1997, but could still be used as travel documents only.

The Exchange of Memoranda was a curious dialogue, one important more in its psychological and moral aspects than in its legal ones, and raising as many questions as it answered. The Chinese memorandum, by declaring that 'All Hong Kong Chinese compatriots . . . are

Chinese nationals', implied a racial basis for nationality which could not be reconciled with Chinese or British law – and yet, China had nothing to say about Hong Kong citizens who were *not* 'Hong Kong Chinese', however that, too, might be defined.[6] Conversely, while Britain insisted on the continuing validity of BDTC passports, it was not easy to see what benefits the holders of those passports were likely to derive from a document which, though issued by the British government, would not confer the right to settle in Britain, and would not, for good measure, confer the right to settle in Hong Kong either.

From the Hong Kong perspective, the best that could be said about the British nationality memorandum was that it undertook to provide a proportion of Hong Kong people, after 1997, with a document which might, conceivably and in extreme circumstances, encourage them to believe that they had some form of moral claim upon the British government.

For Britain, the Exchange of Memoranda was a face-saving exercise, enabling it to maintain that it was not intending simply to desert the British citizens of Hong Kong at the same time as it withdrew from their territory. In that respect, the Exchange probably did more to serve Britain's interests than it did those of Hong Kong, by merely failing to challenge a system of citizenship for which the negotiators of 1984 could scarcely be held responsible.

THE NEXT BIG problem area, land policy, provided the agenda for the twenty-first round of formal talks, on 21–22 August.

The McLaren-Lu working group was already deep into the technicalities of leaseholds and ground rents, Britain and China having established as general principles that the rights of existing leaseholders should be protected. They had also agreed that leases throughout Hong Kong might be written or extended until 2047, fifty years after the British withdrawal, since this was the date until which China was prepared formally to promise that there would be no significant changes to Hong Kong's legal and other systems.

The main stumbling-block was the question of how revenues should be allocated for new leases sold by the government between 1984 and 1997. The sums of money involved were very large: in a good year, one-third of the Hong Kong government's revenues could come from land sales. The Chinese concern was to ensure that Britain could not, in the years before 1997, launch a bonanza sale of land leases running

169

until 2047, and then dissipate or appropriate the revenues before it withdrew.

The initial Chinese proposal was that the Hong Kong government should go on selling land leases as it saw fit but that, since these leases would run until 2047, and since fifty years of each lease would run under Chinese administration, then the pre-1997 Hong Kong government should yield up a corresponding proportion of land sales revenues to be held in trust for its post-1997 successor – a proportion which would be 50/63rds in 1984, 50/62nds in 1985, and so on.

The British countered that the prices paid for land reflected conditions in the market at the time of the sale, not fifty years hence; but there was, nonetheless, a logic in the Chinese argument which was difficult to resist. The eventual compromise reached was one which contained more than an echo of the deceased protocol, in that it created another joint Sino-British body, the Land Commission, though with a remit that was mainly passive in nature.

In principle, the negotiators agreed, a limit would be set at 50 hectares on the amount of land which the Hong Kong government could sell each year prior to 1997. (Actual sales in previous years had typically ranged from 30 to 60 hectares.) The 50-hectare limit could be raised, in a particular year, but only with the Land Commission's agreement; and half the profit from lands sales would go to the Hong Kong government of the day, and half into trust funds which would be released to the Hong Kong government only after 1997.[7]

Aviation was, meanwhile, being settled away from the negotiating table by a political decision within the Chinese government. The Civil Aviation Administration of China, the statutory body which ran China's national airline, had been creating the impasse by demanding control over landing rights at Hong Kong's international airport after 1997. With Hong Kong as a 'Chinese' destination, CAAC would then be able to trade landing rights there against landing rights for CAAC planes in other countries around the world. CAAC was overruled, and the working group proceeded to draft clauses for the Joint Declaration which devolved control of landing rights to Hong Kong itself, stating that it could make or renew air service agreements with other countries, subject to specific authorizations from Beijing. The agreed text also provided for the continuing operation beyond 1997 of 'airlines incorporated and having their principal place of business in Hong Kong', a phrase tailored to the needs of Cathay

Pacific, Hong Kong's main airline and one of its largest companies.

At a photo-call for the Hong Kong media preceding the twenty-second round of formal talks on 5 September, there was a hint in Zhou Nan's opening banter that the end was in sight. Alluding to Evans's arrival in Beijing at New Year, he remarked, 'you have experienced winter, spring and summer. You are now in autumn, a season for harvesting crops.'

On 6 September, the formal talks adjourned without, for the first time since July 1983, a date declared for their resumption. Which was not to say that work stopped: rather, that there was too much of it to permit another round of largely ceremonial talks. In the nine days which followed, the British and Chinese diplomatic machinery hummed informally and continuously at all levels. To the British bewilderment, the Chinese were proposing at the last minute what they called 'stylistic revisions' – 'hundreds of them', recalled one diplomat – to the burgeoning agreement. There were, too, important gaps still left in Annex I, notably as to how the post-1997 legislature would be constituted. Where text had already been agreed, the last 'stylistic revisions' were hammered down. Where text could still not be agreed, the points of obstruction were isolated for a final review at ministerial level. On one such issue, that of the stationing of Chinese troops in Hong Kong after 1997, the British were obliged to concede that the right to garrison the territory was an indivisible aspect of sovereignty. As a partial compromise, however, China accepted a phrase in the Joint Declaration stating that the 'maintenance of public order' in Hong Kong would remain within the competence of the Hong Kong government.

In the last ministerial exchanges of substance, on 15 and 16 September, Sir Geoffrey Howe sent notes to Wu Xueqian seeking China's approval for the insertion of provisions into the Joint Declaration stating that the post-1997 legislature of Hong Kong would be 'constituted by elections', and that the executive would be 'accountable to the legislature'. To both of these points, after two days' consideration, China agreed.

The text was now complete. On 18 September, the negotiators wrote their final telegrams, while the Executive Council arrived in London to review the finished product in Downing Street. On 19 September, the British Embassy in Beijing confirmed that draft texts of the Joint Declaration and its annexes had been 'submitted by delegations on both sides to respective governments for consideration'. Red-eyed diplomats suddenly found their desks clear and their diaries empty. According to one: 'I had never experienced anything like those last six weeks. Total exhaustion. Suddenly, there was an eery silence, as the guns stopped firing.'

On the morning of 26 September, Sir Richard Evans and Zhou Nan met once again, this time in the Great Hall of the People, to initial the draft of their agreement before an audience of Chinese and British diplomats and a invited delegation of Hong Kong VIPs. Apart from the absence of the most senior leaders, the pomp and circumstance of the initialling ceremony were equal to that of a formal signing. According to one British invitee:

In theory, the only significance of the ceremony was to indicate that the texts to be initialled had been agreed by the negotiating teams. Signatures [of heads of government] would still be needed to convert the initial text into a final text, with ratification still to come.

But [the Chinese] wanted a big ceremony. They thought signature and ratification was all rather dreary. They no doubt judged that, once the agreement had been initialled, it would not be re-opened.

Press reaction to the agreement was jubilatory in Hong Kong. The *Far Eastern Economic Review* said in an editorial:

The documents provide the most solid possible foundation on which the community of Hong Kong and those who trade with and invest in Hong Kong can go on building prosperity . . . Cynics have a right to scoff, [but] in doing so they will miss the immense implications of China's agreement to preserve the freedoms and capitalist lifestyle of Hong Kong. It is an augury not just for the people of Hong Kong but for the whole of East Asia, in whose growing prosperity China wants to earn its rightful share.

In London, *The Times* was more measured, saying that:

Just as it would be wrong to celebrate the agreement as a victory, so too it would be wrong to criticize it too severely. It has managed to secure some unusually specific assurances from Peking, and as

172

such holds out the prospect of order, stability and business confidence in Hong Kong, at least for the next few years . . . Given the limits on what could be achieved, it comes close to being as good as Britain and Hong Kong can expect to get. And as such, it should be judged a success.[8]

In New York, Howe, who was attending a meeting of the United Nations, gave a press conference to field questions from international correspondents. Trevor MacDonald, of Independent Television News, raised the most pertinent point now remaining: what if Hong Kong did not *like* the agreement? Could it be changed? Howe gave an answer which was both honest and faintly bleak:

The choice throughout this exercise has been between getting a bad agreement, getting a good agreement, [and] getting no agreement at all . . . We have worked for a good agreement. We are [putting], therefore, to the people of Hong Kong, this question: 'Do you find the good agreement acceptable? Or would you rather take the alternative, which is no agreement at all?'

The Assessment Office, set up by the British government to 'collate' public opinion, duly provided the answer which was to be expected: invited to choose between an agreement and no agreement, Hong Kong favoured an agreement. But the Assessors noted in their report that many of those who accepted the Joint Declaration did so with a very qualified enthusiasm. Among the comments which they cited was this one, from an anonymous respondent:

For the purpose of your statistics, you can classify me as one of those who would accept the draft agreement. But I hope you will also take into account that I only accept it with much reluctance and with many reservations about the feasibility of its implementation. My heart is not truly at ease, and I have no full confidence in our future. The whole thing has not been very fair play to us because we have not had any say and there is no alternative other than not to have an agreement at all.

THE JOINT DECLARATION was debated and endorsed by the Standing Committee of the National People's Congress in Beijing on

14 November, and by the House of Commons in London on 5 December. Mrs Thatcher flew to Beijing for a formal signing ceremony on the morning of 19 December, and for a second, and this time more amicable, meeting with Deng Xiaoping that afternoon. Deng, effervescent, explained that the Joint Declaration, embodying as it did the formula of 'one country, two systems', was a product of 'dialectical Marxism and historical materialism'. Thatcher was more circumspect. It was, she offered, 'an ingenious idea'.

10

Afterwards

One can argue back and forth for hours whether the 1984 Sino-
British Joint Declaration was the best agreement in the circumstances, whether China will honour its promises, whether it is
moral or immoral, good or bad for business. But there is one
point where Britain cannot avoid shame now and in the future:
we have not lived up to our ideals.

David Bonavia[1]

TWO questions have haunted the hiatus between the end of the
negotiations and the beginning of Chinese rule. Could the
Joint Declaration have been different? And was it enough?
It could perhaps have been different only if Britain had thrown the
points at some much earlier junction along the line, and tried to set a
new course for Hong Kong while China was still weak and Britain still
strong. But by the end of the 1970s, when Britain began to press its
case, only the details remained open to discussion. Had Sir Murray
MacLehose not been instructed to raise the lease question in March
1979, and had the British not been so determined then to clarify Hong
Kong's position, the opening of government-to-government negotiations on Hong Kong's future could almost certainly have been delayed
until closer to 1997. If, however, the Foreign Office and others were
correct in their view that confidence in Hong Kong would begin seriously to erode in the early 1980s unless some action were taken on the

lease, then such a delay would have been a very mixed blessing.

And if, three years later, Margaret Thatcher had been more willing to acknowledge some natural justice in China's claim to Hong Kong when she visited Beijing in September 1982, then the formal talks leading up to the Joint Declaration could undoubtedly have begun much sooner and been completed more rapidly. Then, however, the task of 'selling' an eventual agreement to Hong Kong might have been immeasurably more difficult, had Britain not been seen to fight China's embrace as Thatcher did until all was clearly lost. The same argument applied to the prolonging of the British refusal to concede administration of Hong Kong to China, culminating in the currency crisis of September 1983. Such defiance might have achieved nothing concrete; yet attempting it was the only way of proving that it would not work.

However Britain had marshalled its arguments between 1979 and 1984, or, indeed, if it had chosen not to argue at all, it seems simply foolish now to imagine that China might have waived its entitlement to resume the New Territories after 1997, or failed to demand the rest of Hong Kong too. The negotiations of 1982–4 supplied a clear enough view of the historical, cultural and political imperatives which dictated China's demand for Hong Kong's absolute resumption, and which would inevitably have asserted themselves as 1997 approached. The conclusion must surely be that China would still have proceeded to demand resumption of Hong Kong, and to have offered some form of 'one country, two systems' formula of the kind which it had devised at an earlier stage for Taiwan. Against that background, the British negotiating achievement was a very considerable one, inducing China to articulate its general policy into a detailed document capable of persuading large numbers of people, not only in Hong Kong but also around the world, that Hong Kong's future was relatively secure. As the International Commission of Jurists reported after a mission to Hong Kong in 1991: 'Given the assumption – which we do not share – that it was a proper course of action to negotiate the transfer of sovereignty over Hong Kong to the People's Republic of China over the heads of the people of Hong Kong, the Joint Declaration can be regarded as fairly satisfactory.'[2]

The problems arise, however, when an attempt is made to measure the Joint Declaration against the much broader obligations which Britain might be considered to have incurred over 150 years of colonial rule towards those living under its protection in Hong Kong. In effect, the British government found itself signing away to the People's Republic of China 6 million people whom it both claimed and disclaimed as its subjects, having failed in the previous century and a half to endow them with a broadly based representative government which might have disputed the right of Britain or China to treat Hong Kong as a negotiable commodity. It also failed to grant them the capacity to approve or disapprove by referendum the settlement made on their behalf, mainly because it feared the ferocity of China's opposition to anything smacking of 'self-determination' for the territory.[3] Nationality and representative government, separate questions in more ordinary times, were thus fused in the Hong Kong settlement. If Hong Kong people were not British subjects, then how could Britain be in a position to sign them over passively to China? And if they were British subjects, then how could Britain abandon them? As Henry Keswick, of the Jardine Matheson family, argued before the House of Commons Foreign Affairs Committee on 24 May 1989:

> The fact that we have issued a form of British passport means that we must have some obligation, otherwise we would not have given the limited passport at all. The fact is, we have not introduced democracy in Hong Kong, so that Hong Kong [could] choose its own leaders and its own future. We must have a moral obligation, if we have not done that.
>
> What we have done is that we have faced up to *realpolitik*, and we have handed 5 million people over to a sovereign power by negotiation. But that sovereign power is [a] Marxist-Leninist, thuggish, oppressive regime. That is the bottom line.

THE HISTORY OF abandoned attempts to introduce democracy to Hong Kong under British rule, and of the reasons for their failure, is a book in itself.[4] Prior to 1991, when the first direct elections were held for a minority of seats on the Legislative Council, itself little more than a debating-chamber, the constitutional structure of Hong Kong remained largely as it was in the late nineteenth century. Power to make policy rested with the Governor, who appointed a small Executive Council to advise him; responsibility for approving laws and expenditure rested with the Legislative Council, which was entirely appointed by the Governor until 1985, and which in the succeeding six years gained a minority of members elected from trade and professional groups.[5]

177

In Hong Kong's resistance to democracy, three main and mutually reinforcing factors could be identified. The first was pressure from China on Britain not to move Hong Kong in the direction of self-determination and thence independence. The second was the lack of a strong, broadly based demand for democracy from a people whose roots in Hong Kong were often relatively shallow, and whose much more immediate concern was with securing a tolerable standard of living. The third was the inherent conservatism and élitism of senior civil servants, and of the appointed members of the Executive and Legislative Councils, who preferred to govern Hong Kong undisturbed by elected representatives of the governed.

No doubt the limits of China's tolerance could have been tested a little more bravely, and the appetite of the public for self-government awakened, had the civil service and the appointed grandees been at all inclined to forego some of their own power in the interests of democratization. But they were not. An attempt in 1946 by the then Governor, Sir Mark Young, to restructure the government around a new, elected Municipal Council quickly lost momentum when Young left the colony in 1947. The Young Plan was shelved by the (all-appointed) Hong Kong Legislative Council in 1949, and abandoned finally by Britain in 1952.

The antipathy towards democracy shown by the appointed members of the Executive and Legislative Councils was understandable enough. Apart from a purely selfish interest in maintaining their personal power, they believed – as many in Hong Kong still did forty years later – that politics and business were natural enemies, and that business should come first. That senior civil servants should share that antipathy was, however, less defensible, particularly when it extended to propaganda and public relations work in both Hong Kong and London to reinforce the belief that democracy was neither necessary nor useful to Hong Kong. John Walden, who was Director of Home Affairs in the Hong Kong government from 1975 to 1980, wrote after his retirement that:

Throughout the 30 years that I was an official myself, from 1951 to 1981, 'democracy' was a dirty word. Officials were convinced that the introduction of democratic politics into Hong Kong would be the quickest and surest way to ruin Hong Kong's economy and create social and political instability . . .

178

In all those years, civil servants who favoured democratic reform (there were a few, usually from former British colonies in Africa) were regarded as disloyal or even dangerous. Pressure groups advocating political reform or grass-roots democracy were carefully monitored by the Government and the Special Branch of the Hong Kong police, and where possible their activities were discreetly obstructed or frustrated, sometimes by the use of highly questionable tactics. This deliberate and active discouragement of the growth of the democratic processes by the Government continued right up to 1980, to my certain knowledge.[6]

The civil servants might have defended their strategy, if not their tactics, by replying that the China problem was simply insurmountable – that China was sure to see any meaningful democratization of colonial government as the redirecting of Hong Kong along the road to independence, as had, indeed, been the sequence of events elsewhere throughout the British Empire, and would frustrate this process at almost any cost, even to itself. But more than that, defenders of the status quo might have argued, Hong Kong had long enjoyed the best of both constitutional worlds, with the efficiency of executive-led government at a domestic level, and with the sovereign link to Britain and the accountability of the Hong Kong government to the Westminster Parliament ensuring that it simultaneously enjoyed the protection and the stimulant of democratic values at one remove. Hong Kong's own record of economic success was evidence enough that such a combination worked exceedingly well in the territory. So why change it?

Such a reply would have been satisfactory as far as it went, but it was lacking in foresight or imagination. Hong Kong sheltered under the democratic 'umbrella' of Westminster *pro tem*; but the advantage of rooting even a little democracy locally in Hong Kong would have been that it might then still be available to Hong Kong should the British sovereign link ever be broken. For the British, too, there were prospective benefits: should any rendition of Hong Kong eventually occur, the seeding of democracy there would encourage British public opinion and Parliament to feel slightly nobler about the process, and probably also make rendition more acceptable to Hong Kong itself.

It must be considered probable that some perceptions or qualms of this sort underpinned the decision taken in 1980–1, after the lease question had been raised with Beijing but before the formal talks began, to introduce elections by universal suffrage on a constituency basis in Hong Kong for seats on eighteen newly created District Boards. The powers of the boards were very few and very local, and the elected members were in a minority on them. But the importance of the exercise was that it gave Hong Kong an electoral roll, a constituency system and some low-level experience of campaigning and voting. It also enabled British politicians to talk a few years later, as the lease question moved into the public arena, about the 'continued' development of 'representative government' in Hong Kong as though it were a long-standing process rather than merely an adjunct of 1997.

Even within the Sino-British negotiations of 1982–4, and despite the significance which it assumed after the Joint Declaration was signed, the development of 'representative government' for Hong Kong was not a particularly contentious issue. The Executive Council, speaking for Hong Kong's special interests, placed no very high priority on political reform, still less on democratization, in the early stages of the talks, such that the Foreign Office, given China's own preference for the structural status quo, was certainly disinclined to go looking for arguments where none existed.[7] In the later stages of the formal talks, after Britain's *de facto* undertaking to withdraw, it was from London rather than Hong Kong that the main pressure came for a commitment in the Joint Declaration to a more democratic character for the Hong Kong legislature after 1997, the British government's feeling being that a commitment of this kind would be important in securing all-party parliamentary support for the eventual settlement.

The insertion of the phrase 'constituted by elections' to describe the future Hong Kong legislature was one of the very last points to which Britain and China agreed in their drafting of the Joint Declaration, and it was understood by the British negotiators, as well as *a fortiori* by their Chinese counterparts, that it need not mean a legislature elected in its entirety by universal suffrage. The British accepted that 'elections' might include indirect elections and elections through a restricted franchise. In the Chinese political lexicon, 'election' could have meant almost anything; though the Chinese had, in this instance, attempted to make their intentions more transparent by proposing 'election and selection' as the phrase to be used in the Joint Declaration text, before agreeing to the British proposal for 'election' alone.[8]

The phrase 'constituted by elections' supplied, nonetheless, the hook on to which the Hong Kong government, on Britain's behalf, was able to hang a package of inconclusive but very positive-sounding proposals for political reform, in the form of Green and White Papers published in the second half of 1984, as the time approached for presenting the Joint Declaration to Hong Kong and the British Parliament. Even if the exercise was not a wholly cynical one on the part of Britain,[9] it must be presumed, given the timing, that the British government was more concerned at this juncture with the political benefits which would derive from the *idea* of democracy for Hong Kong, than it was with the implementation of democracy as such.

The Green Paper was published in July 1984, before China's agreement to the phrase 'constituted by elections' had been secured, and so was necessarily stronger in general principles than it was in details. The White Paper followed in November 1984, after China's agreement in the Joint Declaration to a legislature 'constituted by elections', and took a more concrete and positive line. It unveiled a planned restructuring of the Legislative Council through the creation of twelve seats for 'functional constituencies' of trade and professional groups, and twelve seats to be returned by an 'electoral college' made up of local government bodies. By these devices, some two-fifths of the Council was to be placed outside the Governor's gift. On direct elections, the White Paper had this to say:

> There was little evidence of support in public comment on the Green Paper for any move towards direct elections in 1985. With few exceptions the bulk of the public response from all sources suggested a cautious approach with a gradual start by introducing a very small number of directly elected members in 1988 and building up to a significant number of directly elected members by 1997.[11]

The White Paper appeared shortly before the House of Commons and the House of Lords debated the Joint Declaration on 5 and 10 December respectively, during which the promises of electoral reform were frequently evoked. Richard Luce, replying to the Commons for the government at the end of the 5 December debate, said: 'The constitutional development of Hong Kong has caused great interest, and a large number of honourable members have expressed legitimate concerns. We all fully accept that we should build up a firmly based democratic administration in Hong Kong in the years between now and 1997.'[12]

Five days later, in the Lords, Baroness Young, also replying for the government, said: 'Almost all of your Lordships referred to the important question of constitutional development in Hong Kong up to 1997. I fully accept the legitimate concerns which have been expressed that we should develop a solidly based democratic administration in Hong Kong in the period up to 1997.'

Undoubtedly, with or without the White Paper, the Joint Declaration would have been overwhelmingly supported.[13] But the apparent prospect of significant Western-style democracy in Hong Kong both before and after 1997 was an important factor in allowing the British Parliament to feel that what had been done for Hong Kong was not merely politically necessary, but also morally adequate.

CHINA, AWARE THAT parliamentary debate and ratification of the Joint Declaration were an inescapable part of the treaty process for the British, said nothing at this time to disabuse any MPs who might have imagined that Beijing was giving its blessing through the Joint Declaration to the bringing of Westminster-style democracy to Hong Kong under British tutelage. It was not until almost a year later that China revealed its true feelings about democracy for Hong Kong, opposing it so relentlessly that the British never quite regained their balance.

In June 1985, China announced the formation of a Basic Law Drafting Committee, the fifty-nine mainland and twenty-three Hong Kong members of which were charged with drawing up a constitutional document for Hong Kong based upon the principles and policies of the Joint Declaration which, when enacted as Chinese law, would regulate the territory after 1997 in its new incarnation as a 'special administrative region' of China. Ji Pengfei, head of the Chinese government's Hong Kong and Macao Affairs Office, was named the committee's chairman. In October, receiving a delegation of Hong Kong architects in Beijing, Ji unveiled China's logic for the transitional period. The political system prevailing in Hong Kong after 1997 would be fixed in the forthcoming Basic Law. Therefore, he said, to ensure a smooth transition, and thus to preserve the stability and prosperity of Hong Kong, as stipulated in the Joint Declaration, the

British Hong Kong government should only alter the Hong Kong political system prior to 1997 in ways which brought it more closely into conformity with the prescriptions of the Basic Law. To this general principle, Ji gave the name of 'convergence'. A month after Ji's low-key warning, Xu Jiatun brought the argument into the public arena with a press conference on 21 November 1985, at which he publicly accused the British of 'deviation from the Joint Declaration' by contemplating political reforms incompatible with the Basic Law. Xu's public attack coincided with private pressure on the British through the medium of the Joint Liaison Group; the matter was probably discussed at a meeting of the JLG in Beijing from 26 to 29 November 1985, if China was following the pattern, developed during the negotiations, of synchronizing its appeals to public opinion with corresponding but confidential diplomacy.

Certainly, by the time that Timothy Renton, newly appointed minister of state at the Foreign Office, visited Beijing in January 1986, the British had decided that their hands were tied by the political realities of the transitional period and by their commitment in the Joint Declaration to seeking a 'solution through consultations' with China on matters relating to 'the smooth transfer of government'.[14] They accepted the principle of 'convergence'. Renton described it as 'important', and later as 'a coming together . . . with the Basic Law'. This was a major victory for China: 'convergence' would regain for it much of the influence over pre-1997 Hong Kong, albeit on an *ad hoc* basis, which it had appeared willing to forego in 1984 by abandoning the protocol. Now, by invoking the Basic Law, China could claim the right to co-determine pre-1997 policy decisions, and also, prior to the Basic Law's publication, to delay any major decisions which Britain might wish to take until China, too, was ready to pronounce on the matter.

The accommodation of 'convergence' produced perhaps the most regrettable action of the British and Hong Kong governments during this difficult period: the publication of a further Green Paper on representative government in May 1987, which was designed to dampen earlier hopes for a brisk pace of democratization, not by an admission of China's successful intransigence, but by a farrago of leading questions designed to insinuate that the change of heart had come from Hong Kong itself.

The Green Paper invited simultaneous public comment on twenty-six main proposals and fourteen sub-options for adjustments to Hong Kong's political system at all levels from the most local to the Legislative Council. Among these, the possibility of introducing directly elected members to the Legislative Council in 1988, by far the most important variable, was ranked as the fifth sub-option of the fourth main option of the fourth chapter of the paper. The obfuscation failed, nonetheless, to deter 368,431 people from registering their opinions with an official Survey Office, of whom 361,398 expressed a view on direct elections: 265,078 in favour, 94,565 against, and 1,755 with no clear preference. Though this was a seemingly unarguable verdict, the Survey Office made it appear otherwise. Most of the views against direct elections had been expressed using pre-printed 'form' letters of a type distributed widely among employees and affiliates of leftist organizations in Hong Kong, who were required to add only a signature and send them to the Survey Office. Much of the support for direct elections, on the other hand, had been co-ordinated by liberal activists who collected large numbers of signatures in the form of petitions and then sent them on to the Survey Office. The Office decided that each signature on a pre-printed letter would be counted as an 'individual submission', while each signature on a petition would not, enabling the Hong Kong government to make the otherwise extraordinary claim, in its White Paper of February 1988, that: 'Among submissions to the Survey Office from individuals, groups and associations, more were against than in favour of the introduction of direct elections in 1988.'[15]

The government duly ruled that the first directly elected seats would not be added to the Legislative Council until 1991 at the earliest, thereby ensuring that the Basic Law would not be anticipated – and also that democracy would gain only a small and fleeting foothold in Hong Kong, in the very last and weakest years of British rule.[16]

IT COULD BE said in defence of Britain's vacillation over democracy in the 1984–8 period that there was at least a significant section of Hong Kong public opinion which approved of the result. Probably not a majority, as the Hong Kong government claimed, but certainly a substantial minority resisted the idea of direct elections in 1988, believing either that democratic politics would be inherently damaging to Hong Kong, or that it was foolish to court China's wrath. But no similar constituency, indeed no constituency of any size, could have

184

been found to support Britain's nationality policy towards Hong Kong. When the House of Commons Foreign Affairs Committee held hearings on Hong Kong in the spring of 1989, in preparation for a report on developments there since the Joint Declaration, it heard from witness after witness denunciations of the 1962 Commonwealth Immigrant Act, which withdrew from Hong Kong citizens (and from most other colonial and Commonwealth citizens) the right to enter and live and work in Britain, and of the 1981 Nationality Act, which articulated this discrimination into new tiers of citizenship, with Hong Kong assigned to the status of British Dependent Territories Citizenship. The view expressed to the committee by Lydia Dunn was among the more moderate: 'I sometimes wonder', she said, 'what the British people feel when they read about Hong Kong British subjects scouring the world to find somewhere else to take them in.'[17]

The answer was, of course, that most British people were scarcely conscious of any connection with Hong Kong at all; and that most of their Members of Parliament felt only a positive sense of relief that the 'scouring' was concentrated somewhere other than Dover or Heathrow. Historical and moral obligations counted, in this context, for nothing. As a member of the Foreign Affairs Committee declared when slapping down a Hong Kong witness who insisted on Britain's moral obligation to offer right of entry to all 3.25 million Hong Kong holders of British passports:

Do you realize, quite apart from principles and morals, the political difficulty of admitting 3.25 million people? That is the way any receiving nation has to view it, whatever the history involved. You talk about allegiance, but can you tell me whether all those 3.25 million have been to England, know England, speak English or have any association with England, or in reality bear any allegiance to it?[18]

Or, as Sir Geoffrey Howe remarked more pithily, in an aside from his own evidence: 'I remember in my Sunday school days, or perhaps a bit later than that, talking about *Civis Britannicus*, which we all know was fine until a huge chunk of the world's population began exercising it.'[19]

In its official formulation, the British position was that the country could not, by virtue of physical and economic constraints, cope with influxes of immigrants from countries which had once been, or even remained, under its rule, and that it was reasonably seeking to with-hold the right of entry into Britain from those who also held citizenship in a separate country which had either achieved or was moving towards independence. Hong Kong, however, sensed keenly two sources of particular injustice in the British nationality regime as it stood after 1981: the first was a strong *de facto* racial bias, favouring for 'first-class' British citizenship those overseas citizens possessing parents or grandparents born in Great Britain; the second was the indisputable fact that Hong Kong was not, so far as anyone knew, heading for independence, and might very well be heading for resumption by China in 1997. As John Swaine, a barrister and member of the Executive Council, said, addressing the same audience as Howe but in a less jocular vein: 'The 1981 Nationality Act . . . created a new citizenship, British Dependent Territories Citizenship, in place of the common citizenship of the United Kingdom and Colonies which people in Hong Kong [had] shared with the citizens of the United Kingdom . . . The belief is widespread that this bill was aimed at Hong Kong and was part of Britain's process of disengagement.'[20]

David Howell, the Foreign Affairs Committee chairman, insisted in reply that: 'The 1981 Act was in no way aimed at Hong Kong, and had nothing to do with the subsequent events which emerged in relation to Hong Kong.'

Similar assurances were repeated at least a dozen times to other witnesses during the committee's hearings. But it was easier, nonetheless, to accept the version of events given a few weeks later by Timothy Raison MP, writing in the *Financial Times* of 14 June 1989, who said of the background to the 1981 Nationality Act: 'The assumption was made that, as and when a dependent territory ceased to be one, its citizens would acquire citizenship in line with the new status – in the case of Hong Kong, Chinese citizenship. Obviously, Hong Kong loomed large in the thinking behind the Act.'

Hong Kong residents supplied, in fact, the overwhelming majority of British Dependent Territories Citizens, the central innovation of the 1981 Nationality Act; and it was, indeed, no more than common sense to presume that legislation devolving the theoretical basis of British Hong Kong citizenship away from Britain and towards Hong Kong, enacted at a time when Britain had already opened talks with China on the colony's future and discovered that China intended to resume it, was tailored to anticipate precisely the severance of Hong Kong which was subsequently agreed.[21] In a technical and political perspective, if not a moral one, British Dependent Territories Citizenship was a most effective invention for domestic British purposes.

In Hong Kong itself, though the right to live and work in Britain had been lost nineteen years earlier, the 1981 Nationality Act reawakened a sense of injury and reinforced a sense of exclusion. Foreign Office and Hong Kong officials lamented the 'unfortunate coincidence' whereby the Act came into force just as Britain and China were approaching the negotiating-table, undercutting the Thatcher government's insistence that Hong Kong was British territory by law and that Britain had a 'moral responsibility' to the Hong Kong people. Yet, though the Nationality Act undoubtedly did damage Britain's credibility in Hong Kong during that time, and created purely tactical difficulties for Britain as it sought to be seen to act in Hong Kong's best interests, the Act probably also worked in Britain's favour in a strategic way, by cutting into such residual attachment as Hong Kong people still possessed towards their sovereign power. It diminished the degree of loss which was felt when Britain's withdrawal from Hong Kong became inevitable, and, by the same token, made the sense of resignation towards resumption by China more complete – all of which is not to suggest that such a detailed consequence was intended or even foreseen by the drafters of the Act, whose interest was limited to keeping 'foreigners with British passports' out of Britain, merely that it was, so to speak, a bonus.

With Britain closed to them, and absorption into China the advancing prospect, increasing numbers of Hong Kong's rich, young, skilled and educated citizens responded to the Joint Declaration by emigrating. According to Hong Kong government estimates, the number of people leaving the territory each year to settle overseas roughly tripled between 1982 and 1991, from 20,300 to about 60,000.[22] According to John Swaine:

Immediately after the Joint Declaration . . . the outflow of people consisted of the very rich, and the ones who were established here went, got their papers and came back to Hong Kong, and we still have them. In the [late 1980s] the profile . . . changed. People in their thirties and forties, middle management, have gone. They have uprooted themselves and taken their families with them. They have sold their homes and re-established themselves in Canada and Australia. They have bought homes and put their children in schools there. We have lost that group for ever.

Almost all middle-class emigrants suffered financial loss by leaving Hong Kong and moving into more junior jobs overseas, drawing more highly taxed wages in more slowly growing economies. They went because they dared not arrive at 1997 with no right of abode elsewhere for themselves and their families should resumption by Communist China prove intolerable. Had these people possessed 'full' British passports, with right of entry into Britain, they would, perversely, not have felt a need to leave Hong Kong at all; in that very direct sense, Hong Kong was obliged to pay the price of Britain's racial intolerance. But it was a situation which, while there were passports available elsewhere in the world, and while there was time in which to secure them, Hong Kong could afford to view pragmatically, more with resignation than with desperation and more with disgust than anger at Britain for espousing a policy which, in Hong Kong's eyes, brought so much shame upon Britain itself.

Canada and Australia were the main beneficiaries of Hong Kong's brain-drain because they stressed professional skills and qualifications more than wealth in their criteria for settlement. For the rich, passports or right-of-residence stamps were available from almost any country in the world, even Britain. But for the rest of Hong Kong, there was no choice but to accept the future as China dictated it. In the loosely translated words of a Cantonese aphorism popular in the mid-1980s:

> Those with cash
> Can always dash;
> And for the poor,
> the Basic Law.

THE PROCESS OF drafting the Basic Law, which had begun with the formation of the Drafting Committee in July 1985, continued with the publication of a first draft in April 1988. Though the draft was a dense and technical document running to some 20,000 words in its English translation, public discussion was plentiful and for the most part constructive in tone. The Basic Law Consultative Committee, set up by

China to co-ordinate local opinion, received 74,000 submissions during the five months designated as a 'consultation period' from May to September 1988.

By and large, the draft Basic Law did what it was supposed to do: it elaborated the provisions of the Joint Declaration into a detailed document considered by China as suitable for enactment into domestic law. Anyone anxious on a point of concrete detail – as to whether, for example, China would indeed commit itself to preserving the convertibility of the Hong Kong dollar, or freedom of speech, or the powers of magistrates' courts – would find reassurance somewhere in the 172 Articles of the Law's first draft.[23]

Where the Basic Law troubled its more politically and legally astute critics, however, was in respect of the foundations, or lack of them, on which it rested. No attempt had been made, for example, to reconcile the Basic Law, a piece of legislation subordinate to China's national constitution,[24] with those articles of China's constitution which it otherwise appeared to contradict – among them, Articles 1 and 5 which stated that: 'The People's Republic of China, is a socialist state . . . Disruption of the socialist system by any organization or individual is prohibited' [Article 1]; and that 'No laws or administrative or local rules and regulations may contravene the Constitution . . . No organization or individual is privileged to go beyond the Constitution or the law' [Article 5].

No less problematic was the vesting of powers of interpretation and amendment of the Basic Law in the standing committee of the National People's Congress, China's rubber-stamp 'parliament'. The standing committee was not a judicial body, but a legislative body under the Communist Party's political control. The standing committee would thus be free, quite legally, to alter the text or meaning of the Basic Law at the will of the Communist Party, all the more so if it chose to exploit inconsistencies between the Basic Law and the constitution.

Finally, though it was not something which could be articulated into any very constructive critique of the Basic Law, there was the concern that the Chinese Communist Party did not have any great respect for laws as such, whatever they might say. Sir Geoffrey Howe and other British politicians had sought to quash similar doubts about China's respect for the Joint Declaration by insisting that China had traditionally shown a very strong disposition to respect international agreements; the Basic Law, however, was not an international agreement, but a domestic law. It could be observed in this context that China's constitution, notably, included many fine-sounding provisions similar to, and in theory of an even more binding nature than, those of the Basic Law – for example, that: 'Citizens of the People's Republic of China enjoy freedom of speech, of the press, of assembly, of association, of procession and of demonstration' [Article 35].

Yet such undertakings were demonstrably not respected within China itself, and the National People's Congress, supposedly also the guardian of the constitution, did nothing whatsoever about violations of it. It was not easy to see why the Basic Law, and Hong Kong, should be any the more respected or protected.

Given the fragile – indeed, the wholly illusory – status of the Basic Law as the principal guarantor of Hong Kong's 'high degree of autonomy' from China, it followed that confidence in the future of Hong Kong could, ultimately, be founded only in a corresponding confidence in the future of China. If, and only if, China was moving towards a new respect within its own borders for enterprise, freedom and the rule of law, could it be expected to respect those commodities in Hong Kong.

Until the spring of 1989, it was possible to argue that such a process was underway, and that Hong Kong was thus relatively secure. But on the night of 3–4 June 1989, such arguments collapsed, and confidence with them, as the People's Liberation Army commenced the suppression of student-led democracy protests in the centre of Beijing, killing hundreds of civilians in the days which followed.[25] After 4 June 1989, it became impossible to argue that the Communist Party of China, so long as it remained in power, would be constrained by any considerations of legality or morality when acting in what it perceived to be the interests of its own survival.

In the weeks before the massacre, Hong Kong had been caught up in the innocence and the optimism of the Beijing protesters. Even usually conservative business figures who had remained silent on democracy for Hong Kong were moved to show sympathy with the campaign for democracy in China. A million people marched through Hong Kong on 21 and 28 May, showing support and collecting money for the Beijing movement. On 24 May, emboldened by the popular mood, unofficial members of the Executive and Legislative Councils unanimously agreed to support an accelerated pace of democratization within Hong Kong itself, calling for half of the Legislative Council to be directly elected in 1995, and the whole of it by 2003.

When the massacre followed, the effect on Hong Kong was convulsive. A million marched once more through the city on 4 June, but in the black silence of mourning; the Governor, David Wilson, flew to London on 7 June, and urged Britain to grant the right of abode to Hong Kong citizens;[26] British participation in the work of the Joint Liaison Group was suspended; and the Hong Kong government, which had temporized for several years over the introduction of a Bill of Rights to the territory, hastened to prepare one.

In Britain, Tiananmen shocked Parliament into some rare moments of emotion about the vulnerability of Hong Kong. Jim Sillars, the Scottish Nationalist MP, reappraising the Joint Declaration, accused government and opposition alike of 'an orgy of self-congratulation. Complacency abounded, the best of all possible solutions had been found . . . They made a monumental error of judgement about the nature and character of the Chinese Communist Party.' But though many must at that moment privately have agreed with Sillars, it was the Conservative voices led by Sir Geoffrey Howe who spoke for British policy, insisting that the spectacle of mass murder by the Chinese government, distressing as it might be, was not of a magnitude sufficient to reverse the historical process which the Joint Declaration had set in motion.

Hong Kong quickly lost the will to keep alive its public anger at the massacre and its hopes for the China which might have been. It was obliged to accept that it lived in the shadow of the Communist Party, however black that shadow might be. The Legislative Council, barely nine months after its declaration for democracy, bowed meekly to the much less liberal model which China adopted in February 1990 for the final text of the Basic Law, and which prescribed, with Britain's acquiescence, that the Legislative Council would have, by or in 1997, 20 directly elected seats, 10 indirectly elected seats, and 30 seats elected by restricted franchise. China was also by then eating its vengeance cold in other ways for Hong Kong's support of the Beijing democracy movement. When the JLG resumed business, it did so on an adversarial basis, with China opposing most British proposals as a matter of principle; and the final text of the Basic Law acquired clauses obliging Hong Kong to suppress 'sedition' after 1997, and promising martial law if 'turmoil' should sweep the territory. This was China's warning that it would not easily forget the whiff of rebellion on the Hong Kong streets, and that, come 1997, opposition to the

Communist Party in Hong Kong would be treated no more kindly than opposition to the Communist Party in Beijing.

THE CONCLUDING PHASE of British rule over Hong Kong began, symbolically, with the arrival of a new and probably final British governor, Christopher Patten, in July 1992. His predecessor, Sir David Wilson, had fallen victim to the reservations of a prime minister, John Major, who, while accepting the need to restore a working relationship with China in the wake of Tiananmen, had also decided that he wanted a governor more responsive than Wilson to the aspirations of democratic and liberal opinion in the colony. When Patten, a former cabinet minister and Conservative Party chairman, lost his parliamentary seat in the general election of April 1992, he was deemed to fit the bill.

The new Governor brought with him to Hong Kong a populism which was a world away from Wilson's fastidious discretion. Patten declined the customary knighthood, discarded the white ceremonial uniform, and drew crowds so large and enthusiastic on his early 'walkabouts' that the police could barely secure his route. Proclaiming himself a democrat by conviction, he proposed in his first major policy speech, on 7 October 1992, a series of measures to broaden the voting base for the next Legislative Council elections in 1995.[27] It was only then that China, having surveyed the newcomer for three months with a quietly baleful eye, erupted.

Patten had not sought China's approval for the proposals which he unveiled; and, had he done so, he would not have received it, since, as China quickly made clear, it regarded the proposals as breaching 'agreements and understandings' which it insisted had been reached between British and Chinese foreign ministers in early 1990, shortly before the Basic Law was published. The essence of these 'agreements and understandings', said China, was that Britain had committed itself specifically to 'converge' prior to 1997 with the formula for the Legislative Council set down in the Basic Law. The Patten proposals were not compatible with that 'convergence', China ruled, and must therefore be withdrawn.

For an interlude of perhaps a fortnight, Hong Kong was inclined to treat China's reaction as pro-forma bluster. But as the Communist press began to hint that it enjoyed the authority of Deng Xiaoping for the saturation campaign of mockery and abuse which it had launched against the new Governor, the severity of the situation asserted itself. China, having reawakened during the Tiananmen crisis its suspicions that Britain might yet try to 'sabotage' the handover of Hong Kong and regretting ever more keenly that it had agreed in 1984 to abandon the 'protocol' to the Joint Declaration which would have given it a much tighter control of Hong Kong during the transitional period, now considered that its fears had been justified and that important principles were at stake. At least three members of the Standing Committee of the Politburo, the apex of the Communist Party leadership, delivered internal speeches denouncing British 'colonialism' during November and December, after Deng himself had reportedly laid down this new general policy line for Hong Kong in late October: 'Should the British Hong Kong government take one false step, we shall issue a reminder. Two false steps and we shall issue a warning. Three false steps and we shall start all over again by asking them to go home.'[28]

If China's early protests against the Patten proposals were the 'reminder' to Britain, then the 'warning' came on 16 November, when Zhu Rongji, a member of the Politburo Standing Committee, said during a visit to London that the Joint Declaration might 'scatter to the winds' if the proposals were not withdrawn. In the weeks which followed, while stopping short of explicitly asking the British to 'go home', China in effect came very close to it by suggesting that parallel institutions of government for Hong Kong might be established by Beijing prior to 1997, and that long-term contracts and obligations of the Hong Kong government might be disowned in 1997 unless China's own separate endorsement for them had previously been obtained.

Yet, even allowing for China's claim that 'agreements' with Britain had been breached, it was difficult to account for the ferocity of Beijing's reaction, extending to its apparent willingness to write off the Joint Declaration and even Hong Kong itself, without invoking causal factors more profound than the Patten proposals alone. Lee Kuan Yew, the former Prime Minister of Singapore, supplied a persuasive diagnosis of the situation during a visit to Hong Kong on 14 December, when he argued that China feared the Patten proposals might prove a stalking-horse for Western pressure on other issues, particularly given the imminence of a new American president, Bill Clinton, whom China had every reason to expect would be less sympathetic to its interests than had been the outgoing President, George Bush. Lee hypothesized:

> I ask myself this question. If I were the Chinese, what would I do? . . . If I give way on Hong Kong to the British, who do not have either the military or the economic clout to hurt me, then I am inviting trouble from Bill Clinton. Chris Patten can only express his exasperation, but Bill Clinton can turn off MFN and with it growth in Guangdong. He might apply pressure in Taiwan, and growth in Fujian is also threatened; then he has Super 301 and so on . . . I think it is highly unlikely, given those stakes, that [China] is going to back off.[29]

Lee's next sentiment could have brought little comfort to Christopher Patten, who sat beside him as he spoke. 'I therefore expect', he said, 'a real scrap in Hong Kong.'

WITH SUCH PASSIONS seemingly unleashed, it is difficult to foresee quite how the tensions between Britain, China and Hong Kong will resolve themselves in the years which remain before 1997, even if Lee's 'scrap' is somehow averted. For if China's leaders now view Britain's presence in Hong Kong with more than a touch of paranoia, it is a paranoia born of their own regime's very real fragility in an otherwise post-Communist world. It is perfectly possible to imagine, on that basis, an escalation of tensions which will force Britain out of Hong Kong before 1997 arrives; or, using much the same arguments, the resumption of Hong Kong by a China in which the Communist Party no longer holds sway.

Perhaps the only certainty about Hong Kong's future is that, whatever course it takes, it will be a future in which Britain has no special part. The city so promiscuously conceived beside the Pearl River in 1841 having lived out its century and a half of borrowed time, the city reborn there in 1997 will be the child of China alone. When the British flag descends by the Hong Kong harbour-front on that sub-tropical summer midnight, it will be the beginning of a new and no doubt equally extraordinary adventure for all who remain. But it will be the end of what has, until that moment, been Hong Kong.

Chronology

1841 20 January
Captain Charles Elliot and Imperial Commissioner Qishan sign the Convention of Chuanbi, ceding Hong Kong Island to Britain. The document is later repudiated by Britain and China.

1842 29 August
Sir Henry Pottinger and Imperial Commissioner Qiying sign the Treaty of Nanjing, again ceding Hong Kong Island to Britain. This treaty is ratified by an exchange of instruments on 26 June 1843.

1860 24 October
Lord Elgin and Prince Gong sign the Convention of Beijing, ceding the Kowloon peninsula to Britain.

1898 9 June
Sir Claude MacDonald and Li Hongzhang sign the second Convention of Beijing, leasing the New Territories to Britain for 99 years from 1 July.

1972 8 March
China tells the United Nations Special Committee on Decolonization that 'the settlement of the questions of Hong Kong and Macao is entirely within China's sovereign right'.

195

1972 13 March
(*cont.*) Britain and China announce normalization of diplomatic relations.

1978 November–December
The Chinese Communist Party holds preparatory meetings, followed by the Third Plenum of the 11th Central Committee, at which Deng Xiaoping's 'reformist' policies are endorsed, and Deng emerges as the Party's unassailable leader.

15 December
The United States and China announce agreement on normalization of diplomatic relations.

1979 1 January
China publishes a 'Letter to Taiwan Compatriots' appealing for peaceful reunification.

29 March
Deng Xiaoping receives Sir Murray MacLehose, Governor of Hong Kong, in Beijing. MacLehose seeks Deng's approval for Britain to issue land leases in the New Territories 'for so long as the Crown administers the territory'. Deng refuses, but says that investors in Hong Kong should 'set their hearts at ease'.

September
The Chinese foreign ministry formally tells Britain that a change in the terms of New Territories land leases would be 'unnecessary'.

29 October–3 November
Hua Guofeng, Chinese Communist Party chairman, visits Britain.

December
Huang Hua, Chinese foreign minister, visits Britain.

1981 March
The British government agrees to guarantee export loans totalling £755 million, to finance construction of a power station in Hong Kong.

3 April
Deng receives Lord Carrington, British Foreign Secretary. Deng declines to pursue a more detailed discussion of Hong Kong's future.

30 September
Ye Jianying, chairman of China's National People's Congress, unveils Beijing's 'Nine-Point Plan' for reunification with Taiwan, an early incarnation of the 'one country, two systems' policy later applied to Hong Kong.

1982   **6 January**
Zhao Ziyang, China's Prime Minister, receives Humphrey Atkins, British Foreign Office minister, in Beijing. Zhao says China will re-establish its sovereignty over Hong Kong, and that Hong Kong will remain a free port. Atkins says Margaret Thatcher, the British Prime Minister, will visit Beijing in the autumn.

6 April
Deng Xiaoping receives Edward Heath, the former British Prime Minister, and asks Heath whether Britain might accept a Hong Kong settlement similar to that proposed by Ye for Taiwan.

20 May
Sir Edward Youde arrives as Governor of Hong Kong, in succession to MacLehose.

15 June
Deng receives a delegation of Hong Kong visitors at the Great Hall of the People, and invites discussion of how China should best resume Hong Kong.

5–6 September
Youde and Executive Council members visit London to discuss Hong Kong with Thatcher prior to her departure for Beijing.

22–24 September
Thatcher meets Deng and Zhao in Beijing. Deng rejects Thatcher's proposal for continued British administration of Hong Kong after 1997, but agrees in principle to open diplomatic negotiations.

26–28 September
Thatcher in Hong Kong. She angers China by telling a press conference that 'if a country will not stand by one treaty, it will not stand by another treaty'.

1982   20 November
(*cont*.)   Liao Chengzhi, head of the State Council's Hong Kong and Macao
Affairs Office, receiving a group of Hong Kong factory owners in
Beijing, says that 'Hong Kong people will rule Hong Kong' after
1997, and that China will have drafted its own blueprint for Hong
Kong in 'about a year'.

4 December
China's National People's Congress adopts a new constitution,
which includes a clause providing for the establishment of 'special
administrative regions' within which socialism need not be practised – the status to be offered Hong Kong.

9–11 December
Lord Belstead, junior Foreign Office minister, visits Hong Kong,
and says a negotiated settlement of the 1997 question must be like a
'three-legged stool', supported by Britain, China and Hong Kong.

1983   9 March
To break a pre-negotiation deadlock with China, Thatcher autho-
rizes a message to Zhao saying that she will be 'prepared to recommend' to Parliament a transfer of sovereignty over Hong Kong if
an acceptable settlement is reached.

May–June
British and Chinese diplomats hold two rounds of meetings in
Beijing, to agree an agenda and to make practical arrangements for
formal negotiations to begin.

10 June
Death of Liao Chengzhi. He is succeeded by Ji Pengfei.

30 June
Xu Jiatun, a member of the Communist Party's Central Commit-
tee, arrives in Hong Kong as director of the New China News
Agency, accompanied by his deputy, Li Chuwen.

1 July
Britain and China announce that formal negotiations on the Hong
Kong question will begin in Beijing on 12 July.

4–5 July
Youde and Executive Council members visit London for discussions with Thatcher and with Sir Geoffrey Howe, the new Foreign Secretary.

12–13 July
First round of formal talks. Britain begins a presentation of papers analysing the need for continued British administration of Hong Kong. The communiqué issued at the close of the talks describes the event as 'useful and constructive'.

25–26 July
Second round of formal talks, described in the communiqué as merely 'useful'.

29 July
A delegation of Hong Kong secondary school students, returning from meetings with Chinese officials in Beijing, publishes an informal draft of China's 'Twelve-Point Plan' for Hong Kong after 1997.

2–3 August
Third round of formal talks. The British presentation ends. China reaffirms its rejection of a post-1997 British administration. Both 'useful' and 'constructive' are omitted from the communiqué.

15 August
Hu Yaobang, Communist Party General Secretary, tells a delegation of Japanese journalists that China will 'recover Hong Kong on 1 July 1997'.

16 September
The *Financial Times* publishes an interview with Zhou Nan, vice-foreign minister, who says 'Sovereignty and administration are inseparable.'

22–23 September
Fourth round of formal talks. Deadlock over Britain's insistence that it should continue to administer Hong Kong after 1997.

24–25 September
The Hong Kong dollar crisis. The exchange rate falls to HK$9.50/US$1 on 24 September, amid signs of social unrest. On

1983
(*cont.*) 25 September, a government statement hints that the Hong Kong dollar exchange rate may be linked to the US dollar.

24–28 September
Richard Luce, junior Foreign Office minister, visits Hong Kong.

27 September
Luce and Sir Percy Cradock, leader of the British negotiating team, meet Youde and the Executive Council. Cradock says the talks may well collapse without a further British concession.

28 September
Luce, at a parting press conference, warns against 'megaphone diplomacy'.

7–8 October
Youde and Executive Council members see Thatcher, Howe and Cradock at Downing Street. They agree that Britain will 'conditionally' shelve its insistence on administering Hong Kong beyond 1997, and instead 'explore' China's plans.

15 October
Hong Kong announces a 'pegging' of its currency at a target rate of HK$7.80/US$1.

19–20 October
Fifth round of formal talks. Britain formally proposes to explore China's blueprint for Hong Kong. The communiqué, and all subsequent ones, restore the terms 'useful and constructive'.

14–15 November
Sixth round of formal talks. Britain says it proposes 'no links of authority' over Hong Kong after 1997.

16 November
Ji Pengfei says China will make no changes to Hong Kong for at least fifty years beyond 1997.

7–8 December
Seventh round of formal talks. China formally tables its blueprint. Discussion of the Hong Kong legal system and government structure after 1997.

1984   13 January
A night of rioting in Kowloon. No deaths, but thirty injuries and much damage to property.

16–17 January
Youde and Executive Council members visit London for a third round of talks with Thatcher. Discussion of the Chinese 'blue-print', which is now being publicly elaborated in interviews by Ji Pengfei.

23 January
Li Chuwen says openly that China will make a unilateral announcement of its plans for Hong Kong, if a negotiated settlement is not reached by September 1984.

25–26 January
Eighth round of formal talks. Both teams have new leaders: Zhou Nan for China, Sir Richard Evans for Britain. Discussion of the post-1997 political system, and of the role of the armed forces in Hong Kong.

22–23 February
Ninth round of formal talks. China urges discussion of 'transitional arrangements', and adoption of a protocol giving it a substantial role in Hong Kong prior to 1997.

26–28 February
Luce, Cradock and Evans hold meetings with Youde and the Executive Council in Hong Kong. Discussion of the September deadline, and of China's insistence on a pre-1997 role.

14 March
The Hong Kong Legislative Council passes the 'Lobo motion', asserting its right to debate any proposals for the future of Hong Kong prior to the concluding of a Sino-British agreement.

16–17 March
Tenth round of formal talks.

26–27 March
Eleventh round of formal talks.

1984   28 March
(cont.) Jardine Matheson, the most famous of the British-run Hong Kong trading houses, announces a plan to move its domicile to Bermuda.

5–6 April
Youde and Executive Council members return to London for talks with Thatcher and Howe, in preparation for a visit by Howe to Beijing.

11–12 April
Twelfth round of formal talks.

15–18 April
Howe visits Beijing for meetings with Deng, Zhao and Ji Pengfei. He persuades Deng that the treaty should be a detailed document, and that only the drafting, not the ratification, need be completed by September 1984.

19–20 April
Howe in Hong Kong. He tells a press conference that it would 'not be realistic' to imagine British administration after 1997.

27–28 April
Thirteenth round of formal talks. Discussion of economic and commercial issues, including trade and shipping.

10 May
A group of Executive and Legislative Council members arrives in London to lobby Parliament for 'adequate assurances' that China will honour a 1997 agreement.

10–11 May
Fourteenth round of formal talks.

25 May
Deng tells Hong Kong television that units of the People's Liberation Army will be stationed in Hong Kong after 1997.

30–31 May
Fifteenth round of formal talks.

12–13 June
Sixteenth round of formal talks. The negotiating teams agree to establish a separate working group to focus on the text of an agreement.

21 June
First meeting of the working group.

23 June
Deng receives a delegation of three Executive Council members from Hong Kong, and rebukes them for failing to 'understand' China. Deng makes the first public reference to the Sino-British Joint Liaison Group which China proposes for the pre-1997 period.

27–28 June
Seventeenth round of formal talks.

4 July
Youde and Evans return for a Downing Street meeting with Thatcher, Howe and Cradock, to plan a second visit by Howe to Beijing.

11–12 July
Eighteenth round of formal talks.

12–13 July
Luce visits Hong Kong to rally the increasingly fractious Executive Council.

24–25 July
Nineteenth round of formal talks.

27–31 July
Howe makes second visit to Beijing for meetings with Deng and other leaders. Several important obstacles are removed, including China's acceptance of a much less prominent role for the Joint Liaison Group.

1 August
Howe gives a press conference in Hong Kong, announcing that a legally binding agreement is now in sight which will preserve Hong Kong's social and economic systems.

1984   8–9 August
(*cont.*)   Twentieth round of formal talks. The discussion narrows to three
major problem areas: land, aviation and nationality.

21–22 August
Twenty-first round of formal talks.

5–6 September
Twenty-second round of formal talks. Agreement that a Land
Commission should be set up as a trustee for pre-1997 land sales
revenue.

6–17 September
Daily informal contacts at all levels to resolve outstanding points.

18 September
The negotiators send drafts of the Joint Declaration to their respective governments.

26 September
Zhou and Evans initial the Joint Declaration at the Great Hall of
the People.

14 November
The standing committee of China's National People's Congress
discusses and endorses the Joint Declaration.

29 November
An official Assessment Office, set up in Hong Kong to sample
public opinion, reports that 'most of the people of Hong Kong find
the draft agreement acceptable'.

5 December
The British House of Commons debates and endorses the Joint
Declaration.

19 December
Thatcher and Zhao formally sign the Joint Declaration on behalf
of their governments, at a ceremony in the Great Hall of the
People.

The Sino-British
Joint Declaration on
the Question of Hong Kong

On 19 December 1984, the Prime Minister of the United Kingdom of Great Britain and Northern Ireland, Mrs Margaret Thatcher, and the Prime Minister of the People's Republic of China, Mr Zhao Ziyang, acting on behalf of their respective Governments, signed the following Agreement on the future of Hong Kong:

JOINT DECLARATION
OF THE GOVERNMENT OF THE UNITED KINGDOM OF
GREAT BRITAIN AND NORTHERN IRELAND
AND
THE GOVERNMENT OF THE PEOPLE'S REPUBLIC OF CHINA
ON THE QUESTION OF HONG KONG

The Government of the United Kingdom of Great Britain and Northern Ireland and the Government of the People's Republic of China have reviewed with satisfaction the friendly relations existing between the two Governments and peoples in recent years and agreed that a proper negotiated settlement of the question of Hong Kong, which is left over from the past, is conducive to the maintenance of the prosperity and stability of Hong Kong and to the further strengthening and development of the relations between the two countries on a new basis. To this end, they have, after talks between the delegations of the two Governments, agreed to declare as follows:

1. The Government of the People's Republic of China declares that to recover the Hong Kong area (including Hong Kong Island, Kowloon and the New Territories, hereinafter referred to as Hong Kong) is the common aspiration of the entire Chinese people, and that it has decided to resume the exercise of sovereignty over Hong Kong with effect from 1 July 1997.

2. The Government of the United Kingdom declares that it will restore Hong Kong to the People's Republic of China with effect from 1 July 1997.

3. The Government of the People's Republic of China declares that the basic policies of the People's Republic of China regarding Hong Kong are as follows:

(1) Upholding national unity and territorial integrity and taking account of the history of Hong Kong and its realities, the People's Republic of China has decided to establish, in accordance with the provisions of Article 31 of the Constitution of the People's Republic of China, a Hong Kong Special Administrative Region upon resuming the exercise of sovereignty over Hong Kong.

(2) The Hong Kong Special Administrative Region will be directly under the authority of the Central People's Government of the People's Republic of China. The Hong Kong Special Administrative Region will enjoy a high degree of autonomy, except in foreign and defence affairs which are the responsibilities of the Central People's Government.

(3) The Hong Kong Special Administrative Region will be vested with executive, legislative and independent judicial power, including that of final adjudication. The laws currently in force in Hong Kong will remain basically unchanged.

(4) The Government of the Hong Kong Special Administrative Region will be composed of local inhabitants. The chief executive will be appointed by the Central People's Government on the basis of the results of elections or consultations to be held locally. Principal officials will be nominated by the chief executive of the Hong Kong Special Administrative Region for appointment by the Central People's Government. Chinese and foreign nationals previously working in the public and police services in the government departments of Hong Kong may remain in employment. British and other foreign nationals may also be employed to serve as advisers or hold certain public posts in government departments of the Hong Kong Special Administrative Region.

(5) The current social and economic systems in Hong Kong will remain unchanged, and so will the life-style. Rights and freedoms, including those of the person, of speech, of the press, of assembly, of association, of travel, of movement, of correspondence, of strike, of choice of occupation, of academic research and of religious belief will be ensured by law in the Hong Kong Special Administrative Region. Private property, ownership of enterprises, legitimate right of inheritance and foreign investment will be protected by law.

(6) The Hong Kong Special Administrative Region will retain the status of a free port and a separate customs territory.

(7)   The Hong Kong Special Administrative Region will retain the status of an international financial centre, and its markets for foreign exchange, gold, securities and futures will continue. There will be free flow of capital. The Hong Kong dollar will continue to circulate and remain freely convertible.

(8)   The Hong Kong Special Administrative Region will have independent finances. The Central People's Government will not levy taxes on the Hong Kong Special Administrative Region.

(9)   The Hong Kong Special Administrative Region may establish mutually beneficial economic relations with the United Kingdom and other countries, whose economic interests in Hong Kong will be given due regard.

(10) Using the name of 'Hong Kong, China', the Hong Kong Special Administrative Region may on its own maintain and develop economic and cultural relations and conclude relevant agreements with states, regions and relevant international organisations.

The Government of the Hong Kong Special Administrative Region may on its own issue travel documents for entry into and exit from Hong Kong.

(11) The maintenance of public order in the Hong Kong Special Administrative Region will be the responsibility of the Government of the Hong Kong Special Administrative Region.

(12) The above-stated basic policies of the People's Republic of China regarding Hong Kong and the elaboration of them in Annex I to this Joint Declaration will be stipulated, in a Basic Law of the Hong Kong Special Administrative Region of the People's Republic of China, by the National People's Congress of the People's Republic of China, and they will remain unchanged for 50 years.

4. The Government of the United Kingdom and the Government of the People's Republic of China declare that, during the transitional period between the date of the entry into force of this Joint Declaration and 30 June 1997, the Government of the United Kingdom will be responsible for the administration of Hong Kong with the object of maintaining and preserving its economic prosperity and social stability; and that the Government of the People's Republic of China will give its cooperation in this connection.

5. The Government of the United Kingdom and the Government of the People's Republic of China declare that, in order to ensure a smooth transfer of government in 1997, and with a view to the effective implementation of this Joint Declaration, a Sino-British Joint Liaison Group will be set up when this Joint Declaration enters into force; and that it will be established and will function in accordance with the provisions of Annex II to this Joint Declaration.

6. The Government of the United Kingdom and the Government of the People's Republic of China declare that land leases in Hong Kong and other related matters will be dealt with in accordance with the provisions of Annex III to this Joint Declaration.

7. The Government of the United Kingdom and the Government of the People's Republic of China agree to implement the preceding declarations and the Annexes to this Joint Declaration.

8. This Joint Declaration is subject to ratification and shall enter into force on the date of the exchange of instruments of ratification, which shall take place in Beijing before 30 June 1985. This Joint Declaration and its Annexes shall be equally binding.

Done in duplicate at Beijing on 19 December 1984 in the English and Chinese languages, both texts being equally authentic.

For the	For the
Government of the United Kingdom	Government of the
of Great Britain and Northern Ireland	People's Republic of China
Margaret Thatcher	Zhao Ziyang

ANNEX I

ELABORATION BY THE GOVERNMENT OF THE PEOPLE'S REPUBLIC OF CHINA OF ITS BASIC POLICIES REGARDING HONG KONG

The Government of the People's Republic of China elaborates the basic policies of the People's Republic of China regarding Hong Kong as set out in paragraph 3 of the Joint Declaration of the Government of the United Kingdom of Great Britain and Northern Ireland and the Government of the People's Republic of China on the Question of Hong Kong as follows:

I

The Constitution of the People's Republic of China stipulates in Article 31 that 'the state may establish special administrative regions when necessary. The systems to be instituted in special administrative regions shall be prescribed by laws enacted by the National People's Congress in the light of the specific conditions.' In accordance with this Article, the People's Republic of China shall, upon the resumption of the exercise of sovereignty over Hong Kong on 1 July 1997, establish the Hong Kong Special Administrative Region of the People's Republic of China. The National People's Congress of the People's Republic of China shall enact and promulgate a Basic Law of the Hong Kong Special Administrative Region of the People's Republic of China (hereinafter referred to as the Basic Law) in accordance with the Constitution of the People's Republic of China, stipulating that after the establishment of the Hong Kong Special Administrative Region the socialist

208

system and socialist policies shall not be practised in the Hong Kong Special Administrative Region and that Hong Kong's previous capitalist system and life-style shall remain unchanged for 50 years.

The Hong Kong Special Administrative Region shall be directly under the authority of the Central People's Government of the People's Republic of China and shall enjoy a high degree of autonomy. Except for foreign and defence affairs which are the responsibilities of the Central People's Government, the Hong Kong Special Administrative Region shall be vested with executive, legislative and independent judicial power, including that of final adjudication. The Central People's Government shall authorise the Hong Kong Special Administrative Region to conduct on its own those external affairs specified in Section XI of this Annex.

The government and legislature of the Hong Kong Special Administrative Region shall be composed of local inhabitants. The chief executive of the Hong Kong Special Administrative Region shall be selected by election or through consultations held locally and be appointed by the Central People's Government. Principal officials (equivalent to Secretaries) shall be nominated by the chief executive of the Hong Kong Special Administrative Region and appointed by the Central People's Government. The legislature of the Hong Kong Special Administrative Region shall be constituted by elections. The executive authorities shall abide by the law and shall be accountable to the legislature.

In addition to Chinese, English may also be used in organs of government and in the courts in the Hong Kong Special Administrative Region.

Apart from displaying the national flag and national emblem of the People's Republic of China, the Hong Kong Special Administrative Region may use a regional flag and emblem of its own.

II

After the establishment of the Hong Kong Special Administrative Region, the laws previously in force in Hong Kong (i.e. the common law, rules of equity, ordinances, subordinate legislation and customary law) shall be maintained, save for any that contravene the Basic Law and subject to any amendment by the Hong Kong Special Administrative Region legislature.

The legislative power of the Hong Kong Special Administrative Region shall be vested in the legislature of the Hong Kong Special Administrative Region. The legislature may on its own authority enact laws in accordance with the provisions of the Basic Law and legal procedures, and report them to the Standing Committee of the National People's Congress for the record. Laws enacted by the legislature which are in accordance with the Basic Law and legal procedures shall be regarded as valid.

The laws of the Hong Kong Special Administrative Region shall be the Basic Law, and the laws previously in force in Hong Kong and laws enacted by the Hong Kong Special Administrative Region legislature as above.

III

After the establishment of the Hong Kong Special Administrative Region, the judicial system previously practised in Hong Kong shall be maintained except for those changes consequent upon the vesting in the courts of the Hong Kong Special Administrative Region of the power of final adjudication.

Judicial power in the Hong Kong Special Administrative Region shall be vested in the courts of the Hong Kong Special Administrative Region. The courts shall exercise judicial power independently and free from any interference. Members of the judiciary shall be immune from legal action in respect of their judicial functions. The courts shall decide cases in accordance with the laws of the Hong Kong Special Administrative Region and may refer to precedents in other common law jurisdictions.

Judges of the Hong Kong Special Administrative Region courts shall be appointed by the chief executive of the Hong Kong Special Administrative Region acting in accordance with the recommendation of an independent commission composed of local judges, persons from the legal profession and other eminent persons. Judges shall be chosen by reference to their judicial qualities and may be recruited from other common law jurisdictions. A judge may only be removed for inability to discharge the functions of his office, or for misbehaviour, by the chief executive of the Hong Kong Special Administrative Region acting in accordance with the recommendation of a tribunal appointed by the chief judge of the court of final appeal, consisting of not fewer than three local judges. Additionally, the appointment or removal of principal judges (i.e. those of the highest rank) shall be made by the chief executive with the endorsement of the Hong Kong Special Administrative Region legislature and reported to the Standing Committee of the National People's Congress for the record. The system of appointment and removal of judicial officers other than judges shall be maintained.

The power of final judgment of the Hong Kong Special Administrative Region shall be vested in the court of final appeal in the Hong Kong Special Administrative Region, which may as required invite judges from other common law jurisdictions to sit on the court of final appeal.

A prosecuting authority of the Hong Kong Special Administrative Region shall control criminal prosecutions free from any interference.

On the basis of the system previously operating in Hong Kong, the Hong Kong Special Administrative Region Government shall on its own make provision for local lawyers and lawyers from outside the Hong Kong Special Administrative Region to work and practise in the Hong Kong Special Administrative Region.

The Central People's Government shall assist or authorise the Hong Kong Special Administrative Region Government to make appropriate arrangements for reciprocal juridical assistance with foreign states.

IV

After the establishment of the Hong Kong Special Administrative Region, public servants previously serving in Hong Kong in all government departments, including the police department, and members of the judiciary may all remain in employment and continue their service with pay, allowances, benefits and conditions of service no less favourable than before. The Hong Kong Special Administrative Region Government shall pay to such persons who retire or complete their contracts, as well as to those who have retired before 1 July 1997, or to their dependants, all pensions, gratuities, allowances and benefits due to them on terms no less favourable than before, and irrespective of their nationality or place of residence.

The Hong Kong Special Administrative Region Government may employ British and other foreign nationals previously serving in the public service in Hong Kong, and may recruit British and other foreign nationals holding permanent identity cards of the Hong Kong Special Administrative Region to serve as public servants at all levels, except as heads of major government departments (corresponding to branches or departments at Secretary level) including the police department, and as deputy heads of some of those departments. The Hong Kong Special Administrative Region Government may also employ British and other foreign nationals as advisers to government departments and, when there is a need, may recruit qualified candidates from outside the Hong Kong Special Administrative Region to professional and technical posts in government departments. The above shall be employed only in their individual capacities and, like other public servants, shall be responsible to the Hong Kong Special Administrative Region Government.

The appointment and promotion of public servants shall be on the basis of qualifications, experience and ability. Hong Kong's previous system of recruitment, employment, assessment, discipline, training and management for the public service (including special bodies for appointment, pay and conditions of service) shall, save for any provisions providing privileged treatment for foreign nationals, be maintained.

V

The Hong Kong Special Administrative Region shall deal on its own with financial matters, including disposing of its financial resources and drawing up its budgets and its final accounts. The Hong Kong Special Administrative Region shall report its budgets and final accounts to the Central People's Government for the record.

The Central People's Government shall not levy taxes on the Hong Kong Special Administrative Region. The Hong Kong Special Administrative Region shall use its financial revenues exclusively for its own purposes and they shall not be handed over to the Central People's Government. The systems by which taxation and public expenditure must be approved by the legislature, and by which there is accountability to the legislature for all public expenditure, and the system for auditing public accounts shall be maintained.

VI

The Hong Kong Special Administrative Region shall maintain the capitalist economic and trade systems previously practised in Hong Kong. The Hong

Kong Special Administrative Region Government shall decide its economic and trade policies on its own. Rights concerning the ownership of property, including those relating to acquisition, use, disposal, inheritance and compensation for lawful deprivation (corresponding to the real value of the property concerned, freely convertible and paid without undue delay) shall continue to be protected by law.

The Hong Kong Special Administrative Region shall retain the status of a free port and continue a free trade policy, including the free movement of goods and capital. The Hong Kong Special Administrative Region may on its own maintain and develop economic and trade relations with all states and regions.

The Hong Kong Special Administrative Region shall be a separate customs territory. It may participate in relevant international organisations and international trade agreements (including preferential trade arrangements), such as the General Agreement on Tariffs and Trade and arrangements regarding international trade in textiles. Export quotas, tariff preferences and other similar arrangements obtained by the Hong Kong Special Administrative Region shall be enjoyed exclusively by the Hong Kong Special Administrative Region. The Hong Kong Special Administrative Region shall have authority to issue its own certificates of origin for products manufactured locally, in accordance with prevailing rules of origin.

The Hong Kong Special Administrative Region may, as necessary, establish official and semi-official economic and trade missions in foreign countries, reporting the establishment of such missions to the Central People's Government for the record.

VII

The Hong Kong Special Administrative Region shall retain the status of an international financial centre. The monetary and financial systems previously practised in Hong Kong, including the systems of regulation and supervision of deposit taking institutions and financial markets, shall be maintained.

The Hong Kong Special Administrative Region Government may decide its monetary and financial policies on its own. It shall safeguard the free operation of financial business and the free flow of capital within, into and out of the Hong Kong Special Administrative Region. No exchange control policy shall be applied in the Hong Kong Special Administrative Region. Markets for foreign exchange, gold, securities and futures shall continue.

The Hong Kong dollar, as the local legal tender, shall continue to circulate and remain freely convertible. The authority to issue Hong Kong currency shall be vested in the Hong Kong Special Administrative Region Government. The Hong Kong Special Administrative Region Government may authorise designated banks to issue or continue to issue Hong Kong currency under statutory authority, after satisfying itself that any issue of currency will be soundly based and that the arrangements for such issue are consistent with the object of maintaining the stability of the currency. Hong Kong currency bearing references inappropriate to the status of Hong Kong as a Special Administrative Region of the People's Republic of China shall be progressively replaced and withdrawn from circulation.

The Exchange Fund shall be managed and controlled by the Hong Kong Special Administrative Region Government, primarily for regulating the exchange value of the Hong Kong dollar.

VIII

The Hong Kong Special Administrative Region shall maintain Hong Kong's previous systems of shipping management and shipping regulation, including the system for regulating conditions of seamen. The specific functions and responsibilities of the Hong Kong Special Administrative Region Government in the field of shipping shall be defined by the Hong Kong Special Administrative Region Government on its own. Private shipping businesses and shipping-related businesses and private container terminals in Hong Kong may continue to operate freely.

The Hong Kong Special Administrative Region shall be authorised by the Central People's Government to continue to maintain a shipping register and issue related certificates under its own legislation in the name of 'Hong Kong, China'.

With the exception of foreign warships, access for which requires the permission of the Central People's Government, ships shall enjoy access to the ports of the Hong Kong Special Administrative Region in accordance with the laws of the Hong Kong Special Administrative Region.

IX

The Hong Kong Special Administrative Region shall maintain the status of Hong Kong as a centre of international and regional aviation. Airlines incorporated and having their principal place of business in Hong Kong and civil aviation related businesses may continue to operate. The Hong Kong Special Administrative Region shall continue the previous system of civil aviation management in Hong Kong, and keep its own aircraft register in accordance with provisions laid down by the Central People's Government concerning nationality marks and registration marks of aircraft. The Hong Kong Special Administrative Region shall be responsible on its own for matters of routine business and technical management of civil aviation, including the management of airports, the provision of air traffic services within the flight information region of the Hong Kong Special Administrative Region, and the discharge of other responsibilities allocated under the regional air navigation procedures of the International Civil Aviation Organisation.

The Central People's Government shall, in consultation with the Hong Kong Special Administrative Region Government, make arrangements providing for air services between the Hong Kong Special Administrative Region and other parts of the People's Republic of China for airlines incorporated and having their principal place of business in the Hong Kong

Special Administrative Region and other airlines of the People's Republic of China. All Air Service Agreements providing for air services between other parts of the People's Republic of China and other states and regions with stops at the Hong Kong Special Administrative Region and air services between the Hong Kong Special Administrative Region and other states and regions with stops at other parts of the People's Republic of China shall be concluded by the Central People's Government. For this purpose, the Central People's Government shall take account of the special conditions and economic interests of the Hong Kong Special Administrative Region and consult the Hong Kong Special Administrative Region Government. Representatives of the Hong Kong Special Administrative Region Government may participate as members of delegations of the Government of the People's Republic of China in air service consultations with foreign governments concerning arrangements for such services.

Acting under specific authorisations from the Central People's Government, the Hong Kong Special Administrative Region Government may:

- renew or amend Air Service Agreements and arrangements previously in force; in principle, all such Agreements and arrangements may be renewed or amended with the rights contained in such previous Agreements and arrangements being as far as possible maintained;
- negotiate and conclude new Air Service Agreements providing routes for airlines incorporated and having their principal place of business in the Hong Kong Special Administrative Region and rights for over-flights and technical stops; and
- negotiate and conclude provisional arrangements where no Air Service Agreement with a foreign state or other region is in force.

All scheduled air services to, from or through the Hong Kong Special Administrative Region which do not operate to, from or through the mainland of China shall be regulated by Air Service Agreements or provisional arrangements referred to in this paragraph.

The Central People's Government shall give the Hong Kong Special Administrative Region Government the authority to:

- negotiate and conclude with other authorities all arrangements concerning the implementation of the above Air Service Agreements and provisional arrangements;
- issue licences to airlines incorporated and having their principal place of business in the Hong Kong Special Administrative Region;
- designate such airlines under the above Air Service Agreements and provisional arrangements; and
- issue permits to foreign airlines for services other than those to, from or through the mainland of China.

X

The Hong Kong Special Administrative Region shall maintain the educational system previously practised in Hong Kong. The Hong Kong Special Administrative Region Government shall on its own decide policies in the fields of culture, education, science and technology, including policies regarding the educational system and its administration, the language of instruction, the allocation of funds, the examination system, the system of academic awards and the recognition of educational and technological qualifications. Institutions of all kinds, including those run by religious and community organisations, may retain their autonomy. They may continue to recruit staff and use teaching materials from outside the Hong Kong Special Administrative Region. Students shall enjoy freedom of choice of education and freedom to pursue their education outside the Hong Kong Special Administrative Region.

XI

Subject to the principle that foreign affairs are the responsibility of the Central People's Government, representatives of the Hong Kong Special Administrative Region Government may participate, as members of delegations of the Government of the People's Republic of China, in negotiations at the diplomatic level directly affecting the Hong Kong Special Administrative Region conducted by the Central People's Government. The Hong Kong Special Administrative Region may on its own, using the name 'Hong Kong, China', maintain and develop relations and conclude and implement agreements with states, regions and relevant international organisations in the appropriate fields, including the economic, trade, financial and monetary, shipping, communications, touristic, cultural and sporting fields. Representatives of the Hong Kong Special Administrative Region Government may participate, as members of delegations of the Government of the People's Republic of China, in international organisations or conferences in appropriate fields limited to states and affecting the Hong Kong Special Administrative Region, or may attend in such other capacity as may be permitted by the Central People's Government and the organisation or conference concerned, and may express their views in the name of 'Hong Kong, China'. The Hong Kong Special Administrative Region may, using the name 'Hong Kong, China', participate in international organisations and conferences not limited to states.

The application to the Hong Kong Special Administrative Region of international agreements to which the People's Republic of China is or becomes a party shall be decided by the Central People's Government, in accordance with the circumstances and needs of the Hong Kong Special Administrative Region, and after seeking the views of the Hong Kong Special Administrative Region Government. International agreements to which the People's Republic of China is not a party but which are implemented in Hong Kong may remain implemented in the Hong Kong Special Administrative Region. The Central People's Government shall, as necessary, authorise or assist the Hong Kong Special Administrative Region Government to make appropriate arrangements for the application to the Hong Kong Special Administrative Region of other relevant international agreements. The Central People's Government shall take the necessary steps to ensure that the Hong Kong Special Administrative Region shall continue to retain its status in an appropriate capacity in those international organisations of which the People's Republic of China is a member and in which Hong Kong participates in one capacity or another. The Central People's Government shall, where necessary, facilitate the continued participation of the Hong Kong Special Administrative Region in an appropriate capacity in those international organisations in which Hong Kong is a participant in one capacity or another, but of which the People's Republic of China is not a member.

Foreign consular and other official or semi-official missions may be established in the Hong Kong Special Administrative Region with the approval of the Central People's Government. Consular and other official missions established in Hong Kong by states which have established formal diplomatic relations with the People's Republic of China may be maintained. According to the circumstances of each case, consular and other official missions of states having no formal diplomatic relations with the People's Republic of China may either be maintained or changed to semi-official missions. States not recognised by the People's Republic of China can only establish non-governmental institutions.

The United Kingdom may establish a Consulate-General in the Hong Kong Special Administrative Region.

XII

The maintenance of public order in the Hong Kong Special Administrative Region shall be the responsibility of the Hong Kong Special Administrative Region Government. Military forces sent by the Central People's Government to be stationed in the Hong Kong Special Administrative Region for the purpose of defence shall not interfere in the internal affairs of the Hong Kong Special Administrative Region. Expenditure for these military forces shall be borne by the Central People's Government.

XIII

The Hong Kong Special Administrative Region Government shall protect the rights and freedoms of inhabitants and other persons in the Hong Kong Special Administrative Region according to law. The Hong Kong Special Administrative Region Government shall maintain the rights and freedoms as provided for by the laws previously in force in Hong Kong, including freedom of the person, of speech, of the press, of assembly, of association, to form and join trade unions, of correspondence, of travel, of movement, of strike, of demonstration, of choice of occupation, of academic research, of belief, inviolability of the home, the freedom to marry and the right to raise a family freely.

Every person shall have the right to confidential legal advice, access to the courts, representation in the courts by lawyers of his choice, and to obtain judicial remedies. Every person shall have the right to challenge the actions of the executive in the courts.

216

Religious organisations and believers may maintain their relations with religious organisations and believers elsewhere, and schools, hospitals and welfare institutions run by religious organisations may be continued. The relationship between religious organisations in the Hong Kong Special Administrative Region and those in other parts of the People's Republic of China shall be based on the principles of non-subordination, non-interference and mutual respect.

The provisions of the International Covenant on Civil and Political Rights and the International Covenant on Economic, Social and Cultural Rights as applied to Hong Kong shall remain in force.

XIV

The following categories of persons shall have the right of abode in the Hong Kong Special Administrative Region, and, in accordance with the law of the Hong Kong Special Administrative Region, be qualified to obtain permanent identity cards issued by the Hong Kong Special Administrative Region Government, which state their right of abode:
- all Chinese nationals who were born or who have ordinarily resided in Hong Kong before or after the establishment of the Hong Kong Special Administrative Region for a continuous period of 7 years or more, and persons of Chinese nationality born outside Hong Kong of such Chinese nationals;
- all other persons who have ordinarily resided in Hong Kong before or after the establishment of the Hong Kong Special Administrative Region for a continuous period of 7 years or more and who have taken Hong Kong as their place of permanent residence before or after the establishment of the Hong Kong Special Administrative Region, and persons under 21 years of age who were born of such persons in Hong Kong before or after the establishment of the Hong Kong Special Administrative Region;
- any other persons who had the right of abode only in Hong Kong before the establishment of the Hong Kong Special Administrative Region.

The Central People's Government shall authorise the Hong Kong Special Administrative Region Government to issue, in accordance with the law, passports of the Hong Kong Special Administrative Region of the People's Republic of China to all Chinese nationals who hold permanent identity cards of the Hong Kong Special Administrative Region, and travel documents of the Hong Kong Special Administrative Region of the People's Republic of China to all other persons lawfully residing in the Hong Kong Special Administrative Region. The above passports and documents shall be valid for all states and regions and shall record the holder's right to return to the Hong Kong Special Administrative Region.

For the purpose of travelling to and from the Hong Kong Special Administrative Region, residents of the Hong Kong Special Administrative Region may use travel documents issued by the Hong Kong Special

Administrative Region Government, or by other competent authorities of the People's Republic of China, or of other states. Holders of permanent identity cards of the Hong Kong Special Administrative Region may have this fact stated in their travel documents as evidence that the holders have the right of abode in the Hong Kong Special Administrative Region.

Entry into the Hong Kong Special Administrative Region of persons from other parts of China shall continue to be regulated in accordance with the present practice.

The Hong Kong Special Administrative Region Government may apply immigration controls on entry, stay in and departure from the Hong Kong Special Administrative Region by persons from foreign states and regions.

Unless restrained by law, holders of valid travel documents shall be free to leave the Hong Kong Special Administrative Region without special authorisation.

The Central People's Government shall assist or authorise the Hong Kong Special Administrative Region Government to conclude visa abolition agreements with states or regions.

ANNEX II

SINO-BRITISH JOINT LIAISON GROUP

1. In furtherance of their common aim and in order to ensure a smooth transfer of government in 1997, the Government of the United Kingdom and the Government of the People's Republic of China have agreed to continue their discussions in a friendly spirit and to develop the cooperative relationship which already exists between the two Governments over Hong Kong with a view to the effective implementation of the Joint Declaration.

2. In order to meet the requirements for liaison, consultation and the exchange of information, the two Governments have agreed to set up a Joint Liaison Group.

3. The functions of the Joint Liaison Group shall be:
  - (*a*) to conduct consultations on the implementation of the Joint Declaration;
  - (*b*) to discuss matters relating to the smooth transfer of government in 1997;
  - (*c*) to exchange information and conduct consultations on such subjects as may be agreed by the two sides.

Matters on which there is disagreement in the Joint Liaison Group shall be referred to the two Governments for solution through consulations.

4. Matters for consideration during the first half of the period between the establishment of the Joint Liaison Group and 1 July 1997 shall include:
  - (*a*) action to be taken by the two Governments to enable the Hong Kong

Special Administrative Region to maintain its economic relations as a separate customs territory, and in particular to ensure the maintenance of Hong Kong's participation in the General Agreement on Tariffs and Trade, the Multifibre Arrangement and other international arrangements; and

(b) action to be taken by the two Governments to ensure the continued application of international rights and obligations affecting Hong Kong.

5. The two Governments have agreed that in the second half of the period between the establishment of the Joint Liaison Group and 1 July 1997 there will be need for closer cooperation, which will therefore be intensified during that period. Matters for consideration during this second period shall include:

(a) procedures to be adopted for the smooth transition in 1997;

(b) action to assist the Hong Kong Special Administrative Region to maintain and develop economic and cultural relations and conclude agreements on these matters with states, regions and relevant international organisations.

6. The Joint Liaison Group shall be an organ for liaison and not an organ of power. It shall play no part in the administration of Hong Kong or the Hong Kong Special Administrative Region. Nor shall it have any supervisory role over that administration. The members and supporting staff of the Joint Liaison Group shall only conduct activities within the scope of the functions of the Joint Liaison Group.

7. Each side shall designate a senior representative, who shall be of Ambassadorial rank, and four other members of the group. Each side may send up to 20 supporting staff.

8. The Joint Liaison Group shall be established on the entry into force of the Joint Declaration. From 1 July 1988 the Joint Liaison Group shall have its principal base in Hong Kong. The Joint Liaison Group shall continue its work until 1 January 2000.

9. The Joint Liaison Group shall meet in Beijing, London and Hong Kong. It shall meet at least once in each of the three locations in each year. The venue for each meeting shall be agreed between the two sides.

10. Members of the Joint Liaison Group shall enjoy diplomatic privileges and immunities as appropriate when in the three locations. Proceedings of the Joint Liaison Group shall remain confidential unless otherwise agreed between the two sides.

11. The Joint Liaison Group may by agreement between the two sides decide to set up specialist sub-groups to deal with particular subjects requiring expert assistance.

12. Meetings of the Joint Liaison Group and sub-groups may be attended by experts other than the members of the Joint Liaison Group. Each side shall determine the composition of its delegation to particular meetings of the Joint Liaison Group or sub-group in accordance with the subjects to be discussed and the venue chosen.

13. The working procedures of the Joint Liaison Group shall be discussed and decided upon by the two sides within the guidelines laid down in this Annex.

ANNEX III

LAND LEASES

The Government of the United Kingdom and the Government of the People's Republic of China have agreed that, with effect from the entry into force of the Joint Declaration, land leases in Hong Kong and other related matters shall be dealt with in accordance with the following provisions:

1. All leases of land granted or decided upon before the entry into force of the Joint Declaration and those granted thereafter in accordance with paragraph 2 or 3 of this Annex, and which extend beyond 30 June 1997, and all rights in relation to such leases shall continue to be recognised and protected under the law of the Hong Kong Special Administrative Region.

2. All leases of land granted by the British Hong Kong Government not containing a right of renewal that expire before 30 June 1997, except short term tenancies and leases for special purposes, may be extended if the lessee so wishes for a period expiring not later than 30 June 2047 without payment of an additional premium. An annual rent shall be charged from the date of extension equivalent to 3 per cent of the rateable value of the property at that date, adjusted in step with any changes in the rateable value thereafter. In the case of old schedule lots, village lots, small houses and similar rural holdings, where the property was on 30 June 1984 held by, or, in the case of small houses granted after that date, the property is granted to, a person descended through the male line from a person who was in 1898 a resident of an established village in Hong Kong, the rent shall remain unchanged so long as the property is held by that person or by one of his lawful successors in the male line. Where leases of land not having a right of renewal expire after 30 June 1997, they shall be dealt with in accordance with the relevant land laws and policies of the Hong Kong Special Administrative Region.

3. From the entry into force of the Joint Declaration until 30 June 1997, new leases of land may be granted by the British Hong Kong Government for terms expiring not later than 30 June 2047. Such leases shall be granted at a premium and nominal rental until 30 June 1997, after which date they shall not require payment of an additional premium but an annual rent equivalent to 3 per cent of the rateable value of the property at that date, adjusted in step with changes in the rateable value thereafter, shall be charged.

4. The total amount of new land to be granted under paragraph 3 of this Annex shall be limited to 50 hectares a year (excluding land to be granted to the Hong Kong Housing Authority for public rental housing) from the entry into force of the Joint Declaration until 30 June 1997.

5. Modifications of the conditions specified in leases granted by the British Hong Kong Government may continue to be granted before 1 July 1997 at a premium equivalent to the difference between the value of the land under the previous conditions and its value under the modified conditions.

6. From the entry into force of the Joint Declaration until 30 June 1997, premium income obtained by the British Hong Kong Government from land transactions shall, after deduction of the average cost of land production, be shared equally between the British Hong Kong Government and the future Hong Kong Special Administrative Region Government. All the income obtained by the British Hong Kong Government, including the amount of the above mentioned deduction, shall be put into the Capital Works Reserve Fund for the financing of land development and public works in Hong Kong. The Hong Kong Special Administrative Region Government's share of the premium income shall be deposited in banks incorporated in Hong Kong and shall not be drawn on except for the financing of land development and public works in Hong Kong in accordance with the provisions of paragraph 7(*d*) of this Annex.

7. A Land Commission shall be established in Hong Kong immediately upon the entry into force of the Joint Declaration. The Land Commission shall be composed of an equal number of officials designated respectively by the Government of the United Kingdom and the Government of the People's Republic of China together with necessary supporting staff. The officials of the two sides shall be responsible to their respective governments. The Land Commission shall be dissolved on 30 June 1997.

The terms of reference of the Land Commission shall be:
- (*a*) to conduct consultations on the implementation of this Annex;
- (*b*) to monitor observance of the limit specified in paragraph 4 of this Annex, the amount of land granted to the Hong Kong Housing Authority for public rental housing, and the division and use of premium income referred to in paragraph 6 of this Annex;
- (*c*) to consider and decide on proposals from the British Hong Kong Government for increasing the limit referred to in paragraph 4 of this Annex;
- (*d*) to examine proposals for drawing on the Hong Kong Special Administrative Region Government's share of premium income referred to in paragraph 6 of this Annex and to make recommendations to the Chinese side for decision.

Matters on which there is disagreement in the Land Commission shall be referred to the Government of the United Kingdom and the Government of the People's Republic of China for decision.

8. Specific details regarding the establishment of the Land Commission shall be finalised separately by the two sides through consultations.

EXCHANGE OF MEMORANDA

(A) UNITED KINGDOM MEMORANDUM

MEMORANDUM

In connection with the Joint Declaration of the Government of the United Kingdom of Great Britain and Northern Ireland and the Government of the People's Republic of China on the question of Hong Kong to be signed this day, the Government of the United Kingdom declares that, subject to the completion of the necessary amendments to the relevant United Kingdom legislation:

(a) All persons who on 30 June 1997 are, by virtue of a connection with Hong Kong, British Dependent Territories citizens (BDTCs) under the law in force in the United Kingdom will cease to be BDTCs with effect from 1 July 1997, but will be eligible to retain an appropriate status which, without conferring the right of abode in the United Kingdom, will entitle them to continue to use passports issued by the Government of the United Kingdom. This status will be acquired by such persons only if they hold or are included in such a British passport issued before 1 July 1997, except that eligible persons born on or after 1 January 1997 but before 1 July 1997 may obtain or be included in such a passport up to 31 December 1997.

(b) No person will acquire BDTC status on or after 1 July 1997 by virtue of a connection with Hong Kong. No person born on or after 1 July 1997 will acquire the status referred to as being appropriate in sub-paragraph (a).

(c) United Kingdom consular officials in the Hong Kong Special Administrative Region and elsewhere may renew and replace passports of persons mentioned in sub-paragraph (a) and may also issue them to persons, born before 1 July 1997 of such persons, who had previously been included in the passport of their parent.

(d) Those who have obtained or been included in passports issued by the Government of the United Kingdom under sub-paragraphs (a) and (c) will be entitled to receive, upon request, British consular services and protection when in third countries.

Beijing, 19 December 1984.

(Stamp of the British Embassy)

222

(B) CHINESE MEMORANDUM

Translation

MEMORANDUM

The Government of the People's Republic of China has received the memorandum from the Government of the United Kingdom of Great Britain and Northern Ireland dated 19 December 1984.

Under the Nationality Law of the People's Republic of China, all Hong Kong Chinese compatriots, whether they are holders of the 'British Dependent Territories citizens' Passport' or not, are Chinese nationals.

Taking account of the historical background of Hong Kong and its realities, the competent authorities of the Government of the People's Republic of China will, with effect from 1 July 1997, permit Chinese nationals in Hong Kong who were previously called 'British Dependent Territories citizens' to use travel documents issued by the Government of the United Kingdom for the purpose of travelling to other states and regions.

The above Chinese nationals will not be entitled to British consular protection in the Hong Kong Special Administrative Region and other parts of the People's Republic of China on account of their holding the above-mentioned British travel documents.

Beijing, 19 December 1984.

(Stamp of the Ministry of Foreign Affairs of the Central People's Government)

Notes

Chapter 1: The Legacy of History

1. An observation borrowed from Felix Patrikeeff, in *Mouldering Pearl: Hong Kong at the Crossroads* (London, 1990), p. 109.
2. Opium was legal in England at this time, and was commonly sold in tincture as laudanum.
3. As Governor-General of Hubei and Hunan, Lin had campaigned vigorously against the opium trade. After his mission to Guangdong, he was dismissed and banished to Xinjiang, but he quickly regained favour and his rank was restored. He died in 1850 at the age of 67 while riding to suppress the Taiping rebels.
4. The principal sources for this account of the seizure and settling of Hong Kong are: Nigel Cameron, *An Illustrated History of Hong Kong* (Hong Kong, 1991); Maurice Collis, *Foreign Mud* (Singapore, 1980); E.H. Parker, *Chinese Account of the Opium War* (reprint) (Wilmington, 1980); Geoffrey Sayer, *Hong Kong, 1841–1862: Birth, Adolescence and Coming of Age* (Hong Kong, 1937); and Jonathan Spence, *The Search for Modern China* (London, 1990).
5. A province roughly contiguous with modern Hebei.
6. Mexican silver dollars, the common currency of the China coast.
7. 'Throughout the whole course of the proceedings', thundered Palmerston, 'you seem to have considered that my instructions were mere waste paper which you might treat with entire disregard.'
8. The Treaty of Nanjing, ratified on 26 June 1843.
9. Hart was appointed Inspector-General of Customs at the age of 29, and held the job for forty-five years. A Chinese contemporary, Chen Zi, wrote of him: 'His counsels prevail at the court and he has gradually

gained control over the conduct of the country's foreign policy. Woe to those who defy his authority! His vast fortune may be compared with the wealth of a nation . . . He looks sincere but is in reality a blackguard. He has been knighted by the British Crown, and this is eloquent proof that he is working for the good of his own country.' Cited in Hu Sheng, *Imperialism and Chinese Politics* (sixth edition, Beijing, 1978; trans. Foreign Languages Press, 1985), pp. 53–4.

10. V. I. Lenin, *The War in China*, 1900, in *Collected Works* (English edition, Moscow, 1960), Vol. 4, p. 374.

11. Apart from works cited, other general sources for those paragraphs dealing with China and Hong Kong in the late 1890s are: Cameron (1991); Jean Chesneaux, Marianne Bastid and Marie-Claire Bergère, *China from the Opium Wars to the 1911 Revolution* (New York, 1976); John Fairbank and Edwin Reischauer, *China: Tradition and Transformation* (Sydney, 1986); Geoffrey Sayer, *Hong Kong, 1862–1919: Years of Discretion* (Hong Kong, 1975); and Spence (1990).

12. Cited in Mary H. Wilgus, 'Sir Claude MacDonald, the Open Door and British Informal Empire in China, 1895–1900' (unpublished Ph.D thesis, Nashville, 1985), p. 104.

13. MacDonald to Salisbury, draft dispatch dated 27 May 1898, in series FO17, Public Record Office, London.

14. Ibid.

15. Balfour to Salisbury, telegram 162, FO17.

16. See Anthony Dicks, 'Treaty, Grant, Usage or Sufferance: Some Legal Aspects of the Status of Hong Kong', in *China Quarterly*, No. 95, London, 1983, p. 97n.

17. Peter Wesley-Smith, *Unequal Treaty 1898–1997: China, Great Britain and Hong Kong's New Territories* (Hong Kong, 1983), p. 143.

18. Ibid., p. 145.

19. Karl Marx, *Revolution in China and Europe* in *The Collected Works of Marx and Engels* (London, 1979), Vol. 12, p. 95.

20. The others were: 'The Movement of the Taiping Heavenly Kingdom, the Sino-French War, the Sino-Japanese War, the Reform Movement of 1898, the Yi Ho Tuan Movement, the Revolution of 1911, the May 4th Movement, the May 30th Movement, the Northern Expedition, the Agrarian Revolution and the present War of Resistance Against Japan.' Mao Zedong, *Selected Works* (Beijing, 1967), Vol. II, p. 314.

21. Hu (1985), pp. 7 and 46. Hu was deputy secretary-general of the committee for revising the Communist Party constitution in 1982.

22. Ibid., p. 6.

23. 'The Opium War', *History of Modern China* (Shanghai, 1976).

24. *Wen Wei Po*, Hong Kong, 6 October 1982.

Chapter 2: The Limits of Possession

1. The words are those of Sir John Pratt, attached to the Far East department of the Foreign Office after consular service in China, in a Foreign Office minute of 1931, quoted in Wesley-Smith (1983), p. 159.
2. Clementi to Amery, 19 January 1927, in series CO129, Public Record Office, London.
3. The Washington Conference on the Limitation of Armaments and Pacific and Far Eastern Questions, November 1921 – February 1922. Walter Ellis, head of the Colonial Office's Far Eastern department, remarked in a Hong Kong file margin note dated 22 January 1927: 'Yes, it is a thousand pities that we promised at Washington to give up Weihaiwei without any such conditions as the conversion of our lease over the New Territories into perpetual sovereignty but we can hardly impose the condition now.'
4. Amery to Clementi, 18 February 1927, CO129.
5. These views were advanced by Clementi during meetings at the Colonial Office on 28 June 1927, minuted in CO129.
6. Minute dated 12 July 1928, CO129.
7. Minute from F. Ashton Gwatkin, 7 November 1928, CO129.
8. Though the Governor of the day, Sir Alexander Grantham, thought that an attack could be resisted. See Grantham, *Via Ports: From Hong Kong to Hong Kong* (Hong Kong, 1965), pp. 140–1.
9. *The Times*, 17 November 1980.
10. Grantham's own published account of the meeting omits the conversation as it touched on Hong Kong. See Grantham (1965), pp. 184–5.
11. The proposal, though not made public at the time, has since been confirmed by British officials and in parliamentary debate (see *Hong Kong Standard*, 9 May 1973). Grantham is said to have replied that there was 'no room for two governors in Hong Kong': see Richard Hughes, *Borrowed Time, Borrowed Place: Hong Kong and its Many Faces* (second edition, London, 1976), pp. 38–9.
12. See Kevin Lane, *Sovereignty and the Status Quo: The Historical Roots of China's Hong Kong Policy* (Boulder, Co., 1990), p. 74; Norman Miners, *The Government and Politics of Hong Kong* (fifth edition, Hong Kong, 1991), p. 6; and Dick Wilson, *Hong Kong, Hong Kong* (London, 1990), p. 196.
13. Cited by Ma Hong in 'How to use the Hong Kong economy to serve the acceleration of China's Four Modernizations', *Economic Studies Reference Materials* (Beijing, March 1979); trans. in Joseph Cheng (ed.), *Hong Kong: In Search of a Future* (Hong Kong, 1984), p. 61.
14. The Central Committee directive and Zhou's encouragement are recorded in Cheng (1984), p. 61.
15. Associated Press, 11 December 1966, reporting a meeting between Chen Yi and a Brazilian lawyer, Carvillo dos Santos. Cited in Gary Wayne Catron, 'China and Hong Kong, 1945–67' (unpublished Ph.D thesis,

Harvard, 1971), pp. 230–1.

16. Cited in Cheng (1984), p. 54.

17. *The Times*, 23 October 1972, quoted in Kevin Rafferty, *City on the Rocks: Hong Kong's Uncertain Future* (London, 1989), pp. 389–90.

Chapter 3: 'A Window of Opportunity

1. White Paper: *A draft agreement between the Government of the United Kingdom and the Government of the People's Republic of China on the Question of Hong Kong* (Hong Kong, Government Printer, September 1984).

2. In 1968, for example, China supplied 19 per cent of Hong Kong's imports, valued at HK$2.4 billion; it was statistically insignificant as a market for Hong Kong's locally produced, or 'domestic', exports; and it was the destination for less than 2 per cent of 're-exported' goods passing through Hong Kong. In 1978, the pattern of the relationship was much the same, though nominal values had increased. China supplied 17 per cent of Hong Kong's imports, valued at HK$10.6 billion; bought 0.2 per cent of its domestic exports, worth just HK$81 million; and was the destination for 1.6 per cent of its re-exports, worth HK$214 million. In 1988, by contrast, after a decade of Deng's economic liberalization programme, China was supplying 31 per cent of Hong Kong's imports, worth HK$155 billion; taking 17.5 per cent of domestic exports, worth HK$38 billion; and was the destination for 34.5 per cent of its re-exports, worth HK$95 billion, making it by far the territory's largest trading partner.

3. The author has not seen these telegrams, but has accepted the accounts of those who have done so. According to one diplomat: 'My abiding memory is of an incredibly intense backwards and forwards correspondence between London and Hong Kong on this whole approach. If ever an issue was exhaustively discussed between the Hong Kong government and the Foreign Office, this was one.'

4. This can be most precisely demonstrated by comparing the movement of property prices on either side of the legal boundary separating Kowloon from the New Territories, using the average prices recorded by the Hong Kong government's Rating and Valuation Department. In 1976, small flats on the very southern fringes of the leased area, immediately to the north of the legal boundary, were selling for 9.5 per cent less per square metre than flats on the south side of the legal boundary, at the very northern fringe of the ceded area of Kowloon. By 1979, not only had prices on both sides of the line risen sharply, but flats to the north of the legal boundary were selling for only 7.3 per cent less than those in the adjacent ceded areas. The discount had narrowed by 2.2 percentage points, or 23 per cent.

5. *Euromoney*, August 1981.

6. Nor, when it came to the crunch, did banks discover any fundamental

legal difficulty in extending mortgage finance beyond 1997 even with the 1997 issue unresolved. In 1982, the Hongkong Bank started offering 20-year mortgages, declaring simply that it would be satisfied with the 'personal assurance of the borrower' that the money would be repaid. Other banks wrote 'balloon' loans with low initial payments but with a large final payment due in June 1997.

7. *Euromoney*, August 1981.
8. From a speech delivered on 16 February 1982. But Wesley-Smith had his own doubts elsewhere. In a footnote to *Unequal Treaty*, p. 240, he writes: 'It is possible that, in law, Britain could merely ignore 1997 and, after that date, rely on the Interpretation and General Clauses Ordinance or on governmental behaviour as an authoritative declaration as to the territory claimed by the Crown. It would be a foolhardy commentator who sought to predict how the courts would react, for we have here advanced into the mists of constitutional theory. The matter is likely to remain hypothetical, for such a "solution" to the problem of 1997 would not be politically satisfactory.'
9. Kadoorie was chairman of China Light and Power, Keswick the retired chairman of Jardine Matheson. Both were veteran Hong Kong figures known and respected in Beijing.
10. Although in practice the lawyers would probably *not* have protested, since English law holds as a matter of principle that a tenant cannot dispute the title of his landlord. This singularity was an essential feature of the Lo scheme.
11. Hong Kong residents who chose to take British citizenship were registered as British Dependent Territories Citizens. From 1985 onward, they could opt to be registered as British Nationals (Overseas), a category created in anticipation of Hong Kong ceasing to be a British Dependent Territory. But neither form of citizenship carried any right of entry to Britain. The Nationality Act of 1981 had no concrete effect on Hong Kong passport-holders, though by restating in new terminology the restrictions imposed since 1962, it was perceived in the territory to be adding insult to injury.
12. See David Owen, *Time to Declare* (London, 1991), p. 407.
13. Ibid.
14. From Han Nianlong and Qian Qichen (eds.), *The Diplomacy of Contemporary China* (Hong Kong, 1990), p. 464. The book's editorial committee includes past and present Chinese foreign ministry officials.

Chapter 4: 'One Country, Two Systems'

1. Deng's remarks were reported by the US delegation in a press statement. Cited in *Facts on File*, New York, 23 January 1979.
2. In January 1979, he embarked at short notice on a rare foreign trip to the United States; in February, he launched a brief war against Vietnam.

3. The proposals for Taiwan were to be publicized in a speech given by Marshal Ye Jianying on 30 September – see p. 65.
4. Founder of the Sun Hung Kai securities and banking group; he died in 1984.
5. As Governor of Sichuan from 1975 to 1980, Zhao Ziyang had successfully pioneered agricultural and factory reforms which became a national model under Deng. Hu Yaobang was a popular, relatively liberal figure who had built up a strong Party base through his leadership of the Communist Youth League. Both later lost Deng's favour.
6. The Taiwan Relations Act, signed into law by President Carter on 10 April, committed the United States to promoting relations with Taiwan through 'unofficial channels', to continuing arms sales to the island, and to unspecified assistance were Taiwan to be attacked.
7. *Ming Pao*, 4 July 1981, from a leader written by the newspaper's editor, Louis Cha, equally eminent as a political journalist and as a martial-arts novelist.
8. New China News Agency, 30 September 1981.
9. 'United Front work', in Communist terminology, means obtaining the co-operation of non-Communist people and organizations which may be useful to the Communist cause. The December 1981 – January 1982 meeting was noted in a New China News Agency bulletin on 15 January 1982.
10. See David Bonavia, *Hong Kong 1997: The Final Settlement* (Hong Kong, 1985), p. 98; *Daily Telegraph*, 7 January 1982; and *Far Eastern Economic Review*, 6 June 1982.
11. *Ming Pao*, 17 March 1982.
12. No attempt was made, however, to reconcile the new clause with seemingly incompatible provisions elsewhere in the Constitution – notably Article 1, which says that 'The People's Republic of China is a socialist state' and that 'Disruption of the socialist system by any organization or individual is prohibited'.
13. The others were recorded as being: Su Wu-tse, wife of Fei Yiming and the Communists' Hong Kong expert on 'women's issues'; Wang Kuancheng and Tang Ping-ta, director and deputy director of the Hong Kong Chinese Chamber of Commerce; Li Tse-chung, publisher of the second main Communist newspaper in Hong Kong, *Wen Wei Po*; Li Hsia-wen, deputy director of *Ta Kung Pao*; Yang Kuang, chairman of the Hong Kong Federation of Trades Unions; Liang Pei, chairman of the Macao Trades Unions; Chen Fu-li, photographer; Wu Kang-min, headmaster; Xu Simin, publisher of *Mirror* magazine; and Chen Hung, assistant general manager of the Bank of China.
14. *Cheng Ming*, Hong Kong, 1 July 1982.
15. *Pai Shing*, Hong Kong, 16 September 1982.
16. *Wide Angle*, Hong Kong, 16 August 1982; translated in Cheng (1984), pp. 69–71.

Chapter 5: Mrs Thatcher Makes a Stand

1. See p. 35.
2. *Ming Pao*, 12 February 1980.
3. *Ming Pao*, 21 February 1981.
4. See, for example, that of *Wide Angle* on pp. 75–6.
5. *Cheng Ming*, the Hong Kong political monthly, reported in its issue of 1 November 1982, apparently drawing on Beijing sources: 'Prior to Mrs Thatcher's visit to China, the foreign ministries of both China and Britain expressed their respective positions through an exchange of official notes. Britain held that the three treaties concerning Hong Kong should still be observed. Communist China did not take umbrage at that time. However, during Mrs Thatcher's visit, her attitude of resting her case on the legality of the three treaties caused resentment within the Communist hierarchy.' The author has not been able to substantiate this 'exchange of notes' from British sources.
6. Hugo Young, *One of Us* (London, 1990), p. 292.
7. *Daily Telegraph*, 24 September 1982.
8. From *The Diplomacy of Contemporary China*, p. 464. As with Deng's statement to MacLehose, this is an edited and polished version of Deng's remarks, but it conforms in its main points to what was said.
9. *Hong Kong Daily News*, 19 April 1983, treats this event from Chinese sources.
10. *Wah Kiu Yat Po*, 9 January 1983.

Chapter 6: The Negotiations Begin

1. China News Service, 20 November 1982; *Hong Kong Standard*, 21 November 1982; *Wen Wei Po*, 22 November 1982; and *Hong Kong Standard*, 2 December 1982. The Royal Hong Kong Jockey Club manages Hong Kong's horse-racing industry, and the on- and off-course bookmaking through which it holds a near-monopoly over legal gambling in the territory.
2. This was the line taken by Yao Guang, China's senior negotiator, when Sir Percy Cradock protested in January 1983 that confidentiality had been violated. See *Hong Kong Daily News*, 19 April 1983.
3. Quoted in the *Far Eastern Economic Review*, 3 December 1982.
4. The fate of Shanghai under Communism was, in fact, the stuff of Hong Kong's nightmares. In January 1983, Liao Chengzhi told another visiting Hong Kong delegation: 'We will not rule Hong Kong like Shanghai.'
5. *Far Eastern Economic Review*, 5 May 1983.
6. Author's italics. According to a report in the *Hong Kong Daily News* of 14 May 1983, the letter 'stressed again that China should not set any precondition to the talks. The talks should not be held merely according to China's position, namely the acknowledgement of China's

sovereignty over Hong Kong. But the letter went on to say that Britain would not object to opening the negotiations, with China adopting the attitude that it held on sovereignty over Hong Kong; and that the sovereignty issue itself should be an item on the agenda.'

7. The unofficials comprised, at the start of 1983, four businessmen, two bankers, two lawyers and a doctor. They were, in descending order of seniority, Sir Sze-yuen Chung (industrialist), Oswald Cheung (barrister), Rogerio Lobo (businessman), Li Fook-wo (banker), Harry Fang (doctor), Michael Sandberg (banker), Lo Tak-shing (solicitor), David Newbigging (company director) and Lydia Dunn (company director).

8. *Far Eastern Economic Review*, 22 September 1983.

9. Quoted in *Mirror*, 10 July 1983.

10. The agenda was set out in English and Chinese versions, of equal validity. Line three caused a certain amount of grammatical deliberation in the British camp, where it was felt that to say '*the* transfer of sovereignty', as China wanted, would yield too much to China's anticipation. Eventually, it was agreed that since the Chinese language did not use articles in this way, the problem could be avoided by using no article in the English text also.

11. Other members, to be announced a week later, included, on the Chinese side, Shao Tianren, legal adviser to the foreign ministry; Ke Zaishuo, counsellor to the western European department of the foreign ministry; and Luo Jiahuan, holding the same rank; and on the British side, the first secretary at the British Embassy in Beijing, William Ehrman; and the two second secretaries, Bob Pierce and Tom Smith.

12. *Wen Wei Po*, 16 August 1983.

13. *Oriental Daily News*, 31 August 1983. The size of the Hong Kong exchange fund was at that time secret. The HK$30 billion claimed here may have been a Chinese guess; or a figure supplied confidentially by Britain; or a confusion between the exchange fund, which was used exclusively for supporting the Hong Kong dollar, and the government's fiscal reserves, which were the accumulated budget surpluses standing then at about HK$20 billion.

Chapter 7: Crisis and Concession

1. *Financial Times*, 16 September 1983.

2. *Cheng Ming*, December 1982, discusses early claims of this type from Beijing sources.

3. *Wen Wei Po*, 21 September 1983.

4. Published with the *Financial Times* of 12 September 1983.

5. Some dealers were offering to sell the Hong Kong dollar at eight to the US dollar and buy it at nine – a 'spread' of 10,000 basis points. In a liquid market for a major currency, spreads are usually quoted in tens of basis points.

6. One unofficial said of the feeling of the meetings: 'I didn't think it was

a finesse, frankly, I thought it was a surrender. We had hoped for miracles, and maybe miracles were in short supply. But we had hoped that a tougher position would be taken. Basically, Mrs Thatcher was being told day after day by Cradock about the way it was going to have to be played. Teddy Youde was fighting hard, but he didn't have the weight that Percy Cradock was able to bring.

'It came to a head in the London meetings. They had decided that it just wasn't possible to continue the battle. And we were still saying "Give it more of a try", and they were saying "No, this is the decision we have reached. This is a dead duck. We must give in gracefully before the temperature rises even higher." We felt we were rubber-stamping a decision which had already been made. We were unhappy with it, but equally, we were not sure we could have pushed it any further.'

But, according to a British source who contests this recollection: 'The Hong Kong representatives were relieved to be offered a way out of an increasingly ugly impasse. They perked up when [told] that there was a formula which would allow [the British side] to explore the Chinese position further without commitment, and they accepted that it would be foolhardy to go into the final confrontation without knowing what the alternatives were.'

7. *Wen Wei Po*, 20 November 1983.
8. The 'mini-constitution' concept was amplified by the *New Evening Post* in a spirited column on 30 November attacking manifestations of Hong Kong's allegiance to the British Crown. It concluded by stating that 'The "Royal Instructions" and "Royal Command" must be replaced by a "mini-constitution" which will be formulated through democratic means.'

Chapter 8: A Matter of Form

1. To the Hong Kong government's silent relief, an assistant director of the NCNA, Qi Feng, declined the bait, saying on 13 January that 'the New China News Agency is not the Government of Hong Kong'.
2. In an interview with Hong Kong visitors, published in *Ta Kung Pao* on 8 January 1984, Ji rehearsed China's known policies, but added new proposals for a post-1997 Hong Kong legislature which he discreetly retracted a month later. He proposed a 'three-thirds' system, whereby 'one-third of its members incline towards the Beijing government, another third incline towards Britain and the remaining third take a neutral stand'.
3. The deadline had been made a matter of public record by Li Chuwen, deputy director at the New China News Agency in Hong Kong, in an interview with *Newsweek* published on 23 January 1984. Li said: 'We hope to work out an agreement with Britain by September 1984. If we cannot, China will make a unilateral announcement within the realm of the Chinese Government's jurisdiction.'

4. And probably never had a Governor worked so hard as Youde did during the negotiations. A close colleague recalled: 'He drove himself. I remember going to London with him on a Monday night, arriving on the Tuesday morning, going straight to the Foreign Office, work work work for two days, leaving on Thursday, back in Hong Kong on Friday, and for him it was straight into an Executive Council meeting on Saturday.' Youde set that pace for himself despite having undergone heart bypass surgery in the year before his arrival in Hong Kong. Few doubted that the workload shortened his life. He died in office, in November 1986.

5. A director of the Jardine group had, in fact, forewarned Youde of the move, but Youde had kept the information to himself or, at any rate, had not circulated it in such a way that it reached the British Embassy in Beijing.

6. Deng talked about this meeting with Howe to Hong Kong reporters on 25 May 1984.

7. The italics are those of the statement.

Chapter 9: The Joint Declaration

1. This remark was omitted from subsequent New China News Agency reports of the dialogue, but preserved in the Hong Kong transcript. See *Hong Kong Standard*, 29 June 1984.

2. The quotation had a curious history. It was also engraved on a fan which Sir Yue-kong Pao, the Hong Kong shipowner, gave to Howe a week before Howe left for Beijing. In an interview with the *South China Morning Post* on 16 September 1985, Pao said that a 'senior British official' asked him to act as an intermediary between Britain and China, clarifying 'two or three points' before Howe's visit. British officials told the author in 1992 that they had no recollection of any such instruction to Pao, while confirming that he offered advice and encouragement of an informal kind.

3. Lu Ping later became director of the State Council Hong Kong and Macao Affairs Office, and McLaren ambassador to Beijing.

4. There is disagreement over the legal force of the Exchange of Memoranda. The International Commission of Jurists, in its Hong Kong report, *Countdown to 1997: Report of a Mission to Hong Kong* (Geneva, 1992), said the memoranda 'are not annexed to the declaration and do not form part of any treaty or other agreement between the United Kingdom and the PRC. As a matter of law, therefore, the UK would not be acting improperly by altering the proposals contained in [its] memorandum.'

   However, in denouncing a British proposal in 1989 to issue 50,000 new passports to Hong Kong residents, and claiming that the Exchange of Memoranda had been violated, the *Beijing Review*, an official Chinese publication, said on 12 February 1990: 'The name given to an international agreement – treaty, convention agreement, accord, exchange of notes, declaration, statement, memorandum of provisional agreement – is decided by its signatories according to its context . . . However, no matter what it is called, it is equally authentic in law and all parties should strictly comply with it.'

5. The term 'an appropriate status' was used because, with Hong Kong ceasing to be a British Dependent Territory in 1997, some new name for BDTC status would have to be devised. That eventually adopted was British National (Overseas). The British had at first tried to persuade China to allow this citizenship to be transmissable by one generation in Hong Kong after 1997, so that those who held British passports in 1997 could obtain them for children born under Chinese sovereignty. But this China refused to accept under any guise, and Britain backed down.

6. By most estimates, 98 per cent of Hong Kong's population of 6 million in the mid-1980s was ethnically Chinese. Some 3.25 million either held or were entitled to obtain British Dependent Territories Citizenship; and those permanent residents who did not qualify for, or did not wish to assume, BDTC status, could obtain a Certificate of Identity which served as a travel document.

Of Hong Kong's non-Chinese 2 per cent, most were long- or short-term expatriates holding the nationalities and passports of countries to which they would probably at some point return, and to whom the Exchange of Memoranda was irrelevant. Where, however, the Exchange of Memoranda fell short was in its failure to provide for those Hong Kong residents who were British Dependent Territories Citizens only, but who might not succeed in acquiring or might not wish to acquire Chinese nationality after 1997.

For those who were ethnically Chinese, and had not obtained a separate nationality overseas, the Chinese memorandum appeared to leave no doubt: they would be treated as 'compatriots', and *ipso facto* as Chinese nationals, whether they wished it or not. But for those who were not 'Hong Kong Chinese compatriots' – for example the 4,500 members of Hong Kong's Indian community who held BDTC documents only – the Chinese memorandum was silent on nationality, although their continued 'right of abode' in Hong Kong was protected by Annex I, Section 14 of the Joint Declaration. This deficiency in the Chinese memorandum could not be made good by reference to China's own nationality law, which would apply to Hong Kong after 1997, since the term 'compatriot' did not occur in the prevailing (1980) Chinese statute.

7. The profit would be calculated by deducting from the gross revenues the average cost to the government that year of 'forming' new land for sale, a process which might include reclamation or levelling, and usually involved the provision of basic infrastructure, such as access roads and drainage.

8. *Far Eastern Economic Review*, 4 October 1984; and *The Times*, 27 September 1984.

Chapter 10: Afterwards

1. In William McGurn (ed.), *Basic Law, Basic Questions* (Hong Kong, 1988), p. vii.
2. International Commission of Jurists (1992), p. 14.
3. This was short-sighted on the part of both Britain and China since, in the atmosphere of relief verging on euphoria which followed the Joint Declaration, its terms very probably would have been approved by a referendum in Hong Kong, to the enormous political advantage of both its principals. The Assessment Office, set up in Hong Kong to collate reaction to the Joint Declaration, reported the receipt of 2,494 submissions, of which 679 came from organizations and 1,815 from individuals, over a seven-week collection period. Of these, only a small minority – 33 organizations and 364 individuals – favoured rejection of the agreement.
4. Literally so. See, notably, Steve Y.S. Tsang, *Democracy Shelved: Great Britain, China and Attempts at Constitutional Reform for Hong Kong, 1945–52* (Hong Kong, 1988).
5. Rate-payers had been allowed since the nineteenth century to elect members to the Urban Council, a body concerned with sanitation and culture on Hong Kong Island; and the first direct elections for District Boards, the most local tier of government, took place as discussed below in 1982.
6. John Walden, *Excellency, Your Gap is Growing* (Hong Kong, 1987), p. 74.
7. According to one Executive Council member: 'MPs who came out used to say how good it would be, how we needed more democracy . . . But there was always Beijing saying "Don't do it, and if you do it we will overturn it anyhow." And so it was very much a question of softly-softly. I am sure we went too softly, and I sure we're going too softly now . . . I think we were really rather foolish not to allow elections sooner [to the Legislative Council] and for a wider number of seats.'
8. The notion of multi-party or otherwise genuinely contested elections has no place in the Chinese political system. At 'elections' for Communist Party bodies, the candidates are pre-selected or approved by the Party hierarchy in numbers equal or almost equal to the posts available. The Communist system favours 'consultation', meaning, in practice, the exercise of the Party's discretion and patronage. In December 1985, during an argument over a gerrymandered 'vote' for office-bearers of the Basic Law Consultative Committee, Xu Jiatun, China's senior representative in Hong Kong, declared consultation to be 'a form of election'.

Xu also reportedly said in an off-the-record briefing in Shenzhen on

20 June 1987 that the phrase 'constituted by elections' was accepted by China in 1984 only for the sake of maintaining good relations with London. The New China News Agency later dismissed reports of this remark as 'inaccurate'. See Peter Wesley-Smith and Albert Chen (eds.), *The Basic Law and Hong Kong's Future* (Singapore, 1988), p. 102; and Ming K. Chan and David J. Clark (eds.), *The Hong Kong Basic Law: Blueprint for Stability and Prosperity under Chinese Sovereignty?* (Hong Kong, 1991), p. 11.

9. John Walden has argued: 'I suspect that the main purpose of the 1984 White Paper was to ensure that the British Parliament endorsed the Sino-British Joint Declaration on the Question of Hong Kong. But I do not believe that the British, Chinese and Hong Kong governments intend to allow the democratic reforms in the White Paper to lead to a situation in which the policies and actions of the government in Hong Kong are determined and controlled by the people of Hong Kong or their elected representatives either before or after 1997.' Walden (1987), p. 73.

10. Green Paper: *The Further Development of Representative Government in Hong Kong* (Hong Kong, July 1984), p. 4.

11. White Paper: *The Further Development of Representative Government in Hong Kong* (Hong Kong, November 1984), p. 8. It was, perhaps, hardly surprising that public opinion should have been so reticent on direct elections in 1985, since the Green Paper on which the public was being consulted had not presented direct elections as a possibility until some time after 1989.

12. When Martin Lee, the Hong Kong liberal activist, quoted Luce's statement in his evidence to a House of Commons Foreign Affairs Committee on 20 April 1989, as part of the argument that Britain should do more to implement its earlier words, he received this lesson in parliamentary procedure from a committee member, Peter Shore: 'I can quote to you what the Foreign Secretary said in the same debate on the same day. He is the senior minister. Mr Richard Luce was then a junior minister. The Foreign Secretary talked about putting "the administration of Hong Kong policy in local hands and for the Executive to be accountable to an elected Legislature". Nothing at all about universal suffrage. If that had been the intention and pledge at that time it would have been stated.'

13. Denis Healey, Labour foreign affairs spokesman, later wrote: 'On issues, like . . . the negotiations with China on the future of Hong Kong, I did my best to help the Government, since it was doing what Labour would have done.' See *The Time of My Life* (London, 1990), p. 507.

14. See the Joint Declaration, Annex II, Clause 3.

15. White Paper: *The Development of Representative Government – The Way Forward* (Hong Kong, February 1988), p. 8. For a discussion of the Survey Office and its methods, see Miners (1991), pp. 26–7.

16. For the subsequent refinements to this formula, see Note 27.
17. Dame Lydia (later Baroness) Dunn, Executive Council member and director of the Swire group of companies, in evidence to the House of Commons Foreign Affairs Committee, 20 April 1989.
18. Peter Temple-Morris to Simon Ip, in evidence given on 19 April 1989.
19. Evidence given on 22 March 1989.
20. Evidence given on 19 April 1989.
21. To protect the loyalty of certain senior civil servants and police officers, a separate and secret scheme was set in motion at about the time of the Nationality Act. They were issued with secret code numbers, which they could use to secure admission to Britain *in extremis*. Henry Keswick referred cryptically to this provision in his evidence to the Commons Foreign Affairs Committee on 24 May 1989, saying: 'There are certain groups in Hong Kong who are at risk if anything goes wrong. As you know, you have at the moment this system of a number. Many people in Hong Kong have a number, but I do not know if one is meant to talk about that. They have a number which, if anything goes wrong, they just use and hope for the best.'
22. Hong Kong's immigration formalities did not require declarations from those who left the territory of why they were leaving and for how long, but plausible emigration figures could be assembled from two main sources: data for 'landings' supplied by the main destination countries, and the number of applications received by the Hong Kong government for 'certificates of no criminal conviction', a document which destination countries almost invariably required of their would-be immigrants. Official estimates of emigration during the period were as follows:

1980	22,400	1986	19,000
1981	18,300	1987	30,000
1982	20,300	1988	45,800
1983	19,800	1989	42,000
1984	22,400	1990	62,000
1985	22,300	1991	60,000 (provisional)

   Source: Hong Kong Government, cited in Sung Yun-wing and Lee Ming-kwan (eds.), *The Other Hong Kong Report 1991* (Hong Kong, 1991), p. 235.
23. The Basic Law is too long and complex to treat here in any detail. For a convenient bilingual edition of the text and related documents, see *The Basic Law of the Hong Kong Special Administrative Region of the People's Republic of China*, published by the One Country Two Systems Economic Research Institute (Hong Kong, 1992). English translations of the first and second drafts were published in Hong Kong by the Basic Law Consultative Committee in April 1988 and February 1989 respectively. For more detailed discussion of the law's provisions, see, in addition to works otherwise cited here: Gladys Li *et al.*, *The Present Situation in Hong Kong*, collated as HK62 in Volume II,

Minutes of Evidence, Hong Kong, Report of the House of Commons Foreign Affairs Committee (London, 1989); and Peter Wesley-Smith (ed.), *Hong Kong's Basic Law* (Hong Kong, 1990).

24. References are to the 1982 Constitution, adopted at the Fifth Session of the Fifth National People's Congress, published in English by the Foreign Languages Press, Beijing, 1987.

25. For first-hand accounts of the massacre, see Michael Fathers and Andrew Higgins, *Tiananmen: The Rape of Peking* (London, 1989); and The Editorial Board of the June 4 Eyewitness Accounts (eds.), *The Eyes Have It* (Hong Kong, 2nd edition, 1990), a verbatim anthology.

26. Britain refused. But it did agree in December 1989 to issue 50,000 full British passports to Hong Kong residents selected by the Hong Kong government through a scheme designed mainly to identify economically important target groups.

27. In addition to the 20 directly elected Legislative Council seats (out of 60) blessed by China in 1990, Patten proposed to attribute 9 seats in 1995 to new and very broadly defined 'functional constituencies', the effect of which would have been to give an additional vote to each worker in Hong Kong; to extend the right to vote in the 21 other, more narrowly defined, 'functional constituencies'; and to invite elected members of District Boards to constitute the 'electoral college' which would choose the remaining 10 members of the Legislative Council who were to be indirectly elected. China said, however, that 'convergence' with the Basic Law required functional constituencies to have only a very narrowly defined franchise, and the electoral college to be a body of appointees.

28. For analyses of the Chinese position, see the *Far Eastern Economic Review*, 17 December 1992; and *Cheng Ming*, January 1993.

29. MFN, 'Most-Favoured Nation' status, gives Chinese exports privileged access to the US market, but is reviewable annually. 'Super 301' is a shorthand term for the power under US law given to the US Congress to demand investigations of – and, where it finds necessary, sanctions against – overseas trading partners. Lee's remarks are taken from the transcript published by *Window* magazine, Hong Kong, on 18 December 1992.

Index

Index

France, 11–12, 13, 162
Friedman, Milton, 125
Fry, Maxwell, 125
Fung King-hey, 63

Galsworthy, Anthony, 159–60
Gang of Four, 31, 37, 63
'Gang ren zhi gang', 99–100, 115, 132
GEC, 92
Germany, 11–12, 13
Gibraltar, 3
Gimson, Franklin, 25
Gladstone, William, 8
Goodhart, Charles, 127
Gordon, Charles, 11
Grantham, Sir Alexander, 27, *226*
Gray, R.W., 84
Great Hall of the People, 54, 85, 86, 87, 99, 132, 156
'Great Leap Forward', 27
Greenwood, John, 124–8
Grey, Anthony, 31
Grindle, Sir Gilbert, 21
GT, 124
Guangdong Province, 25, 27, 37–8
Guangzhou, 6, 7, 8, 9, 21, 92
Guardian, The, 158
Gu Mu, 72

Han Suyin, 4
Hang Lung Bank, 126
Hang Seng Bank, 42
Hang Seng Index, 32, 41, 57, 78, 79, 96–7, 113
Harcourt, Admiral, 25
Hart, Sir Robert, 11, 12, *224–5*
Healey, Denis 153, *236*
Heath, Sir Edward, 34, 50, 70, 71, 117–18, 153
Heren, Louis, 33
Heseltine, Michael, 116
Hollingworth, Clare, 53
Hong Kong:
    currency, 75, 80, 94, 97, 99, 112, 113, 133, 166
        Sept. 1983 'crisis', 120–8, 176, *232*
            'pegging', 124–8
    democracy in, 27, 177–84, 190, *234–5, 235–6*
        Green Paper 1984, 180, *235*
        White Paper 1984, 181, *235*
        Green Paper 1987, 183–4; Survey Office, 184
        White Paper 1988, 184, *236*
        'Young Plan', 178
    emigration from, 187–8, *237*; civil servants' scheme, *237*
    foreign exchange reserves, 116, *231*
    geography, 1–4
    government:
        District Boards, 179, *234*;
        Executive Council, 52, 79, 103–4, 105–6, 116, 117, 143–5, 146, 177, 178, 180, 190; meetings and trips: Jan. 1982, 68; Sept. 1982, 80–1; July 1983, 107;

Sept. 1983, 128–9; Oct. 1983, 130; Jan. 1984, 138; Feb. 1984, 145; Apr. 1984, 149; May 1984 (London lobbying), 152–3, 154; June 1984 (Beijing lobbying), 155–6; 12 July 1984, 157; 31 July 1984, 163–4
        General Duties Branch, 110, 134, 141, 167
        Governor, 76, 89, 100, 176, 192
        Legislative Council, 68, 96, 117, 137, 146, 152–3, 177–84, 190
        Monetary Affairs Branch, 125
        Political Adviser's Office, 37, 110
        Urban Council, *235*
    history:
        colonization, 6–19
        Pacific War, 24–5
        1949, 25–6
        Korean War, 25–6
        Cultural Revolution, 28–32
    land leases, 20, 22–3, 35, 46, 50–2, 55–7, 62, 169–70
    legal system, 76, 112, 133, 134–5, 140, 166
    police, 30, 112, 137–8
    property market, 41–2, 57, 76, 78, 96, 120, *226–7*
    sovereignty, 14–15, 67, 70, 76, 81–2, 84, 87–8, 89, 94, 98, 102–3, 106–7, 109, 113, 116, 119–20, 122–3, 141, 161, 175
    stock market, 32, 76, 78, 80, 93, 94, 96, 120, 165
    taxi strike, 1984, 136–8
    treaties establishing, 5, 19, 32, 70, 71, 90, 92, 93, 94, 95–6, 114–15; *see also*, Chuanbi; Nanjing; Beijing; Conventions/Treaties of
    see also Hong Kong Island; Kowloon; New Territories; Britain, Hong Kong; *and* China, Hong Kong
Hong Kong Chinese Chamber of Commerce, 100
Hong Kong Club, 10
Hong Kong Daily News, 81–2, 121, *229, 230–1*
Hong Kong dollar, *see* Hong Kong, currency
Hong Kong Factory Owners' Association, 99–100
Hong Kong Federation of Trades Unions, *229*
Hong Kong General Chamber of Commerce, 77
Hong Kong International Airport, *see* Kai Tak
Hong Kong Island, cession of, 5, 9, 10, 70; *see also* Chuanbi, Convention of; Nanjing, Treaty of
Hongkong Land Company, 41, 42
Hong Kong and Macao Affairs Office, *see* China, government
Hongkong and Shanghai Bank, 2–3, 42, 125
Hong Kong Society of Accountants, 42
Hong Kong Standard, 230, 233
Hong Kong University, 73
Hong Kong Weekly Press, 14
Howe, Sir Geoffrey, 84, 107, 138, 143, 145, 153, 154–5, 156, 157, 158, 159, 171–2, 185, 189, 191
    in Beijing, Apr. 1984, 148–9, *233*
    in Hong Kong, Apr. 1984, 149–51
    in Beijing, July 1984, 160–3, *233*

241

Index

Index